JAPAN

FROM SURRENDER TO PEACE

General of the Army Douglas MacArthur
Supreme Commander for the Allied Powers in Japan

BARON E. J. LEWE VAN ADUARD

JAPAN

FROM SURRENDER TO PEACE

WITH A FOREWORD BY
JOHN FOSTER DULLES

FREDERICK A. PRAEGER
NEW YORK

BOOKS THAT MATTER

Published in the United States of America
in 1954 by Frederick A. Praeger, Inc.,
Publishers, 105 West 40th Street,
New York 18, N.Y.

Library of Congress Catalog Card Number: 54—6648

*First published in the Netherlands
by Martinus Nijhoff, The Hague*

PRINTED IN THE NETHERLANDS

ACKNOWLEDGMENTS

In the first place I want to express my indebtedness to Ambassador H. Mouw, who introduced me to the fascinating realm of Far Eastern politics. I recall with gratitude our daily discussions on this subject during the years 1949–1952, when he was Head of the Netherlands Mission in Japan, and I had the benefit of profiting from his extensive knowledge and long experience of Far Eastern affairs.

A particular word of thanks is due to Dean A. J. Miller, S.J., Head of the International Division of the Sophia University, Tokyo, for his great assistance in laying the groundwork of this study and for his having encouraged me to write this book.

Gratitude is expressed to Professor H. van Straelen of the Nanzam University, Nagoya; to Professor Shinzo Koizumi, former President of the Keyo University, Tokyo; to Professor Iwao Ayusama, Vice President of the International Christian University, Tokyo, and to Drs. S. Meyer, Chief of the Far Eastern Bureau of the Netherlands Ministry of Foreign Affairs at The Hague, for having read portions of the manuscript and having made valuable suggestions. I alone, however, bear responsibility for the opinions set forth in the book and for its shortcomings.

I am greatly indebted to Mrs. Molly Munters and Miss A. J. H. Visser for their valuable assistance in the preparation of the manuscript.

Yet this book would never have been completed without the great help and the inspiration of my dear companion for life, Krystyna, who has sacrificed so many precious hours of our time together in order to enable me to write these pages.

The Hague, December 1952   L. v. A.

CONTENTS

FOREWORD

The six years between the surrender of Japan on September 2, 1945, and the signing of a Treaty of Peace in San Francisco on September 8, 1951 between Japan and forty-eight of the nations with which she was at war, was a period unique in the history of international affairs. Throughout those six years Japan was occupied by the Allied Powers. Because of what was accomplished during that occupation under the wise leadership of General Douglas MacArthur, it was possible to conclude a peace which showed no trace of angry passion; a peace of reconciliation, not of vengeance.

From its inception the Occupation of Japan was inspired by high moral principles, was governed by the magnanimity that comes from true strength and was carried out in a calm and purposeful manner. Japan's war-making power was destroyed and the influence of those who committed her to armed conquest eliminated. Oppressive laws and restrictive practices were removed and guaranties established for freedom of speech, religion and thought and respect for fundamental human rights. These new freedoms and concepts were planted and nursed with painstaking care by the Occupation. But they would never have taken root at all had it not been for the loyal cooperation of the Japanese people; a cooperation inspired by the very nature of the Occupation. Strengthened and encouraged by the just and fair peace which has been granted them, the Japanese people can be expected to nurture and preserve those freedoms in the light of their own customs and philosophy, and continue in the ways of peace in cooperation with the free world.

The Treaty of Peace with Japan is unique in that it was negotiated and drafted not at a single Peace Conference but through a series of diplomatic conversations and exchanges of memoranda and drafts. As the Special Representative of the President of the United States, I reached agreement with a majority of the nations represented on the Far Eastern Commission as to the principles which should govern the treaty, and later visited the capitals of countries most concerned (including Japan) to negotiate the actual text. I also had numerous conversations in Washington and in New York with the representatives of other States (including the Soviet Union) on the substance and wording of the treaty.

Every nation which constructively interested itself in the treaty can claim authorship of important parts of the final text. Each of these nations can claim the equally honorable distinction of voluntarily subordinating some special interests so that a broad base of unity might be found. The Allied Powers conducted what, in effect, was an eleven months' peace conference participated in by so many nations as to make the treaty the most broadly based one in all history. The treaty, as finally signed, remains as first agreed, a non-punitive, non-discriminatory treaty which restores Japan to dignity, equality and opportunity in the family of nations. No one can predict the future, and no treaty can guarantee the future. But at least it can be predicted that the future will not be worsened because of any of the provisions of the Treaty itself. That is more than can be said for most treaties of "peace".

Baron van Aduard's book is necessarily written without benefit of access to important source material not yet available. Therefore, it cannot be completely authoritative. But it does give a most interesting and, on the whole, reliable account of the Occupation and the steps towards peace as seen by an experienced diplomat in Tokyo. It will, I am sure, help all who read it to understand the philosophy which underlay the Occupation and the writing of the Peace Treaty. It will also, I hope, bring about a better understanding of the problems which face the new Japan as it struggles to achieve a place of dignity within the family of nations and seeks to cooperate in peace and friendship with the Free World.

New York, N.Y., December 16, 1952.

[John Foster Dulles]

INTRODUCTION

On April 28, 1952, Japan regained her status as a sovereign and independent nation, great changes having taken place since she last was her own master.

Japan now finds herself re-entering a world in which the majority of her former enemies extend her a welcome, whilst at the same time, some of the World War II Allies–Russia and China–are opposing the Free World, the world which granted Japan a peace of reconciliation.

During the last few years, 1946–1952, Japan has been introduced to various political, social and economic principles of democracy. Many of them have been readily embraced by her, but whether she will continue to develop along democratic lines and maintain her position among the peaceful and democratic nations, will depend largely upon the future cooperation between Japan and the nations of the free world. Such cooperation presupposes a mutual understanding, based upon a knowledge of the past and an appreciation of the present. My purpose in writing this book is to contribute to this understanding by giving a summary of the years of the Occupation and an estimate of its results.

What was the aim of the Occupation? What role did MacArthur and his advisers play? Did the Japanese cooperate? What was the attitude of the Japanese leaders, their Emperor and his Cabinet Ministers, in particular peace-treaty Prime Minister Yoshida? What considerations guided John Foster Dulles in sponsoring a peace of reconciliation? Were the Japanese sincere in accepting, at San Francisco, a partnership in the free world community? What, in fact, has been accomplished during the years of the Occupation and where will Japan go now?

The subsequent pages will attempt to supply an answer to these questions.

In formulating this answer I have drawn on my experience as Deputy Chief of the Netherlands Mission in Japan during four of the most significant years of the Occupation. My studies during this period have been greatly facilitated by my close personal contact with General MacArthur and the members of his Staff, with the Japanese people and their leaders, and with Mr. Dulles's peace mission.

Four great names dominate the history of post-surrender Japan: Joseph C. Grew, former U.S. Ambassador to Tokyo, who drafted the Occupation directives; General Douglas MacArthur, Supreme Commander for the Allied Powers, who shaped the new Japan; John Foster Dulles, Special Envoy of the President of the United States, who built the Japanese peace treaty; and Shigeru Yoshida, Prime Minister of Japan, who lead his country throughout one of the most difficult and decisive periods of its long existence.

My account presents some of the aspects of their work. It reveals the story of the Occupation, its background, its work and development. It tells how the Occupation faced internal and external difficulties which led to several fruitless peace endeavors, after which failures the piecemeal peace process and the economic reconstruction of Japan were initiated. It describes how this process created circumstances which made peace mandatory. It discloses that this situation resulted in a dilemma which was finally solved through the endeavors of John Foster Dulles, culminating in a peace treaty which restored Japan to full independence. Finally, it gives an estimate of the results of the Occupation and a survey of the circumstances which will influence Japan's attitude towards the Free World.

Without claiming to be a documented study with numerous references to source material, this book is based upon historical data, generally available to those who seriously follow current events. The reader will find in these pages a logical and sequential compilation, and a political analysis, of the events occuring in and around Japan during the years 1946–52. Emphasis has been laid upon the international character of the developments and upon their mutual relationship and interplay. While the following pages, therefore, do not profess to be an exhaustive study of the Occupational years, it is hoped that they may at least be a source of information for some readers, an inducement for others to record their own observations and conclusions about the Occupation, and a challenge to all to stimulate future co-operation between Japan and the other nations of the Free World.

The Hague, December 1952   L. v. A.

Chapter I

THE SURRENDER

General Douglas MacArthur, accepting the surrender of Japan, indicates that the Occupation will be guided by a constructive spirit; he bases his intentions on Potsdam Declaration and Post-Surrender Policy Directive.

1. *The Fate of Japan after the Surrender*

In the clear, early morning of September 2, 1945, the U.S.S. Missouri lay calmly at anchor in Tokyo Bay. Japan's mysterious mountains were to be seen in the distance, topped by a glistening Mount Fuji, the sacred symbol of Japan's hopes and dreams. Why should the famous mountain look so radiant on this fateful September day? There seemed more reason for her to hide in dark clouds of shame and despair, for was it not the first time in Japan's long history that terms of surrender were being dictated on her own soil and foreign troops were standing ready to occupy the Land of the Rising Sun? Might it not be expected that a stern and harsh treatment for the vanquished would follow the four years of bloody, cruel and savage fighting — years which had stirred passions and nourished hatreds? Would not the victorious Allies inflict a program of severe punishment on the Japanese nation? Would they not attempt to destroy the very foundations of Japanese nationhood and to eliminate the best part of its people in order to prevent a return of Japanese imperialism?

Japan had reason to fear such treatment. Only the somewhat vague, though high-sounding promises set down in the Potsdam Declaration of July 1945 indicated that a more lenient attitude could be expected. But Japan had no assurance that the Allies would act accordingly.

Still, the sacred mountain might well look glorious, for the fate of Japan was to prove much happier than could have been anticipated after the many years of brutal and vehement struggle and after Japan's crushing defeat. Accepting the

1

surrender of the Japanese Empire, General MacArthur, the newly appointed Supreme Commander for the Allied Powers, indicated that the Occupation would be guided by an enlightened spirit, declaring:

> "It is not for us here to meet, representing as we do a majority of the people of the earth, in a spirit of distrust, malice or hatred. But it is for us, both victors and vanquished, to rise to that higher dignity which alone befits the sacred purposes we are about to serve, committing all of our people unreservedly to faithful compliance with the undertakings they are here formally to assume".

These solemn words of the Supreme Commander, based on a directive received only a few days before from Washington, ushered in a new era in Japan's history. MacArthur and the people he represented were assuming the responsibility of leading Japan from her erroneous path of conquest and bloodshed to one of peace and world respect.

2. *Supreme Commander Bases Occupation Policy on Potsdam Declaration and Post-Surrender Policy Directive*

What prompted the Supreme Commander to announce this particular course for his new undertaking? Upon what instructions was MacArthur's attitude based?

To answer these questions one must look back to July 26, 1945, when the Heads of State of the three principal Powers waging war against Japan, the United States of America, the British Commonwealth and the Chinese Republic, met at Potsdam to decide the fate of their mutual enemy.

Truman, Churchill and Chiang Kai-shek determined that the surrender of Japan should be unconditional. Basing their conclusions upon the decisions of the Cairo Conference of November 1943, they issued the *Potsdam Declaration,* in which they reiterated their resolve to continue the war against Japan until that country was entirely defeated. They repeated their intention to destroy Japan's warmaking power and to limit Japan's sovereignty to the islands of Hokkaido, Honshu, Kyushu and Shikoku. Their declaration, however, carried a note of hope for the Japanese people owing to the statement that there was no intention of enslaving the Japanese as a race or destroying them as a nation. On the contrary, they promised the people of Japan a peaceful existence as a democratic nation. Obstacles to the revival and growth of a true democracy would be removed. Freedom of speech, religion and thought and respect for fundamental human rights would be established. In short, the Heads of State at Potsdam decided upon a stern but just treatment of Japan.

The Supreme Commander for the Allied Powers was guided by more elaborate directives than those in the Potsdam Declaration. On August 29, 1945, the day before his arrival in Japan, MacArthur received by radio the *Initial Post-Surrender Policy Directive for Japan*. Members of the State, Army and Navy Departments in Washington had been preparing this document months in advance — a document to decide the fate of Nippon for decades to come. Guided by the high ideals set forth in the Charter of the United Nations and with a deep realization of the shortcomings of the 1919 Versailles peace arrangements, the American policy makers had drafted the post-surrender policy with remarkable wisdom. The document proved its soundness throughout six years of occupation notwithstanding the changing circumstances in the world.

The directive stated that the ultimate objective of the United States in Japan is to ensure that the country will never again menace the peace and security of the world. At the same time it indicated that the United States is intent on establishing a peaceful and democratic Japan. It set forth the necessity of destroying the military potential of Japan, as well as limiting it to its four main islands. But the directive also opened the door for the Japanese to rebuild their country as a peaceful member of the community of nations; the Japanese people, stated the policy directive, must be encouraged to develop a desire for democratic values. The directive promised the Japanese that they shall be afforded an opportunity to develop an economy which will satisfy the peacetime requirements of the population. The United States, with prophetic insight, did not set out to destroy Japan, but aimed at reshaping and rehabilitating the country so that it might be worthy of a place in the family of nations.

The United States decided that the basic structure of the

Japanese State should remain intact. The authority of the
Emperor and the Japanese Government, however, would be
subjugated to the Supreme Commander. MacArthur, on the
other hand, was advised to exercise his authority through the
Japanese governmental machinery and its agencies, including
the Emperor.

The Post-Surrender Policy Directive for Japan is a comprehensive, yet concise, statement. Its nine chapters contain, first
of all, an outline of its ultimate objectives. Secondly, they give
directives for establishing a military occupation — the relation
of the Occupation to the Japanese Government, the handling of
publicity, the encouragement of individual liberties and democratic processes and the disarmament and demilitarization of
Japan. Thirdly, they deal with the economic demilitarization
of Japan, the promotion of democracy in the economic field and
the resumption of peaceful economic activity. Further, the
directive prescribes the policies for reparations, for restitution
of property and for fiscal, monetary and banking activities. It
deals with the international aspect of trade and finance and
with Japanese property abroad. It even considers the property
of the Imperial Household.

3. *MacArthur's Personal Approach to Japanese Problem in Line
   with Official Directives*

Notwithstanding the explicit character of the post-surrender
policy directive, however, one might doubt whether a man who
did not fully comprehend its meaning or clearly evaluate its
fundamental issues, could have acted in conformity with its
spirit and accomplished its ultimate aim. Guiding the defeated
Japanese nation was a tremendous task indeed. MacArthur was
not a man to execute instructions without further questioning.
He had to understand their meaning fully — to agree completely with their purpose — before complying with them. A
task of so challenging a nature as directing the Occupation of
Japan could only have been undertaken by MacArthur when
he had a firm belief in his mission and after he had formed a
clear picture of how to discharge his duties. One can visualize
MacArthur, pacing the floor of his temporary headquarters

during those difficult days on the road back to Manila and Tokyo. One can imagine how he struggled with the question: „What shall we do with Japan?" In view of MacArthur's nature the question must have been a very personal and direct one. „What shall *I* do with Japan?" was probably how he put it. He had undoubtedly formulated the answer long before receiving the directives of the Joint Chiefs of Staff. MacArthur was convinced of the historic importance of the Allied undertaking; he understood the necessity of punishing the aggressor and of limiting the possibilities of a renewed imperialistic adventure. But he was opposed to the annihilation of the Japanese nation; he did not want to destroy the country; his desire was to take the Japanese people by the hand and lead them up the road to freedom, self-respect and recovery. Therefore, when on September 2, 1945, from aboard the U.S.S. Missouri, the Supreme Commander announced that it was his firm intention to proceed with justice and tolerance in the discharge of his responsibility, he was not merely speaking euphemistically. The main actor in this coming drama was conscious that history would judge how he played his role, and that the fate of Japan, in fact the future of the entire Far East, depended on his decisions and the way they were carried out.

4. *Allied Nations as well as Japan Fail to Grasp Intended Implementation of Chosen Policy*

Aboard the Missouri, three admirals and six generals, representing Australia, Canada, China, France, the Netherlands, New Zealand, the Soviet Union, the United Kingdom and the United States, put their signatures to the instrument of surrender, thereby formally accepting the Japanese surrender under the terms of the Potsdam Declaration. At the same time they expressed the agreement of their respective countries that the Occupation be guided by this declaration. Yet, one might doubt whether they and their Governments grasped the full significance of their promise — whether they foresaw in what spirit the Supreme Commander planned to comply with the surrender terms. Had they had a clear idea of MacArthur's intentions, they might have given their adherence more hesitatingly, their signature less willingly. In that case, some of these emissaries might — there and then — have been suspicious or mistrustful of the American attitude toward the former enemy. The developments, however, which were to create these sentiments still lay hidden in the future. The general satisfaction at the victory that had been won and the happiness that the costly and bloody campaign was ended, prevailed over any differences of opinion as to Japan's future.

In the distance, however, the rumbling of a new and much greater conflict in Asia could be heard. Where Japan's imperialism had been crushed, Soviet expansionism stood ready to take its place. The Russian delegate aboard the Missouri, by his stiff and rather cold attitude, hinted at his country's regret at the Allied refusal to appoint General Vasilevsky as Commander-in-Chief in Tokyo, with a rank equal to that of General MacArthur. This incident was one of the first of the long series of Allied disagreements which were to follow.

The Japanese representatives on board the American battleship in Tokyo Bay — where less than 100 years before Commodore Perry's ships had forced open the doors of Japan — must have realized clearly that their great adventure to conquer the world had ended in utter defeat. It will remain open to doubt whether the Japanese, who accepted the provisions of the surrender by command and on behalf of the Emperor and the Japanese Government — as well as on behalf of the Japanese Imperial General Headquarters — apprehended the meaning of General MacArthur's words. Certainly they did not realize that this new era in the history of Japan would be as dramatic in its changes and as creative in its implications as had been the Meiji Restoration, which followed the opening of Japan in the middle of the 19th century by the Western powers. Did the Japanese experience any feeling other than deep shame, sullen resentment, doubt and fear for the future? The suddenness and completeness of their defeat had doubtlessly numbed their minds and spirits. On the other hand, a certain amount of hatred toward the victors must have prevailed in their hearts. The humble attitude of the Japanese delegates, however, served as an effective cloak to hide their true inner sentiments.

5. *The Curtain Rises*

Notwithstanding the feelings, the hopes and the considerations of the men present at that significant ceremony aboard
the mightiest of America's warships in early September 1945,
the curtain of history was raised for a new act, revealing the
stage for one of the most spectacular dramas in the history of
Japan and of the world.

CHAPTER II

THE AMERICAN CHARACTER
OF THE OCCUPATION

The predominantly American character of the Occupation is contrary to the wishes of some other Allies, in particular the Soviet Union. Yalta Conference gives Stalin hope of realizing Soviet plans in Japan. After Potsdam Conference, however, Stalin's hopes are gradually frustrated, notwithstanding Russian participation in war. The claims of the Soviet Union and the British Commonwealth to participate in Occupation is voiced during London Conference. At Moscow Conference, however, preponderant position of United States in Japan is retained.

1. *Allied Occupation of Japan Implemented by United States*

At approximately the same time as the protocol of surrender was signed, the occupation of Japan actually began. By combined air and seaborne landings MacArthur's combat troops invaded Japan's major ports, industrial areas and population centers, while naval and air forces patrolled, prepared to support if necessary. No resistance was offered. The purely military phase of occupying the enemy country was brought to an end smoothly and quickly.

On October 2, 1945, MacArthur's field headquarters was reorganized and the General Headquarters of the Supreme Commander for the Allied Powers, usually called GHQ, SCAP, was established in Tokyo. This organization was to serve the Supreme Commander in implementing the occupation policies. It was staffed chiefly by Americans and remained so during its existence.

The preponderant role of the United States in fighting World War II in the Pacific made it clear that the United States would take the most important and decisive part in determining the fate of post-surrender Japan.

The United States Army furnished the bulk of the occupation units, while powerful elements of the United States Navy and Air Force were stationed in and around Japan. By

November 15, 1945, about 400,000 American troops were participating in the Occupation.

So far as the other Allies were concerned, only a relatively small number of British Commonwealth forces took part in the Occupation. These forces were composed of Australian, New Zealand, British and a few Indian units, and some ships and planes of the Royal Navy and the Royal Australian Air Force. The Commander-in-Chief of the Commonwealth Forces, General Robertson of Australia, was justly proud of the favorable impression his troops made in Japan. The popularity of their colorful regimental band and of their marching soldiers on the Tokyo parade-grounds was matched only by their efficiency in executing their occupation duties. Yet, as mere token forces their political influence was negligible. The British Commonwealth units were integrated in the American occupation army. Their commanders served, for all practical purposes, under the American field commanders. The Commonwealth troops, organized as part of the U.S. Eighth Army, occupied a section of southern Honshu, their main garrisons being in Kure and atombombed Hiroshima. The military government teams in this zone, which constituted the only official contact between the Occupation and the Japanese, were however, exclusively American and directly subordinated to the General Headquarters in Tokyo. The Commonwealth forces played no part except in the purely military phase of the Occupation and their number remained small throughout. The first contingent of Australians arrived in Japan in February 1946. By the middle of 1946, Commonwealth troops numbered 39,000. As of February 1947 their strength was reduced substantially, and their participation would have been terminated in the summer of 1950, but for the outbreak of the Korean war.

Because of the intermittent war between the Chinese Communists and the Nationalist Government, the Chinese did not take part in the Occupation.

The Russians abstained from sending troops to Japan when the United States declared that they would be accepted only as an integral part of MacArthur's occupation forces. Officials in Moscow, who had hoped to occupy independently the island of Hokkaido, grudgingly shelved their plans.

The largely American character of the Occupation was further emphasized by the dominating personality of the Supreme Commander, General MacArthur, who acquired a special position in Japan by exercising a very personal and powerful influence on the Occupation. This Allied undertaking was, indeed, an American undertaking, and even more, a MacArthur "show". The Supreme Commander was, in practice, the American proconsul in Japan.

2. *American Character of Occupation contrary to Wishes of Some of the Other Allies; Stalin's Plans Regarding Japan*

The American-staffed headquarters, the numerical superiority of American troops in Japan, and the dominant position of the Supreme Commander symbolized the decisive role the United States was to play in post-surrender Japan. This, however, was not in accordance with the plans and wishes of several of the other Allied Powers. Only after a long diplomatic struggle did the Allies concede to this status.

The Soviet Union, principally, objected to the preponderant position of the United States in Japan. The U.S.S.R. had quite different plans for Nippon's future. In order to understand the attitude and aims of the Kremlin in this matter, one should review the Soviet policy in East Asia. One should remember that Stalin, pursuing the imperialistic plans of the Russian Czars, had cherished for many decades the dream of a great Soviet empire in the Far East. He had tried, time and time again, to expand Soviet influence in the Pacific region. He had envisaged incorporating Japan into the sphere of communist influence and had played with the idea of constructing a mighty Soviet fleet in the Japanese shipyards, by which he hoped to gain ascendency in the Pacific.

When Stalin, during the course of World War II, recognised the inevitability of the collapse of Japan, no doubt he felt that the chances of realizing his Far Eastern dreams had never been more promising. His main problem was in executing his plans. Stalin had the choice of acting independently, neglecting his wartime Allies, or cooperating with the Great Powers, fighting Japan. Stalin preferred the second choice. As early as January 1943, and again in October of the same year, the

Soviet leader secretly informed the Allies that Russia would join in the war against Japan after Germany's defeat. In October 1944, those assurances were repeated to the American Ambassador in Moscow.

3. *Outcome of Yalta Conference Favorable to Soviet Far Eastern Policy*

During the Yalta Conference, in February 1945, Russian participation in the war against Japan was one of the main topics of deliberation between Churchill, Roosevelt and Stalin. The agreements reached during this conference reveal that the American and British leaders at that time were of the opinion that compliance with Stalin's desires regarding the Far East constituted a reasonable compensation for Soviet contribution to the war. They agreed to restore Sakhalin, the Kuriles and Port Arthur to the Russians; moreover they recognized the pre-eminent position of the Soviet Union in Dairen and, more important, in Outer Mongolia and Manchuria. In fact, they assented to practically all of Stalin's wishes, and offered no resistance to a considerable extension of Soviet influence in Asia. They certainly were not cognizant of Stalin's secret desires and plans.

The American attitude in Yalta has been seriously criticized in recent years. In the light of present circumstances this criticism is not unwarranted. The strategic pattern, however, as it presented itself to the Allied leaders in the beginning of 1945, was quite different from the situation today. At that time the agreement seemed quite reasonable — even desirable. The war in Europe had not yet reached its climax; victory in the Pacific appeared far away. Russian participation was considered necessary in order to crush Japan's resistance without an enormous and undue sacrifice of American lives. This, also, was the opinion in Army circles, sponsored by General Marshall and endorsed by the American and British Combined Chiefs of Staff. Admiral Leahy, the Chairman of the United States Joint Chiefs of Staff, had held a different point of view; he believed that Japan could be defeated by sea and air power alone. But the Army won the day, and the Combined Staffs recommended that Russia should also join in.

Today we know that Leahy was right and that the armed might of Japan, and in particular the strategic potential of the Japanese Empire at that time, was greatly overestimated by the military advisers. But who can blame the President of the United States for following the explicit advice of the combined American and British military advisers on such a technical question, particularly in view of the then prevailing political climate in Washington and London. Consequently, it was decided that during the discussions with the Soviet leaders at Yalta, the United States and Britain would seek Russia's cooperation in the war against Japan. This was the underlying policy which guided the Allied leaders during Yalta as far as the Far East was concerned. They accepted in good faith the Soviet intentions and trusted Stalin as being sincere in his professed aims. The secret plans and dreams of the leaders of the Kremlin were safely hidden behind friendly and cooperative smiles.

Unfortunately, the Western leaders turned a blind eye to the fundamental issues of Soviet policy. They were too busily engaged in the immediate problem of victory in battle, and they were deceived by Stalin's apparently cooperative attitude. In the course of history, the Yalta Agreement will figure as a great diplomatic victory for the Kremlin. Stalin legalized his first and most important step on the road to the conquest of East Asia.

In some circles it is still believed that Stalin at Yalta was sincere in his endeavor to cooperate with the Western Powers — that he was truly convinced of the desirability of establishing peace and order in the Far East after Japan's defeat. There is, however, no great evidence for such a belief. On the contrary, the developments indicate that Stalin was waiting for the most opportune moment to pave the way for further Soviet conquests in the Far East. If he ever had intended to forsake his Far Eastern dreams and to favor the establishing of peaceful and independent nations in Asia, why did he keep secret the information he received from his Tokyo Embassy in the course of 1944 — that circumstances in Japan were deteriorating? Why did he fail to inform his Allies that in early 1945 the Japanese Government had requested Jacob Malik, the Russian Ambassador in Tokyo, to mediate in an armistice between Japan and her enemies? The only answer is that Stalin needed to wage war with Japan in order to realize his secret dreams. But in the spring of 1945 he was not yet prepared to enter the campaign. Moreover, he was only too glad that the American forces were bearing the brunt of crushing Japanese resistance. It suited the Kremlin for Japan to be severely defeated and for the United States to pay a high price for that defeat. Stalin aimed at creating a power vacuum in Japan, which could rapidly and easily be filled by Soviet communism.

4. *Stalin's Hopes Gradually Frustrated*

The foregoing shows that in the first half of 1945 the Soviet leaders were hopeful of carrying out their imperialistic plans in the Far East. A study of further developments, however, reveals that these hopes were gradually frustrated, especially so far as Japan was concerned. Slowly and hesitatingly Washington realized the deep significance of the Soviet wishes with regard to the Far East and, in particular, to Japan. It would, however, take four high-level international conferences in all to make Washington realize that it had to adopt a firmer attitude if it wanted to retain its position in Nippon, and it would take still longer to firmly convince the American Government of this necessity, as subsequent chapters will reveal.

The *Yalta* Conference of February 1945 was followed in July of the same year by a conference at *Potsdam*. Notwithstanding the fact that in some Allied circles a slight feeling of hesitation had been awakened, the net result of this conference was again a major victory for the Soviet Far Eastern policy. During the third of these international meetings, the *London* Conference of the Foreign Ministers of the Big Four in September of the same year, the first indications of America's reluctance and unwillingness to agree to the wishes of the Kremlin became apparent. And in December 1945, during the Foreign Ministers Conference at *Moscow*, the fourth and last international meeting of that year, a definite stand was taken by the United States; in theory the United States compromised, so far as the Allied participation in the Occupation of Japan was concerned, by agreeing to the establishment of the Far Eastern Commission and the Allied Council. In reality, however, this compromise was an American victory. The agreement reached in Moscow left the United States in a powerful and dominating position in Nippon.

To understand this development clearly a closer consideration of the events at these international conferences and the agreements reached is advisable. Moreover, such consideration will reveal to what extent the United States were willing to grant its Allies a voice in the Occupation of the former enemy country.

5. *Potsdam Conference Still Russian Victory.*

Some months after Yalta — which conference has been described above — the war in Europe was brought to a victorious conclusion. Germany was defeated. In order to settle the problems resulting from her surrender the Potsdam Conference was convened for July 6, 1945, and was attended by the Heads of State of America, Britain and Russia. By that time, Truman had succeeded Roosevelt, and Potsdam was the first international appearance for his new Secretary of State, Mr. James Byrnes. Moreover, during the conference, the British elections swept Churchill and Eden out of office, Attlee and Bevin taking their places. These changes placed the Western Allies, diplomatically speaking, in a rather weak position. Their spokesmen lacked the experience of the wartime leaders. The Allied policy was but a faithful continuance of the one followed in previous years. It failed to recognize the great changes in international relations. Moscow, on the other hand, had already reversed its apparent policy. The Soviets were about to return to their prewar course of action. For Moscow, the danger seemed to have passed. The German aggressor was crushed; Japan's resistance was soon to be broken. Russian leaders saw little reason to seek the friendship of the Western democracies. Although their open activities were still limited to the establishing of satellite governments in countries bordering the Soviet Union, they had already broken with their wartime policy of cooperation with the Allies. The Kremlin was back on its way to world domination. As a first step, Stalin hoped to achieve a political vacuum in Germany and Japan, into which Soviet power could easily flow. Stalin was willing to cooperate with the

Western Allies only in punishing and destroying the former enemies, thereby helping Moscow to create and to expand this vacuum.

Unfortunately, the people of the Western world did not realize this hard and cynical truth. In Britain and in the United States the Russians were greatly admired for their heroic part in the war against Germany. The Red Army had fought amazingly well. Stalin figured as a great wartime leader who had inspired the Russian people to stand firm in the dark days of the Moscow battle — perhaps saving the fate of the democratic world. A genuine feeling of good will toward Russia prevailed in the West. No wonder, then, that the leaders of the Western world were willing and even eager to continue the wartime cooperation with the Soviets in the post-surrender days. The creation of the United Nations at San Francisco gave reasons for high hopes. The Western Powers either were not aware of the changes in the Russian attitude, or preferred to ignore them.

The foregoing considerations are important in order to understand what happened at Potsdam. They describe the political climate which prevailed at the conference — a climate which greatly influenced the attitude of the American Secretary of State, Byrnes. On the one hand his decisions were governed by his wish to continue the wartime alliance with the Soviet Union; on the other hand he was reluctant to encourage the Soviets in their plans. He had seen enough of Soviet actions in eastern Germany and the violation of the Yalta Agreement in Poland, Rumania and Bulgaria. Byrnes would have preferred the Russians not to enter the war against Japan. He believed, however, that the Western Allies were compelled by the Yalta Agreement to accept Russia's participation. The Allies, according to the American Secretary of State, were bound to their wartime promises.

Stalin shrewdly discerned the American and British hesitation and the weakness of their position. He feigned reluctance to enter the war against Japan and to violate the Soviet-Japanese neutrality pact without open Allied backing. He induced the Allies to send him an official letter, requesting him to declare war upon Japan and he persuaded the Western Powers to urge Chiang Kai-shek to comply with the Russian wishes as stipulated at Yalta. The attitude of the Western Powers at the Potsdam Conference was very passive and weak, and their determination to maintain their position in the Far East was at its lowest ebb.

This is the more evident when one realizes how strong the American position in fact was. During this conference President Truman was informed of the successful completion of the atomic bomb experiments; the United States were ready to deliver the last shattering blow to Japanese resistance. Moreover, this resistance was already collapsing.

In July 1945 the Japanese approached the Kremlin anew, requesting the Russians to mediate in arranging an armistice. This time Stalin informed Washington and London of the Japanese move. The American and British reaction revealed how wrongly the West judged the situation; notwithstanding the fact that the atomic bomb could be expected to crush the last remnants of Japan's will to fight, and notwithstanding the fact that the Allies had proof that Japan's power of resistance was practically exhausted, Truman and Attlee formally asked the Soviet Union to take part in the war. Stalin did nothing to enlighten the Western leaders as to the Japanese situation. He deliberately made very little of the Japanese appeal for an armistice in order to be able to act as if, in his opinion, the matter was not worth investigating further. A Japanese armistice at that time would not have suited the Russians; the Kremlin did not want to lose the opportunity to share in the spoils.

6. *Russians Join Fighting Against Japan*

During the Potsdam Conference the United States and Britain, with the consent of China, issued a last appeal to the Japanese to surrender. This appeal, known as the Potsdam Declaration, had been made without Russian knowledge. When the Russians heard of it they became alarmed, lest the Potsdam Declaration should result in the war ending without their participating in the fighting. Molotov tried to delay the release of the Declaration. The Russian Minister for Foreign Affairs, however, was too late; the appeal already had been made public. Stalin was obviously annoyed. The Russians left Potsdam and hastened back to Moscow to declare war on Japan. On August 8, 1945,

Stalin proclaimed that, at the request of the Allies, he had decided to join the battle against the Japanese Empire. The war between Russia and Japan, however, turned out to be a very short one. On August 14, 1945, an armistice between the Japanese and Allied forces was agreed upon. The unconditional surrender of the Japanese followed, just six days after the Russian declaration of war.

On several fronts the actual fighting still continued for some days. Manchuria was one of them. The Russians made the most of this fact in order to magnify their active participation in the Far Eastern conflict. One communique after another appeared in the Moscow press, telling of sweeping victories of the Red Army over the Imperial Japanese forces. The Emperor eventually dispatched a special envoy to Manchuria to inform the Japanese Commander-in-Chief of the surrender. On August 22, 1945, Japan's Manchurian army also ceased its resistance. The Japanese forces were imprisoned by the Russians, and later were lead away as slave laborers. Japan's possessions on the mainland of Asia were taken over by the Russians. The Soviet armies, penetrating Japanese continental territory, rushed eastward to the Pacific coast line.

The developments in August 1945 resulted in a situation whereby, for the first time in history, Russia and the United States faced each other in the western Pacific as the only two major contestants. A new period in Russian American relationship in Asia had begun. Antagonism sprang up almost immediately between the two wartime Allies. The first difference of opinion concerned the occupation of Japan and the position of the Allies in that country after its surrender. It has since been revealed that as early as August 10, 1945, two days after the Russians joined the war, the Russian Government approached the American Ambassador in Moscow, suggesting that a Soviet general be appointed Co-Commander-in-Chief in Tokyo with a rank equal to MacArthur's. This proposal had been turned down. The Russians, however, evidenced that they would insist on a decisive voice in the occupation of Japan.

In this endeavor the Soviets found sympathy and support from the British Commonwealth. Immediately after the armistice it became clear that London and Canberra shared the Russian objection against the proposed American position in post-surrender Japan. Australia, in particular, hoped for an important role in the Pacific and desired an active part in the Occupation of the enemy country. Following the surrender the British, at the instigation of its Commonwealth members, asked that an Allied Commission be established in Tokyo. On August 21, 1945, the State Department invited the 11 main Powers in the war against Japan to an autumn conference in Washington in order to draft the policies for the occupation and to discuss the organization of an Allied Commission for the Far East. Washington obviously hoped that by taking the initiative it would strengthen its position in Japan.

7. Japanese Question Informally Discussed at London Conference

In September 1945 the third international conference of that year, a meeting of the Foreign Ministers of the Big Three, was held in London to study the problems resulting from the war in Europe. The Occupation of Japan was not included in the agenda. However, Molotov, the Russian representative, immediately raised the Japanese question and requested the establishment in Tokyo of a Four Power Allied Control Council, similar to the occupation control machinery in Berlin. He angrily accused the United States of failing to execute the surrender terms in Japan as had been decided at Yalta and Potsdam. Molotov charged the United States with being much too lenient toward the former enemy. Why not use the Japanese prisoners of war as slave laborers? Why not embark on a program of heavy punishment and thorough demolition of Japan? Such were the questions in the mind of the Soviet Minister of Foreign Affairs.

However, the American Secretary of State, Byrnes, refused to discuss Far Eastern questions. At first he was backed by Britain. Under pressure of the Commonwealth representatives — the Australian Minister of Foreign Affairs, Evatt, in particular — the Foreign Office, unfortunately, reversed its point of view and sided with Moscow in trying to persuade the United States to admit Allied participation in the formulation and execution of occupation policies for Japan. The British advocated the setting up of a Control Commission on which the most important nations of the Pacific war were to be represented.

Washington was reluctant to make any concessions; recent disappointing experiences in Hungary, Rumania and Bulgaria with similar international organs had put the State Department on its guard. Moreover, Byrnes was hesitant in agreeing to foreign interference in Japan, because of MacArthur's refusal to allow the slightest encroachment on his powers, especially when Russian-endorsed. The Supreme Commander had already taken a firm stand against granting the Soviets a separate occupation zone, and the State Department was certain of serious trouble if it acted against MacArthur's outspoken desires. In addition, Washinton was cognizant of the Soviet Union's intention to follow a harsh and vindictive policy in Japan. The Americans resisted such a course of action; they were resolved that the humane approach, advocated by the Potsdam Declaration, was sound and logical. They let it be known that they would adhere to their original policy. As soon as the Russians realized that the United States was a serious obstacle to the accomplishment of Soviet aims in Japan, Moscow set out to thwart America's predominant influence over the occupation of that country. The cold war about Japan cast its shadow ahead.

As a result of these developments, the London Conference ended in a deadlock, not only with regard to settling the European questions, but also with regard to the Far East. Britain and the United States reached some sort of compromise to set up a Far Eastern Advisory Commission, but the Russians rejected it. Molotov stated that in view of what had happened in Japan he doubted the use of their keeping a representative in Tokyo. When the Russians left London the problems under discussion remained unsolved.

The Americans had not purposely created this deadlock. On the contrary, Washington had sincerely tried to reach an agreement. It was still willing to go a long way in meeting the wishes of its wartime Allies. Although the United States had become suspicious of Stalin's aims and was less inclined to yield to the ever-increasing demands of the Soviets, Washington had not yet realized how very important the Far Eastern question was to Moscow. The deep interest of Russia in the Orient would, however, soon become more evident. In October 1945 the American Ambassador to the Kremlin, Averell W.

Harriman, visited Stalin at his summer resort on the Caspian Sea to discuss certain European problems. The Russian leader gave Harriman little opportunity to state his case. He immediately remarked that the American envoy had not touched upon the Japanese question. He told Harriman that the Soviet Union was seriously concerned about the manner in which the surrender policies were being implemented in Tokyo, and about MacArthur's treatment of the Soviet representative. As the Supreme Commander seemed to consider the Russian General Derevyanko "a mere piece of furniture", Stalin saw little reason for keeping him in Tokyo.

Stalin's remarks to Harriman were a revelation to the State Department. Was Moscow really so seriously interested in the Far East? Would a further exploration of the Russian wishes in this field clear the clouded sky of American-Soviet relations? Byrnes did not want to neglect any possibility of saving the gradually deteriorating wartime alliance. He suggested that another Foreign Ministers Conference be held in Moscow in December 1945.

8. *Moscow Conference Settles Problem of Occupation in Favor of United States*

In the meantime the State Departement convened the Far Eastern Advisory Commission, as agreed in September during the London talks. Immediately upon returning from London to Washington, Mr. Byrnes had issued invitations to the 11 Pacific nations to form a commission for the formulation and execution of the post-surrender policies for Japan. All the nations invited, with the exception of the Soviet Union, appeared in Washington on October 23, 1945. Moscow, persisting in its attitude, did not agree with the anticipated advisory nature of the envisaged commission.

One of the first actions of the newly installed Far Eastern Advisory Commission was to decide on a visit of orientation to Japan. The members left Washington in November 1945, returning in February 1946.

During this time the Conference of Foreign Ministers in Moscow, the fourth important international meeting held during 1945, took place, and the question of Allied participation in the Occupation of Japan was finally settled. Russia apparently realized that further obstruction would not enhance her opportunities of playing a more important part in the Japanese Occupation. She hoped that by agreeing now, she would get a change of pursuing her aims later. Consequently, she yielded to Allied pressure and consented to the American plans for the organisation of the Occupation. After long discussions a compromise was reached by the Big Four, by which a policy-making body, the Far Eastern Commission, was established in Washington, superseding the Far Eastern Advisory Commission. The Far Eastern Commission was to be the most important international organ on post-surrender policies for Japan. It consisted of 11 members: Australia, Canada, China, France, India, the Netherlands, the Philippines, the Soviet Union, the United Kingdom and the United States; later, Burma and Pakistan joined the Commission. An Allied Council — a purely advisory body — was set up in Tokyo, composed of members of the British Commonwealth, China, the Soviet Union and the United States.

The decision regarding the organization of the two international bodies constituted an American victory. During the conference it had become evident that the American attitude had stiffened. The United States was more determined than before to oppose any interference in Japan that would endanger the ultimate objectives of the Occupation. Consequently, Washington agreed only to the establishment of organizations definitely restricted in their powers. Allied pressure for a decisive voice in Japanese affairs had been successfully sidetracked at the Moscow Conference.

At first sight the *Far Eastern Commission* appeared to have been granted impressive powers — formulating the policies and setting forth the principles and standards for the obligations to be fulfilled by Japan under the terms of surrender. It had the right to review any directive and any action of the Supreme Commander involving policy decisions. It had, however, to respect the existing control machinery in Japan, including the chain of command from the United States Government to SCAP, and it had to accept the United States Government as the agency designated to transfer policy decisions to the Supreme Commander. Further, SCAP would remain the sole authority charged with the implementation of these decisions. In addition to this, the Far Eastern Commission had to accept the right of the United States Government to issue so-called interim directives, which could be issued whenever urgent matters arose not covered by policies already formulated by the Commission. By means of these provisions Washington hoped to overcome possible difficulties arising from the fact that the four Great Powers were virtually holding a right of veto in the Commission. The great authority which appeared at first sight to be vested in the Commission was in practice nullified by these arrangements. During the meetings of the Commission a lengthy debate would often develop, without any decision on the more substantial questions forthcoming. Then Washington would decide the issue by an interim directive. And the Far Eastern Commission, after some time, would endorse the American decision and adopt it as a policy statement of the Commission.

It is to the credit of the representatives in the Far Eastern Commission that notwithstanding the many controversial questions with which they had to deal, a great number of agreements were reached at a time when international commissions had become notorious for their disagreements. One of the most indicative examples of the working method of the Far Eastern Commission is the practically unaltered adoption of the American post-surrender policy directive as the Far Eastern Commission's official post-surrender policy in September 1947. The fact remains, however, that by using its prerogative to issue interim directives, Washington retained, during the entire Occupation, its right to take any action it deemed necessary.

Consequently, the actual influence of the Far Eastern Commission on major policy decisions was very slight. The Commission, however, exercised an indirect restraining influence on the handling of occupation problems by the United States and provided the major Powers with a legal channel through which to voice their opinions on the progress of the Occupation. Partly as a result of the Commission's wise decision to confer with closed doors, and partly as a result of some sort of gentlemen's agreement between the representatives on this Commission, it avoided becoming one of the numerous inept international agencies as have unfortunately sprung up since World War II. The Far Eastern Commission managed to remain a dignified institution, whose members devoted considerable time and energy to studying Japan's postwar problems. Its discussions were instrumental in convincing several of its members of the correctness and necessity of the American policy and its execution. It gave its members the opportunity to consider these measures and after due consideration to adhere to them. Its position, however, gradually but inevitably deteriorated into that of a high-level debating club.

The fate of the *Allied Council for Japan* was even less inspiring. Very soon after its establishment, this organization degenerated into complete sterility. The Council had been constituted as the eyes and ears of the Far Eastern Commission in Tokyo. It had been entrusted with certain definite powers. The purpose of its establishment had been to exercise control authority over Japan, together with the Supreme Commander, who was designated as its chairman; the Supreme Commander had to consult with the Council in advance of the issuance of orders on matters of substance and on any change in the regime of control. Fundamental changes in the Japanese constitutional structure and changes in the Japanese Government as a whole had to be submitted to the Council for consideration and advice; a dissenting opinion of a member of the Council could, according to its terms of reference, forestall the issuance of orders on such questions, pending agreement thereon in the Far Eastern Commission. This seemed to imply that the Council had almost permissive prerogatives.

But if any member of the Council had ever had the illusion that he could exercise any real power in Tokyo, his dreams were shattered during the first Council session. As has already been said, the Supreme Commander evidenced that he would tolerate no interference with the execution of his task or with the way he saw fit to implement his directives.

General MacArthur, in his welcoming address to the Council members on April 3, 1946, stated clearly that he considered the Council's powers to be limited to consultation and advice. No reference was made to any control authority of the Allied Council or to its relations with the Far Eastern Commission. During the second meeting, the Chief of SCAP's Government

Section, who had been admitted to answer a question put by the Soviet member, stressed the completely negative attitude of General Headquarters toward the Council. ,,The Allied Council", he remarked, ,,is not set up for the purpose of prying into SCAP affairs, attempting to find some weak point in SCAP armor".

In the beginning some serious work was done by the members of the Council. After some months, however, it became a forum for public attacks on SCAP. The Commonwealth representative frequently sided with his Soviet colleague in criticizing the Occupation. The gradual deterioration of the relations between the United States and the Soviet Union was reflected in increasing clashes between the American and Russian representatives on the Council. The other members, embarrassed by this situation, retreated to neutral positions. Only a very few examples of constructive advice can be cited. The most important were the recommendations on land reform and on wages and prices — both by the Commonwealth representative, Macmahon Ball. In later years the sharp tone of the discussions between the Soviet representative and the American delegate became notorious, particularly on the question of the repatriation of Japanese prisoners of war from Manchuria. Russia's failure to return those prisoners became the subject of a sort of cold war, fought in the Council's conference room in Tokyo. Both countries used the Allied Council as a public forum for their political propaganda campaigns. More often, however, the chairman, SCAP's highly competent Diplomatic Adviser, William J. Sebald, closed its weekly session after a one-minute reading of the agenda.

The foregoing pages show that the two official organizations created to exercise Allied influence on the Occupation of Japan were actually neutralized and made powerless. The policy decisions of the United States alone were to decide the fate of Japan. Furthermore, the actual leaders of the Occupation — the members of General Headquarters in Tokyo (where the Australian Brigadier John O'Brien was the only non-American General) the government teams in the country and the occupation troops — were principally American.

Consequently, the Occupation of Japan became an American undertaking. Although it was an Allied commitment, the

Allies took only a limited part in its execution and had hardly any voice in the implementation of its policies. This development was the logical consequence of a growing American suspicion as to the sincerity of the aims of the Soviet Union with regard to Japan. Yet, the undivided authority of General MacArthur and the unified command of the Occupation under American leadership saved Japan from many of the misfortunes which befell Germany as a result of its fourheaded control during post-surrender days.

CHAPTER III

THE WORK OF THE OCCUPATION BEGINS

MacArthur decides on rapid and drastic reforms which subsequently descend as an avalanche on Japan. Japan's prewar government system is overhauled; a new Constitution is promulgated; old leaders are purged; press and religion are freed; education is reformed; public health and welfare are encouraged; a land reform is effectuated; the economic structure is democratized; the Zaibatsu is liquidated; labor is organized, and women are emancipated. By the spring of 1946 the groundwork for the reformation has been laid, but the upper structure has still to be erected. Gradually, however, a tendency from correction and reformation toward reconstruction becomes discernible.

1. *MacArthur, Entering Tokyo, Contemplates Accomplishment of First Phase of Occupation; Decides on Rapid and Drastic Reforms*

MacArthur, accompanied by his wife and eight year old son, arrived in Tokyo on a hot, cloudy September day in 1945. A heavy, depressing atmosphere hung over the capital; the streets were desolate and silent. The few cars of the Supreme Commander and his personal staff were the only vehicles on the road from Yokohama to Tokyo. They moved through the war-devastated suburbs of the Japanese capital, where previously the sprawling industrial center of this widespread metropolis had been.

The Japanese people, stunned by the blow of the sudden surrender and sullen under the strain of living in their flattened city, hid from the entering conqueror. Doubtlessly they feared and hated the victorious enemy. Could it be that the Japanese Empire had been defeated? Was it possible that the mighty Japanese Army had been beaten and the Imperial Navy destroyed? The inhabitants of Tokyo remembered with horror the fire bombings, in which tens of thousands had been burned alive. With equal horror they heard the tales of the atomic bombing of Hiroshima and of Nagasaki — tales that slowly filtered through to the capital. What were the Japanese to think of this opponent who had forced the divine

Emperor to surrender, who had defeated the invincible Japanese warrior, who had destroyed so many historical landmarks of their beloved country and who had dared to enter their sacred land?

Not only did the Japanese fear, and perhaps hate, the invader; they deeply mistrusted his intentions. Uncertain about the behavior of the victorious soldiers entering their country, they hid their wives and daughters and locked themselves and their children behind the wooden enclosures of their humble homes. Not even a few of the thousands of ever present children were out on the lonely streets.

MacArthur, driving through the desolate city, may have pondered over the reasons for this complete silence. Was it fear? Was it smoldering hatred? Or was it the result of a well-organized demonstration, staged by the Japanese leaders, who, notwithstanding their humble bows aboard the U.S.S. Missouri, had decided on a program of secret sabotage? Or did it indicate a huge trap prepared for the army of occupation? Perhaps it was only mistrust and uncertainty about the future! MacArthur definitely hoped that feelings of doubt, and not of hatred and cunning prevailed; his conception of his occupation duties envisaged the eventual cooperation of the Japanese people. He hoped that the Japanese would learn to consider the occupation forces as the advocates and sponsors of a democratic way of life. MacArthur's aim was to reshape Japan into a free and democratic nation, where people would understand, cherish, and — if necessary — defend the high values of human liberty and individual dignity won at such a staggering cost in bloodshed and defeat. He saw his task as constructive rather than destructive, reformative rather than punitive.

When the September sun went down bloodred on the horizon in one of those gorgeous sunsets so well-known in Japan, MacArthur's mind, however, may have turned back to the fierce battles just fought and to the immeasurable loss of human lives in the struggle against the Japanese Empire. The Supreme Commander may have realized, more than ever before, that the Japanese people would have to remember forever that aggressive war does not pay. He may have felt that it should be made clear to the Japanese that the deep distress of their nation had been brought about by their own totalitarian leaders. MacArthur must have realized that stern and drastic measures of a punitive character had to precede any reformative action. The forces which had led Japan to war had to be crushed; the state of mind which had bred the imperialistic militarism of the preceding decade had to be annihilated. The enemy had to be prevented from ever returning to aggression.

In this state of mind the Supreme Commander set out to implement his occupation directives. The Japanese armed forces had to be demobilized, the country demilitarized and its military installations and war industries disassembled. The political institutions and philosophy of Japan had to be changed completely. The feudalistic structure of the Japanese State had to make place for that of a modern, peace-loving democracy. In the economic field the old bastions of concentrated power, which could so easily be used for the execution of totalitarian and warlike policies, had to be demolished. The Japanese economy had to be reshaped into a democratic and free system of enterprise — a system in which every citizen could take part, and which would be dedicated to benefit all people — not merely to profit a few. Culture, education, religion, the social system — the entire complex structure of Japanese nation-hood — had to be examined, had to be partly destroyed and reshaped to serve a new and peaceful Japan.

Although the road to peace was obstructed by mountainous difficulties, the Supreme Commander embarked upon the fulfilment of his task with amazing zest and vigor.

2. An Avalanche of Reforms Descends on Japan

An avalanche of orders and instructions constituting sweeping changes was launched. In rapid succession one old institution after another was liquidated, and new ones were created. The work continued day by day without interruption. This breath-taking pace was to be kept up for many months. Never before in history had any nation received such a thorough and swift overhauling; never before had a peaceful revolution been more drastic.

A brief enumeration of these reformations follows below; later on a more detailed study will be made.

On September 29, within three weeks of the arrival of the Supreme Commander in Japan, the program was initiated by restoring complete freedom to the press and other organs of public information.

On September 30 the Japanese Army and Navy General Staffs were abolished, and as early as October 15 the Japanese armed forces were liquidated as an organization. By November 30, 1945, 7.000.000 servicemen from the Japanese Army, Navy and Air Force had been disarmed and demilitarized. On that date it was officially announced that the demobilization of all armed forces within Japanese territory had been completed. In the meantime, on October 31, the Big Four reached an agreement on the destruction of what was left of the once proud Imperial Japanese Navy. The ships of the Rising Sun disappeared from the waters of the sea, where until recently they had created havoc and distress. The War and Navy Ministries were abolished and reinstituted as demobilization bureaux, with the task of taking care of the remaining administrative problems. In an amazingly short time, without any bloodshed and without even any serious disturbances, the mighty Imperial forces of Japan were disbanded and their members returned to civilian life. "Japan is unable to stage a military comeback for the first hundred years", declared the Supreme Commander in the spring of 1946 . With due consideration of oratorical effect, this declaration was true. The proud Imperial Army and Navy and its nerve center, the Japanese Imperial Staff, had indeed been liquidated.

On October 4, 1945, all laws restricting political, civil and religious liberties were suspended, thereby freeing the Japanese individual from the shackles which had been imposed on him by the totalitarian regime. In addition, many political prisoners were released, and the Government received orders to liquidate its secret police. These measures were followed by an announcement on October 31 that all militaristic and ultra-nationalistic organizations had to be disbanded immediately.

On October 13, 1945, the Japanese women were enfranchized. On the same date a commission for the revision of the Japanese Constitution was established. As early as January 31, 1946, a tentative draft of a revised Constitution was made public.

On July 3, 1946, the Far Eastern Commission in Washington unanimously approved the basic principles of the new Japanese Constitution; a milestone had been reached in the liberalization of Japan and in the creation of a new and democratic State. On August 24, 1946, the new Constitution passed the House of Representatives, and on August 26 it was accepted by the House of Peers. It was promulgated October 3, 1946, and the basic law of the new Japan became effective as from April 1, 1947.

The march toward freedom continued. Japan's economic strongholds did not escape SCAP's attention. On October 15, 1945, a spokesman for the Supreme Commander warned the ten prominent business families in Japan, the famous Zaibatsu, that the dissolution of their organizations could soon be expected. On November 6 the liquidation of the Zaibatsu was initiated. SCAP ordered the immediate dispersal of the Mitsui, Mitsubishi, Yasuda and Sumitomo holding companies. On March 16, 1946, the reorganization of the remaining six large holding companies, controlling 139 major and minor industrial companies, followed. A major attack on one of Japan's foremost bulwarks of concentrated and excessive power had been launched.

The educational system of Japan was not left untouched. On October 25, 1945, a thorough survey of educational institutions was ordered, followed by far-reaching changes in the entire educational system.

The arrest of war criminals, started immediately after the surrender, proceeded swiftly. By October 5, 1945, 1,000 had been taken into custody. On November 19 the arrest of 12 high-ranking Japanese officials suspected as war criminals followed. Between December 3 and 6 a further 100 prominent Japanese were arrested. On January 15, 1946, 110 high army officials, including seven lieutenant-generals, were taken into custody. On February 15 of the same year the installation of the International Military Tribunal of the Far East for the trial of Class-A war criminals was announced. Twenty-five of Japan's highest officials, including Premier Tojo and several of his ministers, were to be tried by this court. Early in March 1946 the Tribunal began its momentous task.

Japan's industrial potential had to be curbed. On November

15, 1945, President Truman's personal envoy, Ambassador Edwin W. Pauly, returning from Japan, declared with reference to the anticipated reparation policy for Japan: "We will remove everything that is not needed for a useful minimum economy". On January 22, 1946, the dismantling of 400 Japanese aircraft factories, army and navy arsenals and munition industries was ordered as part of the reparations.

On November 21, 1945, the Imperial Household was affected; its funds were frozen.

"War does not pay", said General MacArthur on November 25, 1945, ordering the Japanese Government to impose severe war taxes, stripping Japanese firms and individuals of profits gained during World War II.

On December 10, 1945, two sweeping programs for agrarian reform were initiated by MacArthur.

On December 16, 1945, Shintoism was dissolved as the State religion.

On January 4, 1946, the so-called "purge" was initiated by a directive ordering the Japanese Government to remove from public office and to exclude from government service all persons who had actively engaged in militaristic and ultra-nationalistic activities.

On February 1, 1946, the wings of the Japanese Foreign Office were clipped: its political and economic bureaux were abolished, and only a general affairs and an information bureau were allowed to continue.

3. *Groundwork for Reformation of Japan Laid by Spring 1946; Upperstructure Still to be Erected*

During the following years of the Occupation many further additions were to be made to this impressive list of activities. By the spring of 1946, however, it could be said that the groundwork for the reformation of Japan had already been laid. MacArthur brought this fact to the attention of the world by stating, at the opening session of the Allied Council for Japan on March 12, 1946, that most of the reformative directives required by the Potsdam Declaration had been issued to the Japanese Government. The demilitarization of Japan was progressing rapidly. The destruction of militaristic organizations

had been commenced. The feudalistic and totalitarian structure
of the Japanese Government had been demolished, and a new
pattern had been set. A beginning had been made with the slow
and difficult process of building a new Japan and of preparing
the minds and hearts of the Japanese people for their task as
worthy citizens of a democratic and peaceful nation.

Of course, all these changes and reforms were only the
first steps on a long and difficult road. "Much has been
accomplished, much still remains to be done", remarked the
Supreme Commander in his address to the Japanese on September 2, 1946, one year after the signing of the surrender
terms. The coming years were to bring many more changes. The
framework of the new Japan, however, had been erected; the
basis of the work to be done had been laid. The future task
would be one mainly of elaboration and maturation.

In order to judge the over-all results of the Occupation and
to evaluate objectively Japan's present position in international
relations, a deeper understanding of the changes wrought in
Japan in the first years after the surrender should be gained. A
more detailed review of the measures taken by the Supreme
Commander in demilitarizing and democratizing Japan is
therefore desirable.

The foremost objective of the Allied policy with regard to
Japan was to make sure that Japan would not again become a
menace to the peace and security of the world. To attain this
aim, a thorough demilitarization of the Japanese nation had to
be undertaken simultaneously with the democratization of the
Japanese people and their political, social and economic institutions. This constituted a comprehensive task. Japan had to be
completely disarmed and demilitarized; the basis of her militarism and the influence of her totalitarian leaders had to be
eliminated. Drastic political reforms had to be effected, and
sweeping changes in the social and economic fields had to be
made in order to assure a lasting effect of the reformations.

The initial post-surrender policy directive for Japan was
very explicit with regard to the reformative actions to be taken
in Japan. It prescribed that high military officials and leaders of
ultra-nationalistic and militaristic organizations had to be
taken into custody and held for future trial. It ordered the
removal of people who had been active exponents of militarism

and militant nationalism from public offices and other responsible positions. It prescribed that ultra-nationalistic and militaristic societies and institutions in the political, social, educational and economic fields were to be dissolved. Laws, decrees and regulations which implied discriminations had to be abrogated. Agencies which interfered with the freedom and liberty of the individual had to be abolished or modified. In short, a complete housecleaning of all totalitarian and militaristic organizations and institutions had to be accomplished.

Besides this initial task, MacArthur's directives emphasized the constructive aims of the Occupation. The judicial, legal and police systems had to be reformed and thereafter progressively influenced to protect the civil rights and liberties of the individual. The democratization of Japan had to be encouraged in as broad and varied a field as possible. A far-reaching political reform was anticipated in order to change the prewar Japanese government structure, which was of a frankly totalitarian character. In short, everything contrary to the aims of the Occupation had to be destroyed; everything acceptable had to be kept or modified. New ideals, a new conception of life and new political, economic and social institutions had to be introduced.

The most important part of this huge occupation task was the political reform of the Japanese nation — of its government and basic laws. This reform will be studied first.

4. Japan's Pre-War Government System Overhauled

The initial post-surrender policy states that one of the ultimate objectives of the Allies with regard to Japan was eventually to establish a peaceful and responsible Government which would respect the rights of other States and support the objectives as reflected in the ideals and principles of the Charter of the United Nations. The post-surrender policy desires that the new Japanese Government should conform as closely as possible to the principles of democratic self-government. On the other hand, it clearly states that the Allied Powers are not responsible for imposing upon Japan any form of government not supported by the freely expressed will of the people. The post-surrender policy directive stipulates that the Japanese people should be "encouraged" to develop a desire for individual liberties and respect for fundamental human rights, particularly for the freedom of religion, assembly, speech and the press; they should be inspired to form democratic and representative organizations and political parties. A special chapter of the directive elaborates on the necessity of encouraging in the Japanese people the desire for individual liberties and for democratic processes.

The implementation of this part of the post-surrender directive was a tremendous undertaking. In order to assist the Supreme Commander in executing the anticipated political reformations, a special staff section of the General Headquarters, the Government Section, was organized. It began its work on October 2, 1945. All problems of political administration were entrusted to this Section.

Japan's prewar Government was a national bureaucratic oligarchy, exercising the three powers of government — legislative, executive and judicial — in the name of the Emperor. The Imperial institution formed the top of the pyramidal structure of the Japanese State. All authority was concentrated in the Emperor. A rather cumbersome and obscure law, known as the Meiji Constitution, adopted in 1890, formed the basis of the Japanese State. The bureaucracy represented the most powerful influence in the Government, with the Army and Navy Ministries exercising an unrestricted control, — in fact holding some sort of veto over the legislative branch. The Government had no independent judiciary branch. Local governments, moreover, were merely administrative subdivisions. Since 1890 Japan had known a bicameral representative institution, the Imperial Diet. Its position and influence, however, had grown insignificant. Between 1890 and 1920 fair progress toward parliamentary government had been made, notwithstanding the legal and institutional disabilities of the Diet. But in the late 1930's the totalitarian influence in Japan, exercised mainly by the Army, wrecked parliamentary progress. The country was rapidly reverting to totalitarianism, and the theory of government which saw in parliament the real center of power, was completely rejected. A huge police organization backed the Japanese Government in its totalitarian aspirations; the prewar police system in Japan was a single, nationwide force which controlled the daily

life of every Japanese. A separate and independent chain of
communication ran from every police box in Japan to the Home
Ministry in Tokyo. Through this system every move of the
80,000,000 Japanese was controlled by the central government,
in the name of the Emperor.

The foregoing summary evidences that Japan had a government of men, and not a government of law. The Japanese, in
fact, formed an extremely regimented nation, governed by an
oligarchic dictatorship.

The first step toward political reformation, therefore, was
to remove the restrictions to the freedom of thought, religion,
assembly and speech, and to restore the basic concepts of
freedom and human dignity. On October 4, 1945, a directive
was issued which freed the Japanese people from these restrictions.

The question then arose as to how the political structure
should itself be reformed. The post-surrender policy directive
only stated that the Japanese people should be "encouraged"
to form a democratic government. It had, however, purposely
avoided ordering the Supreme Commander to impose such
a government. On the contrary, it stressed that the Japanese
had to remain free to choose the form of government they
wanted. It even went so far as to say that in the case of the
Japanese people reverting to force in their desire to change the
form of government, the Supreme Commander should only
interfere when it was necessary to ensure the security of his
forces and the accomplishment of the other objectives of the
Occupation.

The instructions of the Supreme Commander, however,
were so broad that in practice MacArthur was left to decide
how the political democratization of Japan should be realized.
MacArthur could choose between two extreme solutions of
this problem. He could wait for a basic constitutional reform
in Japan to result from the gradual changes which the Occupation would try to induce in the social and political make-up
of the Japanese people. Or he could direct the Japanese to
make immediate basic changes in their constitutional law,
and thus impose a series of basic reforms; in that case he would
depend on these reforms to create an environment in which a
democratic conception of life could develop.

MacArthur chose the second method. Under the circumstances of the Occupation the process had to be swift if any enduring results were to be expected. The second method was the quicker and therefore seemed the better way. Consequently, after the Japanese had been freed from all political restrictions, three consecutive steps were taken to initiate a basic reform: (1) The governmental structure was redesigned and based on a radically amended Constitution; (2) new political leadership was fostered by the removal and exclusion of prewar and wartime politicians, and (3) the interest in political life was awakened by the sponsoring of nationwide elections.

5. New Constitution Promulgated

The main step was the introduction of a new constitutional law. As early as September 1945 the Prime Minister of Japan was informed by General MacArthur that complete democratization of the structure of the Japanese Government was required, beginning with the liberalization of the Constitution. Constitutional reform was considered by SCAP of first importance. On October 11, 1945, the Supreme Commander's viewpoint in this matter was repeated more forcefully. He directed the Japanese Cabinet to initiate measures for the complete reformation of the Constitution. The Emperor ordered Prince Konoye to form a constitutional investigation committee, within the office of the Lord Privy Seal. In line with the basic concept of the Occupation, it was considered preferable that the reform of the Japanese Constitution be commenced and executed by the Japanese themselves.

A period of study and widespread discussion followed. Tangible results, however, were lacking. SCAP became impatient, and early in February 1946 the problem of drafting a revised Constitution was taken over by the Government Section of MacArthur's Headquarters. On March 6 the American draft was completed, and, after it had been translated, was issued by the Japanese Cabinet as an original document, MacArthur placing behind it the weight of his personal approval. Inevitably, some Japanese criticized its un-Japanese character. After a thorough debate, however, and after some amendments, the new Constitution passed the Diet. It was promulgated on October 3, 1946, and became law May 3, 1947.

The "modus operandi" of introducing this new law perhaps was not exactly forthright. Its strict compliance with the directives as issued to SCAP in regard to political reforms in Japan was also open to doubt. The Supreme Commander obviously had done more than merely encourage the Japanese. They had been more or less compelled to accept MacArthur's vision of the new Constitution. The free expression of their will had been strongly influenced. The procedure, however, was the logical outcome of the method chosen for implementing the Occupation reforms; a set of basic reforms had been incorporated; a procedure whereby such reforms would have been allowed to grow and develop as the minds of the Japanese gradually became adjusted to the new social and political ideas, would probably never have led to concrete results. Looking back, the way followed was the only practicable one to provide Japan with a new constitutional law. The sharp edges have worn off; most of what seemed incomprehensible has become understood; a great part of what seemed foreign and unacceptable has become familiar and desirable.

The new Constitution drew on the experience of many other countries and incorporated the essentials of modern representative democracy. The Imperial institution underwent a complete change of character. The Emperor no longer formed the source of all sovereignty. Under the new Constitution sovereignty resided with the people. The Emperor was retained as a constitutional monarch to serve as a symbol of the State and of the unity of the people.

A bicameral national Diet was established as the highest organ of state power and as the sole law-making organ of the State. Both Houses were to be elected by universal adult suffrage. The executive power was to be vested in a Cabinet collectively responsible to the Diet. An independent judiciary branch of the Government was created, with the Supreme Court as its highest organ. The principle of local government was recognized. Fundamental human rights were guaranteed to the people, and the spheres of individual freedom, into which the Government could not move without the individual's consent, were designed in a chapter which has become known as the Japanese "Bill of Rights", As an innovation in the history of human relationships, the threat or use of force as a way of settling international disputes was officially renounced. Undoubtedly this Constitution provided Japan with a strong base upon which to build a peaceful and democratic nation.

6. *Old Leaders Purged; New Leaders Elected*

It is highly questionable whether the political reformation could have endured, except as a theory, had not a new leadership — sympathetic to the movement and devoted to its support — emerged, along with the renovation of the Government.

The development of such a new leadership, therefore, had to be encouraged.

Two major actions were undertaken for this purpose. The first was the removal of the undesirable former leaders. Those persons who had been instrumental in shaping and executing Japan's prewar course of aggression and totalitarianism were ordered removed and excluded from public life. The second action aimed at sponsoring a new leadership. Popular elections were fostered to offer the people an opportunity to bring forward new leaders.

The first measure is known as the purge. It was initiated by a SCAP directive, issued January 4, 1946, directing the Japanese Government to remove and exclude from public office all persons who in one capacity or another had been influential in promoting militarism. Under the close supervision of GHQ, SCAP the purge was carried out in several phases and finally completed in May 1948. A total of 202,000 persons — bureaucrats, politicians, militarists, diplomats, educators, journalists, and business, finance and industrial magnates — were designated as purgees.

No other aspect of the Occupation aroused more controversy than this nationwide purge. Some people criticized it as being too lenient; others feared that the best brains of Japan had been removed from public service. In a program of such scope, mistakes inevitably were made. Undoubtedly some hard-core ultra-nationalistic leaders escaped the purge. Surely many fine minds were denied participation in directing post-surrender Japan. The program as such, however, was essential in order to implement the reforms desired by the Occupation. In view of the fact that the Occupation, in its reformative operations, worked with, and through, the existing machinery of the Japanese Government, the necessity of removing from public life those persons who were likely to sabotage any change or reform cannot be questioned.

In judging the results of the purge one has to remember that this drastic interference in Japan's public life inevitably called for the rise of new leaders in the political, social and economic fields, leaders free from the suspicion of wishing to return to prewar totalitarianism or militarism, desirous of building a new Japan.

In order to give the people an opportunity to bring forward these new leaders, nationwide elections were sponsored by the occupation authorities. Based on a liberalized General Election Law, promulgated in December 1945, an election of members of the Diet was held in April 1946. Contrary to the opinion of the Far Eastern Commission and of many other authorities who considered the holding of general elections premature, the Supreme Commander insisted on having them. He believed that if the Japanese Government was going to be utilized in the advancement of the occupation's objectives, it had to work with and through a constitutionally elected Diet, rather than through the remainder of wartime elected representatives.

The April 1946 elections were a success. Seventy-two percent of the electorate exercised their right to vote. The new General Election Law extended the franchise to women and lowered the voting age to 20. As a result of these new regulations many people previously excluded from voting participated in the elections. A more representative Diet came into being. From then on, real vigilance in exercising their newly won political rights and liberties was maintained by the Japanese people, not only on the national, but also on the prefectural and local levels. The April 1946 and following elections were highly instrumental in awakening and kindling their interest in the political problems of their country.

The crucial question, however, was: How deeply would the political reformations penetrate into the Japanese way of life? How much would these newly acquired liberties and rights, these new duties and responsibilities, become an acknowledged part of Japanese nationhood? How much would remain foreign and superimposed; how much would be genuinely accepted and become an inherent part of the Japanese way of thinking and acting; how essential would this new conception of political life become to the Japanese; how sincerely would it be cherished; how vigorously would it be defended? Obviously, in 1946 and 1947, it was impossible to estimate the long-term influence and the results of those political reformations. Only a framework had been erected; only a basis had been laid. Most of the work had yet to be done.

MacArthur was convinced that, for the political reforms to endure, parallel reformations in all social and economic aspects of Japanese life had to follow — in press and public relations, in religion, in education, in health and welfare services, in the status of the agricultural and industrial workers, in labor relations — in short, in the over-all structure of the economic and social system of Japan. The success of these key reforms would largely determine how great a part of the political reforms, initiated by the Occupation, would become permanent in Japan.

7. *Press and Religion Freed; Education Reformed*

A democratic reform, in order to be permanent, has to be based upon the people's deep understanding of the free and democratic conception of life. Reformations in the spiritual and cultural sphere were therefore of great importance to Japan. Their attainment, moreover, was one of the most difficult and complex tasks of the Occupation.

A prerequisite was the dissemination of information regarding the rest of the world. Japan had been closed for a long period; the people had been denied the possibility of learning of the happenings and changes in other countries. This had to be remedied. The Occupation abolished all restrictions on the press and on the relaying of news in the widest sense of the word. An enormous informational program was launched, covering such broad fields as political education, the emancipation of women, labor-management relations and several other spheres of political, economic and cultural life. Seventeen information centers were organized, divided over the four main islands of Japan. The reading and reference material in each consisted of at least 6,000 books in English, 400 periodicals and several thousand documents and pamphlets covering a wide variety of subjects. The improvement of the Japanese broadcasting system was encouraged; a variety of radio programs became available to the Japanese; the number of radio sets was estimated in 1949 at one for each four families and is steadily increasing. Newspaper circulation increased greatly after the end of the war. By December 1949 the total circulation was more than 27,900,000 copies a day, or one copy for every 2.9 persons. Daily papers were supplemented by numerous magazines of a popular and specialized character. At the end of 1949 the circulation was estimated at 55,000,000. The Japanese press generally adopted a code of ethics modeled after that of the American Newspaper Publishers Association and began to show a greater objectivity and accuracy in news reporting. Freedom of the press became a zealously guarded privilege of the Japanese people.

Another important cultural reform was the liberation of religion. In prewar Japan, Shintoism as the State religion formed an important instrument for maintaining a strictly controlled totalitarian regime. Through it the leaders of Japan had controlled the spiritual life of the Japanese people; it had served to encourage ultra-nationalistic aims and had permeated these aims with a spiritual purpose. The predominant influence of Shintoism, therefore, had to be broken. On December 16, 1945, Shintoism was disestablished as the official State religion and freedom of religion was proclaimed.

The task of accomplishing these reforms was entrusted to the Civil Information and Education Section, established September 22, 1945. Its most important duty, however, was to free Japanese education from its former feudalistic and militaristic influences. A daring program was launched, and Japan's educational system was completely reorganized. A new educational law, passed by the Japanese Diet in 1947, abolished the old discriminatory educational ladder. Replacing the old system by the so-called 6–3–3 system, it assured the perpetuation of educational privileges to all Japanese children, boys and girls alike. The 1947 Educational Law was based on the new Constitution of Japan, which states, specifically:

"All people shall have the right to receive an equal education, correspondent to their ability, as provided by law.
All people shall be obligated to have all boys and girls
under their protection receive ordinary education as provided by law. Such compulsory education shall be free".

The implementation of these principles opened a new chapter
in the history of Japanese education.

Simultaneously, the Ministry of Education, a bastion of
rigid control and regimentation, was reorganized from an
agency of centralized administration into an effective professional service agency to assist institutions and educators
in their manifold problems. Furthermore, textbooks were
liberalized, the training of educators was initiated and school
buildings were erected throughout the country. The completion
of this ambitious program would take a long time, but the
pattern had been set, and the basis for free and constructive
education in Japan had been created.

8. *Public Health and Welfare Encouraged*

The foregoing pages show that in the political and cultural
spheres a much more thorough work had been undertaken
than the mere encouragement of the Japanese people toward
democracy. The occupation authorities, during the first year
of the occupation of Japan, had not only launched severe
attacks on the militaristic and ultra-nationalistic tendencies
of Japan, but also had initiated a huge constructive and reformative program.

Among other endeavors, the work done in public health
and welfare must be mentioned in particular. This has proved
to be a real blessing to Japan. It was started with a view to
safeguarding the Occupation against widespread disease and
unrest, which would inevitably follow in the war's wake; but
it was rapidly expanded into a large-scale program of fostering
and preserving the public health and welfare of the Japanese
people. The execution of this task was the responsibility of the
Public Health and Welfare Section, which accomplished it
in a most thorough manner. Inspired by the highest ideals of
their medical profession, Brig. General C. F. Sams, the Chief
of this Section, and his staff erected a lasting monument to the

unselfishness and benevolence of the American Occupation of Japan.

Before World War II health and welfare activities in Japan were primitive and ineffective, and the state of public health had deteriorated even further under wartime conditions. In order to carry out health and welfare programs, a sound organization from the national to the local level had to be established. Under American guidance the Japanese Ministry of Welfare was reorganized, and in 1946 and 1947, health and welfare departments were set up in all prefectural governments. A large program of preventive medicine was introduced and medical institutions were modernized. Social security was expanded to include the total working population. Such sweeping reforms and changes, as represented by these public health and welfare programs, needed time, patience and perseverance to develop and mature. The basis was laid, but much advise, guidance and training were necessary to implement these reformations. The benefit of this undertaking will probably not be fully realized for years to come.

9. *The Agrarian Problem*

Another major role in initiating reforms and promulgating democratic principles for the Japanese people was played by the Natural Resources Section. The work of this Section touched chiefly on the agrarian population of Japan. Its responsibilities were very large. Yet the success with which this relatively small but efficiently directed staff section of GHQ, SCAP accomplished its extensive mission was prodigious. Under the exceptionally competent leadership of Professor H. G. Schenk, formerly of Michigan University, this Section displayed a great interest in and devotion to its work. Far-reaching reforms in agriculture, fisheries, mining and forestry were effected, in both the political and social, and technical fields. A thorough survey of Japan's natural resources was made — in fact Japan may be the most elaborately described country in the world — and highly important innovations were introduced — which proved of incalculable value in preserving and cultivating Japan's natural resources.

About 18,300,000 Japanese workers are engaged in agriculture and forestry, 608,000 in fulltime fishing activities and related pursuits, and 501,000 in mining and metallurgy. Fifty-four percent of the total adult working population of Japan are engaged in farming, fishing, forestry or mining. All these aspects of Japan's economic life were the concern of the Natural Resources Section. Its part in democratizing this large percentage of the Japanese labor force must be considered one of the most important in the political reformation of Japan.

Furthermore, one has to realize that a solution of the agrarian problem is, in general, decisive for any political development in Asia. Stability in Asia is remote until some settlement of the land question is reached. The typical pattern of farming in Asia is that of the individual family farm unit. It is a very old pattern, and farmers cling to it tenaciously. The greatest aspiration of the Asiatic rural masses is simply the security of owning a farm. Their wishes are deeply rooted and constitute a potential source for great emotional movements. Land reform is probably the main prerequisite to a solution of the problem of political unrest in Asia. A successful agrarian reform in Japan, therefore, was a not only of decisive influence on the success of the Occupation but also of the utmost significance to the political prestige of the Western democracies in Asia.

In Japan the need for agrarian reforms undoubtedly was great. Although Japan began accepting modern ideas in 1868, the farm population remained practically unchanged, a very reservoir of the life and customs of the earlier feudalistic system. Their working conditions were extremely poor. More than 70 percent of all Japanese cultivators were wholly or partly tenants. More than one-third were landless tenants. Forty-six percent of the Japanese farmland was tenant-operated. The land rent was exorbitant. It had to be paid in kind. From one half to two-thirds of the farmer's crop had to be delivered to the landowners. Scarcely 19,000,000 of Japan's 91,000,000 acres is agricultural land. Yet, about 36,000,000 of the 82,000,000 Japanese live on this land and must extract from it a living for themselves and their families. They consist of approximately 6,500,000 farming units, sharing the arable land. Forty percent of the Japanese farmers cultivate 1.2 acres or less. The average sized farm unit is 2.5 acres. With 70 percent of all farmers partly or wholly tenants, and with rentals averaging about one half of the gross crop, these tiny farms created a very grave problem. The Japanese farmer was land hungry and he was completely dependent on the landowner; in fact, he was only a poor and backward slave laborer. No wonder that the history of Japan records many examples of agrarian unrest. The discontent of the farm population, depressed by hopelessness, and restless as a result of its tragically low economic status, had provided no small part of the stimulant to Japan's aggressive foreign policy. Army circles had abused the misery and poverty of the farmers to achieve their imperialistic aims. The Army's power was built mainly on this section of the population; it had fed the farmers on false promises of a better livelihood and a higher economic standard if the Army's ambitious projects should be realized. Thus the feudalistic agrarian community had always been an attractive basis for a totalitarian regime; it would, accordingly, remain a potential danger so long as its low standard of living and its insecurity existed. Indeed, land reform could be considered a prerequisite to the success of the Occupation reformations in Japan.

10. *MacArthur's Land Reform*

General MacArthur issued his famous Rural Land Reform Directive on December 9, 1945. The Japanese Government was instructed to take measures "to ensure to those, who till the soil of Japan, the enjoyment of the fruits of their labor". The directive called on the Japanese Government to present, within four months, a program providing for transfer of land ownership from landlords to tenants and for protecting the new owners from reversion to tenancy. The significance of this program can hardly be overestimated. One of the basic ills in the structure of the Japanese nationhood was about to be remedied. One of the most promising avenues for a communist attack on the Japanese population was to be closed.

Notwithstanding the enormous difficulties involved in the execution of the land reform plan, a sizable measure of success was achieved during the initial transfer phase, which was virtually completed by December 31, 1949. Almost one-third of the cultivated land in Japan, nearly 4,650,000 acres involving about 3,000,000 separate tracts, had been purchased by the

Government from former landowners for resale to cultivators. As has already been stated, previous to MacArthur's land reform, 54 percent of the farm land was cultivated by the private owner, 46 percent was cultivated by the tenant; after December 31, 1949, 89 percent of the Japanese land was operated by the owners, and only 11 percent remained in the hands of small landowners.

The vast scope of this undertaking becomes clear when one realizes that a village-by-village election in about 12,000 communities had to be held to elect the 120,000 village commissioners and the 900 prefectural commissioners needed for the huge task of effecting the purchase and sale transactions of the roughly 5,000,000 acres of land involved.

In the following years additional reformative measures were taken in order to stimulate the organization of agricultural cooperatives, necessary to strengthen the legal and financial position of the Japanese farmer.

This challenging reform, executed under the direct orders and with the great personal interest of General MacArthur, stands out as an example for similar adjustments elsewhere in Asia. The extent to which the agricultural reforms in Japan are maintained will serve as an indication of the endurance and effectiveness of the democratization of Nippon.

Similar reforms were initiated for the large fishing industry. In Japan, most fisheries were operated under a system of fishing rights. This system paralleled land ownership in agriculture. On November 27, 1948, after elaborate preparative work, the Diet passed legislation to free the Japanese fisherman. Although the fishing industry reform has not been as successful as the land reform, the social changes in the countless fishing villages, resulting from this reform, have been appreciable.

The Natural Resources Section, consequently, can rightly claim that it played a major part in the liberation and democratization of the Japanese rural labor force, and by so doing contributed greatly to the endurance of the political reforms in post-surrender Japan.

In addition, the Natural Resources Section was charged with many other responsibilities. Supervision of the Japanese food supply from indigenous sources must be mentioned as the most important of these. Japan is a country which has been and will be dependent on importation of about 18 percent of its food. This imposes a heavy burden on its balance of payment. The preservation and extension of the agricultural production of Japan must, therefore, be considered as an extremely important aspect of the Japanese economy. The Natural Resources Section successfully sponsored a program of intensification of agriculture in Japan.

In addition to a food shortage, Japan has a shortage of wood and pulp; the country also lacks essential raw materials, particularly high-grade iron ore, coking coal and oil. Several measures, designed to improve this situation, constituted another notable achievement of the Natural Resources Section.

The enlargement and modernization of Japan's agricultural and fishing industry, the modernization of Japan's mining techniques and mineral research work, the introduction of more scientific and efficient ways of preserving and utilizing Japan's natural resources stand together as an outstanding feature in the constructive reformations initiated and sponsored by the Occupation.

11. Democratization of the Economic Structure

As has been described above, the task of the Natural Resources Section comprised many of the economic activities of the Occupation. But the actual economic problems were primarily the concern of the Economic and Scientific Section of GHQ, SCAP — the largest and probably the most controversial Section of MacArthur's Headquarters.

The post-surrender policy directive stipulates that the basis of Japanese military strength had to be destroyed. The directive outlines an elaborate program of demolition and reconversion. It emphasizes that the pre-surrender policies of Japan had brought down on the people great economic destruction and had confronted them with staggering economic difficulties and suffering. But it was not the duty of the victorious nations to restore this destruction. "The plight of Japan", states the post-surrender policy directive, "is the direct outcome of Japan's own behavior, and the Allies will not undertake the burden of repairing the damage". The directive prescribes, on the other hand, that the Japanese people should be given the opportunity to develop for themselves an economy which would permit the peacetime requirements of the population to be met. The accomplishment of this aim, however, would be a problem to be solved by the Japanese themselves. The initial approach of the Occupation to the economic problems of Japan was, therefore, exclusively concerned with the demilitarization and democratization of Japan's economy, and with the fulfilment of the responsibilities of the United States as an occupying Power. Under the Geneva Convention, this included the prevention of disease and unrest.

The demilitarization and democratization of Japan's economic structure, as outlined in the post-surrender policy directive, was in itself an enormous task. The Japanese economy had for many decades been dominated by the so-called Zaibatsu, a group of powerful families who controlled most of Japan's industry, raw materials, finance, shipping and commerce. For mutual advantage they had been closely connected with influential elements in the military and political sphere. The Zaibatsu almost completely controlled the standard of living in Japan. It exercised this control through international and domestic cartel arrangements, through pyramidal-constructed holding companies, and through monopolies of basic resources, key services, major banking and insurance institutions. The Zaibatsu formed, in fact, a system of private internal economic empires, which dominated the economic life of Japan.

The Allied directives for the Occupation included disposing of the influence of these families, liquidating their preponderant position and breaking their economic strongholds. An economy of free enterprise and of fair competition had to be created. The ordinary business man had to have a stake in the economic life of new, democratic Japan.

It must be remembered, however, that the Zaibatsu system was the outcome of a process of economic growth in Japan.

Many people advocated the theory that the extreme concentration of economic power which these concerns represented was an integral feature of Japan's peculiar economic system, and that it would be impossible to destroy the Zaibatsu's organization and leadership without dislocating the entire economy. The circles holding this view were opposed to complete liquidation of the Zaibatsu influence. These considerations however, were overruled by the policy-makers who drafted the post-surrender directives. In Chapter V a more elaborate description of the controversies and of the consequences of the economic deconcentration of Japan will be given. For the present it suffices to state that the dissolution of the Zaibatsu was a difficult, if not a hazardous task, which the occupation authorities had to approach with caution.

The program gradually got underway. In the first months of the Occupation 57 members of 11 different families were designated as Zaibatsu; their securities were taken over for disposal, and their active participation in economic activities was restricted. Following a policy directive of the Supreme Commander, issued November 6, 1945, a Holding Company Liquidation Commission was organized, which took over the securities of the Zaibatsu for eventual dissolution and disposal. The liquidation commission held its inaugural meeting in August 1946. Its task was one of baffling complexity.

Several other measures were taken to unravel and to dissolve the great economic enterprises of Japan. In 1947 a law for the Elimination of Excessive Concentration of Economic Power was passed by the Japanese Diet. Two basic permanent laws followed: the Anti-Monopoly Law of 1947 and the Trade Association Law of 1948, designed to eliminate the concentrated power of Japan's economic empires and to prevent the re-creation of monopolistic controls. A Fair Trade Commission was established for the purpose of administering these laws.

Questions may arise as to the success of the liquidation program. In order to judge, one should realize that the occupation authorities had to execute this complex task with only a handful of economists and technical assistants. Consequently, most of the work had to be entrusted to the Japanese — and here again only a few, outside the former economic circles, were competent to cope with the manifold problems of this undertaking. Inevitably, most of the actual work was done by former Zaibatsu employees themselves. In addition to these circumstances, hardly inducive to a thorough execution of the dissolution program, the attention of the occupation authorities shifted in later years to other more immediate problems, and interest was lost in the complete liquidation of the Zaibatsu system. Moreover, the necessity of Japan's economic rehabilit-

ation made it less desirable to carry the entire program into
effect. Notwithstanding these circumstances, radical changes
in the economic structure were made, and the concentrated
and practically totalitarian power of the Zaibatsu was substantially diminished.

12. *The Organization of Labor*

Another important aspect of the democratization of Japan was
the encouragement to develop democratic labor organizations
in industry and agriculture. This task was entrusted to the
Labor Division of the Economic and Scientific Section. This
Division was concerned primarily with creating conditions
under which a free and democratic labor movement could
come into being. It aimed at encouraging sound relations
between labor and management, and it initiated a very useful
system of labor legislation. On October 4, 1945, the Supreme
Commander issued a directive establishing civil liberties and
ordering the immediate abrogation of all legislation restricting
labor organizations and collective bargaining. This directive
was followed, October 11, by an instruction to the Japanese
Government to encourage labor organizations in Japan. As
early as December 21, 1945, a Trade Union Law was passed by
the Diet. For the first time in Japan's history the workers were
guaranteed the right to organize and bargain collectively. With
unexpected enthusiasm the workers took to their newly
established rights and liberties. By the end of 1945, 509 local
unions had been formed, counting 381,000 members. By the
end of 1946 this number had increased to 17,000 local unions
with 4,900,000 members and by the middle of 1949 nearly
56 percent of the paid industrial workers of Japan were organized into labor unions.

The local unions immediately began to group themselves
into national industrial unions. In the beginning a large
percentage of organized labor was under communist influence,
but during 1948 a trend to the right became clearly discernible. In the course of that year so-called Democratization
Leagues were organized in a score of unions. These leagues
formed anti-communist centers. In September 1949 the
Democratization Leagues organized the National Federation of

Industrial Unions, which includes the main part of the Japanese labor movement. The organization of this Federation has given the labor movement of Japan a definite anti-communist character; the majority of Japanese labor today provides a strong anti-communist front.

It is beyond the scope of this work to give a more elaborate survey of the postwar labor movement in Japan. Undoubtedly, the standard of Japanese labor organizations is not yet comparable to that of similar institutions in Western democracies. The paternal relationship between worker and management was not removed immediately. The influence of management in the labor unions remained quite large. However, an impressive array of labor laws was introduced in Japan, and the workers acquired a thorough comprehension of, and a just pride in their newly gained rights and liberties. If the economic situation in Japan remains favorable to a permanent democratic system, the further development of a Japanese pattern of labor organization can be expected. This, in turn, will favor the democratic influences in the country. Certainly any government would have difficulty in depriving Japan's industrial workers of their newly won democratic rights and in bringing them back to their pre-surrender status of a strictly regimented and underpaid labor force.

In order to give a balanced judgment on labor standards and labor organizations in Japan it must be borne in mind that the skilled Japanese laborer constitutes one of Japan's most important economic assets. Japan's main source of income springs from the use of its huge and relatively highly trained labor force. Cheap labor was one of the corks on which the very unbalanced Japanese economy was kept floating. A highly developed system of social legislation, based on a strong labor movement, might look attractive from a modern sociological point of view or might be welcomed by those who fear Japan's industrial competition; in how far it will prove too costly for Japan, however, is an open question. Those responsible for the management of the Japanese export-industry might consider such a system less attractive, even an irresponsible luxury. On the other hand, those responsible for the well-being of the Japanese people, might entertain a different point of view. As political considerations will therefore play an important part in deciding the question of labor standards and labor organizations, the answer will be a compromise; whatever the outcome, it will greatly affect the future of democracy in Japan.

13. *The Emancipation of Women*

In the early period of Japan's history men and women held a practically equal status in society. In later periods the position of Japanese women retrogressed, chiefly because of the influence of Buddhism and Confucianism. In the middle of the 19th century the women of Japan had practically no rights; they were at the mercy of their husbands or the heads of their families. The best woman was the one who acted as a perfect servant.

The enormous changes in the period after the Meiji Restoration obviously affected the position of Japanese women. The influence of Western culture led to a gradually increasing criticism of women's subordination. Some changes were effected, the most important of which was the opening of schools for girls.

Notwithstanding the fact that a reactionary trend at the end of the century seriously hampered the process, a gradual emancipation of the women of Japan got underway. In 1911 the first feminist organization was established.

The industrialization of Japan and the employment of women in factories and offices, where they worked with men, inevitably changed their position. In the late 1930's many Japanese women had become members of some organization. These organizations were soon brought under government control, and from then on they served nationalistic purposes only — the interests and welfare of the women playing but a secondary role. No political rights had been granted to the women of Japan by the end of World War II, and their legal status had not improved. Japan had definitely remained a man's country.

Early in the Occupation, SCAP ordered drastic reforms in the position of the women of Japan. Pursuant to a directive from the Supreme Commander, the Japanese Government, on October 13, 1945, enfranchised all women above the age of

20 and granted them the right of suffrage and of holding political office. In the following months, full equality was officially granted to women in legal and other aspects. The new Constitution, promulgated in 1946, guarantees the fundamental rights of the women of Japan and establishes a legal basis for equality of the sexes.

Based upon the principles of the new Constitution:

(1) The Civil Code was revised to grant women full civic rights.

(2) The Fundamental Law of Education was passed providing the extension of compulsory education from six to nine years and providing an opportunity for co-education in secondary schools and universities.

(3) The Labor Standards Law was enacted, setting forth the principle of equal pay for equal work, and also offering special maternity facilities.

A girl of 20 years can now vote, marry whom she wants, choose a career and be independent of her family, obtain a divorce on equal grounds with men, act as guardian of her children and be elected or nominated to practically all public offices.

The women of Japan have rapidly and eagerly accepted this new position of freedom. Obviously, the reform needs time to mature, particularly in the social field. Certainly the process has been relatively slow in the villages.

Japanese women have displayed more interest in the political affairs of their country than was expected. In the three general elections since women acquired the vote, 66 women have been elected to the Diet. At the time of the signing of the peace treaty, 24 women were in office — 12 in the Lower House and 12 in the House of Councillors. Feminine members of local assemblies total 961, and 5 hold the office of village chief.

It is estimated that some 10,000 women's organizations, with a membership of 6,000,000, have sprang up. There was danger, however, that those organizations, through lack of democratically trained leaders, might fall into the hands of political bosses from either the extreme right or left. To prevent such a development, a large-scale educational program in the political and social fields was undertaken by several prominent leaders of the Japanese women's movement, with the aid of such organizations as the Y.W.C.A., Japan's League of Women Voters and the League of Democratic Women. In 1947 the Government established the Women's and Minor's Bureau in the Labor Ministry to promote the interests of women and children. This bureau is engaged on information and education work and research concerning women, in cooperation with other governmental and non-governmental agencies.

The advancement of Japanese women has made amazing progress in a short time. They have already contributed to the establishment of a vigorous and healthy democracy in their country. Given time and a fair chance, the emancipation of Japanese women promises to become one of the most important contributions to the building of a new, peace-loving and democratic Japan.

14. *Modus Operandi*

This chapter would be incomplete without consideration of the "modus operandi" followed by the occupation authorities in executing their task. The post-surrender policy directive stipulates that, subject to his right and duty to act directly when necessary, the Supreme Commander is to exercise his authority through the Japanese governmental machinery and agencies, including the Emperor. This was the most logical course of procedure. The United States did not have at its disposal enough trained personnel to organize a complete military government in Japan. Moreover, the insufficient knowledge of Japanese among the occupation staff members made the chosen procedure practically imperative.

Guided by the decision to work through the Japanese Government, General MacArthur organized a broadly based staff in Tokyo, composed of many different sections, in order to deal with such divergent tasks as political reformation, social welfare and restitution of property. The most important of these sections have already been mentioned. From the Tokyo Headquarters the directives and instructions were issued to the Japanese Government for execution. In each prefecture a local military government team was stationed, serving as part of the army of occupation. They did not have any executive power, but served as a control agency only. They were the eyes and ears of the Tokyo Headquarters. Generally speaking, one can say that these teams have done excellent work. The officers serving on military government duty have proved themselves real standard-bearers of a free and healthy democracy. Their tactful guidance and wise restraint have been very helpful in accomplishing the difficult task of the Occupation of Japan.

This system inevitably led to a highly centralized form of government, and, as such, was in contradiction with one of the aims of the Occupation — the decentralization of the Japanese governmental structure. Furthermore, it made the Occupation virtually dependent on the Japanese authorities. The possibility of sabotaging the occupation directives was ever present. On the other hand, as a consequence of the chosen system, the Japanese Government had to work, from the outset, according to the new rules and regulations, and thus it automatically became familiar with them.

Both the advantages and the disadvantages influenced the Occupation. Some reforms were attained rather slowly and less thoroughly than desired; other measures gained significance through their implementation by the Japanese themselves. In general, one can say that the best possible use was made of a system which for sheer physical reasons was the only workable one. The Occupation handled it with tact. After the first avalanche of directives hardly any written order of real significance was issued. SCAP exercised its influence by persuasion, indirect leadership, enlightenment and subtle pressure, preferably on a personal and unofficial basis. The occasions for direct action were limited to some outstanding issues: controversies between GHQ, SCAP and the Japanese Government or changes in policy and in former directives.

One of the outstanding features in this connection was the retaining of the Imperial system and of the Emperor himself. The United States, acting on behalf of the Allied Powers, had stipulated that the authority of the Emperor and the Japanese Government should be subject to the Supreme Commander for the Allied Powers and that the ultimate form of government for Japan had to be determined by the freely expressed will of the Japanese people. For the time being, however, the Allies left the governmental structure of Japan, and also the Emperor, untouched. This was a particularly wise and useful decision. It considerably lightened the task of effecting the surrender and of demilitarizing the Japanese forces; in fact, it may have prevented a suicidal, last-ditch fight by the Japanese. Furthermore, the Emperor was the only symbol of faith and unity left to the Japanese people in the cataclysmic moral collapse of the surrender days. He was a vital stabilizing factor, of a strictly Japanese character, in the turmoil of postwar Japan. Emperor Hirohito himself acted in an exemplary way, accepting his new status as a constitutional monarch in the most graceful manner and gaining in popularity and actual influence. The Emperor may in the future be recognized as having played one of the most important roles in preserving the true values of the Japanese nation, stimulating and not impeding the process of assimilating the Western ideas and philosophy, and as such having exercized an influence of great significance in post-surrender Japan.

15. *From Correction and Reformation to Reconstruction*

In judging the accomplishments of the first years of the Occupation one must realize that in the beginning the reformative, even punitive, character of the Occupation was stressed. The measures taken aimed primarily at preventing Japan from staging a comeback as an imperialistic and aggressive power. The military potential of Japan had to be reduced and permanently restricted; imperialistic and militaristic trends had to be eliminated.

The long lists of war criminals and the accounts of their trials bear out the foregoing statement. Many high-ranking Japanese officers were tried and executed in Japan and neighboring countries. The news of these executions was a grim reminder to the Japanese that they had lost their imperialistic war and that their leaders carried the guilt for the acts of aggression. The long sessions of the International Tribunal of the Far East, where the complete and previously secret story of Japan's aggression was revealed, drove home this truth. More than 20 of Japan's foremost wartime leaders stood before the world as criminals who had violated the laws of humanity and civilization. Japan had surrendered unconditionally, and a stern, righteous treatment by the Allies had been decided upon and was to be executed.

This however, did not change the fact that, as the Occupation progressed, more emphasis was laid upon the constructive aspects of this Allied undertaking. The reforms instituted by the Occupation were in themselves of a positive character. In executing these reforms the Occupation showed an unmistakable trend toward a more lenient attitude. This was not only a normal development but it was in accordance with the original occupation directives, which aimed at the reformation of Japan and the establishment of a trustworthy democracy. Moreover, as the situation developed, a combination of circumstances in and outside of Japan called for a more benevolent attitude toward the former enemy.

CHAPTER IV

FROM REFORMATION TO RECONSTRUCTION

The critical economic situation of Japan requires far-reaching measures, which Washington hesitates to take. MacArthur tries to solve the dilemna by a peace appeal. Australia sponsors the peace idea and convenes the Canberra Conference. Peace for Japan, however, remains a forlorn hope. Consequently, SCAP is faced with the problem of improving the economic situation in Japan; the Occupation will take an active part.

1. *Japan's Food Situation Critical; America Sends Foodstuffs*

The account of the occupation reforms, as given in the previous chapter, has carried the reader far into the post-surrender years and has revealed the many positive attainments of the Occupation.

Immediately upon the cessation of the hostilities, however, the circumstances in Japan were far from favorable; misery and poverty prevailed, intensified by the evergrowing scarcity of practically all the prime necessities of life. The unfavorable economic situation of postwar Japan hardly seemed likely to improve matters; on the contrary, early in 1946 the latent economic difficulties came to a head and threatened the work of the Occupation. Hunger and unrest reared up their dreaded heads. The Japanese nation seemed incapable of coping with the situation. Even though the farmlands had escaped actual war damage, crops were scanty. Fertilizers were scarce, and the food distribution system had been severely disrupted. But still, apart from these unfavorable circumstances, Japan would not have been able to produce enough food for her 80,000,000 people. Roughly 18 percent of Japan's food supplies have always had to be imported. The population cannot be fed from the food produced in Japan itself and that derived from adjacent waters.

In those post-surrender days the situation was even more serious. The Japanese lacked the foreign exchange necessary to buy foodstuffs abroad. The export trade, which provided these funds, had broken down, first as a result of the war and secondly as a result of SCAP's orders. Stocks were depleted, and reserves were exhausted. The food situation deteriorated rapidly, and the dark prospect of starvation haunted the Japanese.

Fortunately for Japan, the Supreme Commander felt that it was incumbent on the Occupation to prevent large-scale hunger and famine, which would inevitably result in unrest and disease and thus threaten the Occupation. Consequently, MacArthur decided that measures should be taken to improve the food situation. As a first step, a certain amount of foodstuffs would have to be imported. This would require the permission and cooperation of the U.S. Government.

MacArthur, early in Januari 1946, sent a report on Japan's grim food situation to Washington. "Thirty million people are threatened by starvation", he warned; "unrest and disease will endanger the work of the Occupation".

The Supreme Commander was concerned not only about the fate of the Japanese people, and the prevention of unrest and disease, as specified in the post-surrender directive, but he feared also that widespread famine would seriously impair the more constructive side of his work in Japan. He considered the safeguarding of the first successes in democratizing Japan of primary importance.

SCAP, therefore, urged the War Department to provide 2,250,000 tons of rice and wheat for distribution to the Japanese. Washington, however, was reluctant to comply with MacArthur's request. Instead it decided to send to Japan an International Investigation Commission, composed of an American, a Britisher and a Canadian, to study the problem. The commission concluded that there was no question of actual starvation in Japan, but that serious food shortages had to be expected in May of that year, and would become more serious during the summer of 1946. The former United States President, Mr. Herbert Hoover, who visited Japan on a trip to the Far East in connection with similar matters, added the weight of his authority to MacArthur's demands. He made a somewhat alarming statement, declaring that: "Japan must have some food imports, if that country will not fall down to the level of existence comparable to the Buchenwald concentration camp". As a result of the survey and of these statements, Washington decided to dispatch several shiploads of rice and wheat to Japan. The quota requested by SCAP was not filled, but substantial support was given to the Japanese in their distress. Large-scale famine and serious troubles were avoided.

2. *Permanent Improvement Implies Rehabilitation of Economy*

These food imports, however, were obviously insufficient to provide a permanent and satisfactory solution to the Japanese food problem. Japan could not be fed for any length of time at the expense of the American taxpayer. The mounting burden on the United States Treasury, if America were to continue supplying food for Japan, was unacceptable. Something more positive had to be done. The steadily deteriorating economic situation of Japan, which was the basic reason for the unusually serious food shortage, had to be improved. The only practical measure to solve the problem was the reshaping of the Japanese economy, followed by the revival of some of Japan's export trade. This would enable Japan to gain the foreign exchange needed for buying necessary food supplies abroad.

The rehabilitation of the Japanese economy, however, constituted a complicated problem. At the end of World War II Japan's economic position was desperate. Japan's overseas territories, which previously had supplied large amounts of food and raw materials, were lost. The Japanese mercantile marine lay at the bottom of the Pacific Ocean. Japan's industrial centers were flattened, and most of the factories had been destroyed by the Allies. What remained of Japan's industrial capacity rumbled to a virtual standstill at the time of the armistice. The equipment was worn out, raw materials were lacking and the workers had left the coal shafts and the machine shops. Moreover, apathy and hopelessness had numbed the Japanese people. The industrialists and the Japanese trade firms lacked the will and incentive to rebuild their factories and re-establish their business. Shipping companies had no ships to sail, banks no money to loan. The economic potential of the country had been dangerously exhausted. It was not, and never had been the intention of the Allies to rebuild and reshape Japan's devastated economy. The Potsdam Declaration and the Post-Surrender Policy Directive were very explicit in this matter. The rehabilitation of the war-torn Japanese economy was a problem for the Japanese themselves.

Not only war-weariness caused the negative attitude of the Japanese toward reviving their industries. The uncertainty of the future, resulting from the fact that the Far Eastern Commission in Washington could not reach a decision as to which factories and utilities were eventually to be dismantled and shipped abroad as reparations, was another important factor. The severe limitations imposed by the Occupation upon Japan's import and export trade formed another. A speedy decision on reparations and removal of some of the controls maintained by the occupation authorities, were, therefore, as necessary to the improvement of the economic situation of Japan as were drastic measures and courageous initiative by the Japanese themselves.

MacArthur, acknowledging all this, took several measures to improve matters. Some of the restrictions imposed on one of Japan's most important food resources, the deep-sea fishing industry, were lifted. The area which Japanese fishermen were allowed to fish was extended. Simultaneously, Japanese whaling activities in the Antarctic were resumed — although still under strict Allied supervision. Furthermore, the export trade of Japan was revived. On March 18, 1946, the U.S. War Department, on General MacArthur's recommendation, granted permission for the reopening of Japan's overseas trade. A Foreign Trade Board was established and, as a first step, the export of Japanese goods to British and Dutch territory in Southeast Asia was resumed.

3. Peace Arrangement is Real Solution

After further study of the problem, however, MacArthur concluded that a satisfactory revival of Japan's economy was, in fact, not possible under an occupation. Consequently, he decided that the speedy conclusion of a peace treaty with Japan was the only real solution. This was his answer to the question of how to feed the Japanese people without imposing an undue burden on the United States.

The Supreme Commander had further reasons for advocating a Japanese peace treaty. In his opinion Japan was ready for peace; the Occupation had achieved all that was practicable under occupation circumstances. A long occupation would only alienate the Japanese and endanger the work already done in democratizing Japan. MacArthur had always favored a radical and spectacular, but short occupation. He was of the opinion that the Japanese were now ready to be left alone.

As early as September 2, 1946, in his message to the Japanese on the occasion of the first anniversary of the Occupation, MacArthur had stated that a spiritual revolution, unknown in history, had changed the spirit of the Japanese people. Said the Supreme Commander: "Japan is now underway to real democracy". In his New Year's message for 1947, MacArthur had been even more outspoken. On that occasion he remarked: "Major advances have been made toward the development of a social system in Japan, designed along the most progressive and liberal lines". He had stressed that it was now the responsibility of the Japanese to grasp and explore this opportunity to create an enduring and real democracy. According to MacArthur, the foundations for the new Japan had been laid; the framework had been erected; but the Japanese themselves had to raise the building; it was clearly his opinion that in order to get lasting and real results, the Occupation had to step back.

Thus, he favored a complete change — a speedy withdrawal of the military occupation and the organization of some sort of international supervising council. MacArthur hoped that he could lay down his function as Supreme Commander of the Allied Powers at the time of this reorganization. The bold and pioneering spirit of the first occupation months, resulting in speedy and dramatic accomplishments, had been to his taste. It had been work which suited the dynamic and powerful character of the Supreme Commander. To play the role of the guardian, however, was a task MacArthur preferred to avoid. He therefore considered that the time for a change in the Occupation and a change for him personally had come.

MacArthur had not kept these ideas to himself. When at the end of February 1947 the Secretary of the Interior, accompanied by some members of Congress, visited Tokyo, he told them that the speedy conclusion of a formal peace treaty would promote the democratization of Japan. Delay, said MacArthur, would handicap the recovery of that country. With prophetic clear-sightedness, the Supreme Commander warned the visiting Americans that the longer the Occupation continued, the more dependent Japan would become upon the United States. MacArthur earnestly, although not yet publicly, advocated the speedy convening of a peace conference for Japan.

Obviously, MacArthur needed the endorsement of the American Government for his plans. The best way for the Supreme Commander to advance his ideas in Washington was to send a personal envoy to the United States for the purpose of explaining the situation in Japan and exploring the possibilities for a satisfactory arrangement. So MacArthur ordered his political adviser, Ambassador Acheson, to proceed to Washington in order to explain to the U.S. Government and the Far Eastern Commission the necessity of solving the reparations deadlock and of lifting some of the occupation controls. Simultaneously, Acheson was to sound the authorities on MacArthur's ideas concerning a peace for Japan. Acheson visited Washington in the early months of 1947. His trip was unsuccessful. The State Department, having failed to reach an agreement with regard to a German peace treaty, was not willing to consider the convening of a Japanese peace conference.

Neither the warnings of MacArthur nor the pleadings of Ambassador Acheson could convince Washington. Even the immediate problem of deciding the scope of the reparations remained unsolved. Acheson returned from the United States empty-handed. Washington was not prepared to take definite steps in promoting a speedy Japanese peace treaty. Only the food imports would continue. A more definite solution for the problems had not been provided.

4. *Washington Reluctant to Make Decision, so MacArthur Voices Peace Appeal*

Thereupon MacArthur took the situation in his own hands.

"The time has now approached that we must talk peace with Japan", sounded the sonorous voice of the Supreme Commander on March 17, 1947.

Thus began a new period in the Occupation.

After having called news correspondents together in an

unprecedented manner, MacArthur personally made his spectacular statement. No one expected such news, even though it was not the first time that an Allied authority had suggested peace for Japan. As early as February 1946, the American Secretary of State, Byrnes, had declared that he expected peace treaties with Japan and Germany to be concluded soon. Following this announcement the State Department had drafted a treaty for the disarmament of Japan, which on June 21, 1946, was submitted to the Far Eastern Commission countries. This American suggestion closely resembled a similar draft for Germany. The proposal did not envisage an actual peace treaty but a far-reaching change in the Occupation and in the supervision of Japan. No definite results were attained, however, and the proposal was shelved. Peace for Japan was, according to the official view held by Washington, to remain a thing of the future.

It was therefore quite understandable that MacArthur's statement came as a complete surprise. "Peace for Japan" was a new idea for the world. The Supreme Commander, elaborating on his startling pronouncement, said that the Occupation could be designated as falling roughly into three phases — military, political and economic. The military work had been done; the political work was approaching such completion as was possible under an occupation. So far as the economic phase was concerned, however, the Supreme Commander believed that hardly anything had changed since the end of World War II. Japan was still blockaded by the Allied Powers. MacArthur warned that hundreds of thousands of Japanese were on the verge of starvation and that food supplies were being exhausted. He emphasized the fact that the gap between available food and necessary food had to be filled by the Allies. He said that if the economic blockade continued, increasing support would have to be given. He termed this an expensive luxury, but pointed out that the United States would have to pay for it, or let millions die. He reminded the press that no clear-cut policy for the economic phase of the Occupation had been established. Furthermore, he stated that he believed the Occupation could not solve the several problems resulting from the economic situation. A prolonged occupation would only cause economic strangulation. He, therefore, urged the speedy conclusion of a peace treaty. He said that he realized the necessity for continued control and guidance for Japan, and suggested that the country be put under the direct supervision of the United Nations.

MacArthur's peace move set the world speculating. How many of his statements about the accomplishments of the Occupation were really true? How much of his plan for the future of Japan could possibly be realized? What was the attitude of Washington toward his suggestions?

5. *Washington's Reactions to MacArthur's Peace Move*

In how far MacArthur had consulted Washington on his sensational remarks remains doubtful. Possibly the Supreme Commander took the initiative when Washington failed to make a decision; in the next few years there would be a number of similar cases. The fact is, however, that on March 24, seven days after MacArthur's statement, the U.S. War and State Departments revealed that they were preparing to open negotiations for the drafting of a peace treaty. Washington emphasized that the Big Four — the United States, the United Kingdom, Russia and China, and possibly Australia — should take part in the negotiations, which should be followed later by consultations with the other members of the Far Eastern Commission.

Although Washington made these peace plans public, it was greatly displeased with MacArthur's far-reaching peace proposal. The State Department foresaw serious difficulties in any endeavor to comply with the suggestions of the Supreme Commander. In order to appreciate these difficulties, one must remember that those were the days when the Foreign Ministers of the United States, the United Kingdom, the Soviet Union and China were assembled in Moscow discussing the problem of a German peace treaty, a problem which had proved within previous years to be practically unsolvable. At the time of MacArthur's peace appeal for Japan the prospects were no better. It looked as if the Moscow Conference would be a failure. The international atmosphere in those early days of 1947 was tense. The mounting communist threat to Greece and Turkey was about to lead to a far-reaching change in U.S. foreign policy. By the end of April 1947 hundreds of millions of dollars had been allocated to help those two countries resist communism. This significant move was the beginning of

5

that historical American undertaking which would result in large-scale economic help to Europe in her battle for rehabilit-ation and for the preservation of her freedom and independence. These new developments in the foreign policy of the United States, however, were obviously not appreciated in Moscow. The relations between the Soviet and the Western world deteriorated further and further. A friendly settlement of the outstanding questions between the United States and Russia proved to be unobtainable. On April 15, 1947, the Moscow Conference ended in deadlock. This made the outlook for a Big Four agreement on Japan practically hopeless.

In order to avoid sole responsibility for the expected failure of the Japanese peace plans, the State Department decided that the question of a peace treaty for Japan would hereafter be the exclusive concern of the Far Eastern Commission. The future would show that this decision made the achievement of peace for Japan even more difficult.

There were still additional reasons which prompted the State Department to shift Japan's peace deliberations to the 11 nations of the Far Eastern Commission. The smaller Common-wealth countries, Australia in particular, had made it clear that they wanted to take part in any talks on Japan. Pressed by the Australians, the British Foreign Secretary, in May 1947, publicly stated that a peace treaty for Japan should be discussed by the 11 nations of the Far Eastern Commission. The Ameri-cans were only to willing to comply with the wishes of their British Allies and to leave the deliberations about the eventual holding of a Japanese peace conference to the members of this Commission.

6. *Evatt Suggests Commonwealth Talks on Japan Peace*

Just at that time, when the world was waiting for the outcome of the informative talks concerning Japan, a new complication was about to develop, resulting from the initiative of the Australian Minister of Foreign Affairs, Evatt. Mr. Evatt was not satisfied with Australia's comparatively unimportant position in the Far Eastern Commission. In his opinion, Australia had the right to play a much bigger, in fact a major role in the Pacific. A welcome occasion to emphasize Australia's position in that part of the world seemed to present itself in connection with the Japanese peace treaty. By the end of June 1947 Evatt had persuaded his Government to invite the other Commonwealth nations for a conference in Canberra to be held in July or August of that year. The agenda included such general topics as the defense of the Pacific and peace for Japan.

An additional reason for Evatt's unexpected initiative was undoubtedly his increasing irritation about America's position in Japan and the dominating role MacArthur continued to play in the Far East. In the opinion of her Minister for Foreign Affairs, Australia had not been sufficiently consulted about Japan. Evatt set out to remedy the situation. Simultaneously with his plan for a Commonwealth conference, he announced his intention of visiting the Japanese capital to see for himself what the Occupation had accomplished.

The Australian plan for the Canberra Conference was not favorably viewed in Washington. The State Department, already weary with the prospect of an endless peace conference for Japan to be attended by the Soviet Union and Nationalist China, feared the consequences of a preliminary Commonwealth line-up. It expected that Evatt's plan would unnecessarily stiffen the attitude of both Moscow and Nanking.

Moreover, in view of the general developments in international affairs, Washington preferred the Japanese peace conference to be postponed for some time. It had to reconsider its position before making new decisions. Many important events had changed the international situation. The breakdown of the Moscow Conference and the growing threat of Russian imperialism had led to far-reaching American commitments in Europe. On June 11, 1947, Marshall had announced his momentous plan to grant assistance to Europe in her endeavors to recover from her wartime scars and to resist imperialistic threats. Marshall had made it clear that he expected the European nations to pool their efforts and resources. The response from Europe had been overwhelming. Bevin and Bidault, the British and French Foreign Ministers, had enthusiastically endorsed the American plan. East European countries hastened to show sympathy. Even Russia announced it would attend the Marshall Plan Conference in Paris at the end of June. Hopes were rising that the deadlock between the Iron Curtain countries and the West could be broken.

But all expectations were in vain. The Soviets left the Paris Conference after serious differences of opinion had wrecked all hopes of conciliation. The controversy between Moscow and the West was sharper than before. Under such circumstances the problem of trying to agree on such a disputed question as the Japanese peace treaty seemed hopeless.

This was to be borne out by the facts. On July 14, 1947, the Soviet Foreign Minister announced that Russia was opposed to any conference of the 11 Far Eastern Commission nations on the Japanese peace treaty. Moscow was of the opinion that to arrange a peace for Japan was the prerogative of the Big Four. As the United States knew beforehand what it could expect from a Big Four Conference, it was not willing to repeat such fruitless talks. Under those circumstances, it seemed opportune to shelve the Japanese peace plans for a while.

On the other hand, Washington felt that it had to take some definite step, notwithstanding its hesitation of the previous months. While others were clamoring for peace, the United States could not remain silent. Hoping to side-track the Australian initiative for the Canberra Conference, it decided upon a rather clumsy course of action. In spite of the plans of the Australian Foreign Minister and although it could not expect any results in view of Moscow's attitude, the State Department on July 14, 1947, nevertheless issued official invitations to the 11 Far Eastern Commission countries to attend a conference on the Japanese peace problems to be held in Washington on August 19, 1947 — a date which obviously conflicted with the scheduled Canberra Conference. Washington apparently hoped to prevent the Commonwealth talks and, at the same time, to induce Moscow to attend. Both hopes were frustrated. The Russian answer to the American invitation came within a week; the Soviet Union would not attend the conference. London and the other Commonwealth capitals politely refused the invitation, pointing out the impossibility of attending simultaneously a conference in Canberra and a conference in Washington.

MacArthur himself, in a last effort, tried to convince the Australian Foreign Minister that he had better cancel his Canberra meeting. During Evatt's visit to Tokyo, the Supreme Commander exercised all his powers of persuasion and charm in trying to win him over to his point of view. He did not fail altogether; Evatt departed full of praise for MacArthur and his work. But the plans for the Canberra Conference remained unchanged.

7. *The Canberra Conference*

The Canberra Conference opened on August 26, 1947, and was attended by the United Kingdom, Canada, Australia, New Zealand, South Africa, India, Pakistan and Burma. Evatt was chosen as chairman. The conference as such was a success for the Australian Minister of Foreign Affairs. The discussions served to explore the attitude of the Commonwealth countries in regard to the Japanese peace problem and were very useful as a preparation for the anticipated 11 nations peace talks, which the participants recommended should be held as soon as possib le. They favored the plan proposed by Washington for the two-thirds majority voting procedure.

The United Kingdom and Canadian representatives, on the other hand, made it clear that the views expressed at Canberra should not be considered the ultimate and definite standpoint of their respective governments concerning the Japan peace. They did not want to commit themselves; moreover, they were anxious to avoid anything which could be interpreted as the formation of a pre-peace conference Empire bloc — obviously in order not to hurt America's feelings. Besides this, the United Kingdom delegation emphasized that the fact of the talks being held in Canberra should not be interpreted as meaning that the leadership of the British group at the full-scale conference would be entrusted to Australia. Britain had no intention of agreeing to a secondary role in the Pacific. If Australia had hoped to have a decisive voice with regard to the Pacific affairs of the British Commonwealth, it had made a miscalculation. In this respect, the conference was not so successful for the Australians.

Evatt, however, took the good with the bad; in fact he displayed considerable restraint and sobriety of judgment. Obviously he endeavored not to spoil his chances for the Presidency of the United Nations General Assembly meeting, convening in the autumn of 1947. Furthermore, his approach to the Japanese problem was clearly influenced by his recent experiences in Tokyo, for his proposals at the Canberra Conference approximately paralleled MacArthur's plans for Japan. The conference revealed no evidence of resentment or vindictiveness toward Japan. A speedy and just peace, including the organization of an Allied control agency to supervise the fulfillment of the treaty provisions, was advocated. Japan, moreover, should be given self-government. No harsh treatment or excessive reparation payments were counseled. It was clear that the Empire countries deliberately refrained from adopting a hard and fast attitude until they had heard the views of the United States.

Obviously, the American position in Japan was recognized by the Canberra Conference. It was unavoidable, however, that the conference led to a certain stiffening of the attitude of the British group toward Japan. This would constitute a problem when, in later years, a constructive approach toward Japan became a prerequisite for a sound and unified Western policy in Asia.

8. *Washington's Endeavors for Convening a Peace Conference Fail; Peace Plans Shelved*

In the meantime, Washington pursued its latest plans for a conference of the 11 Far Eastern Commission countries on the Japanese peace problem. In the middle of August 1947, it clearly and bluntly told Moscow that it would insist on an 11 nations conference in order to avoid the deadlock that had resulted with regard to the German and Austrian peace questions.

With characteristic stubbornness Moscow, on August 29, 1947, answered that the Soviet Union insisted on primary talks by the representatives of the Big Four. Washington, this time, did not change its plans; it continued its preparations for the 11 nations conference. The Supreme Commander for the Allied Powers, in his second report on the work and achievements of the first years of the Occupation, warned again that an early peace was necessary to ensure the gains which had been achieved. It looked as if Washington, through force of circumstances, would go ahead with a peace conference, notwithstanding the practically insurmountable difficulties which the Soviet Union advanced.

On September 11, 1947, however, a new element entered the deliberations. China warned the world against the attempt of any country to hold separate peace talks with Japan. The indication was clear. In an unexpected move Nanking had sided with Moscow. It informed the State Department that it would boycott any Japanese peace talks that did not include the Soviet Union. What reasons had the Kuo Min-tang Government to act thus? Did Nanking hoped to come to some sort of agreement with Russia? It was, undoubtedly, seriously concerned about the manner in which the Soviets had deviated from the Chinese-Russian Agreement of July 1945. Was China trying to demonstrate that she strictly adhered to previous agreements? Or did she fear the consequences of a peace conference in which she did not hold a veto — a fear enhanced by the Commonwealth attitude? The arguments and the motives of the Chinese Government remain unknown. Washington opened new negotiations with Nanking in order to settle the differences of opinion. But the efforts of the State Department failed once more. On February 19, 1948, the Chinese Foreign Minister publicly declared that China would reject an invitation to an 11 nations peace talk. The hope for a compromise on the Japanese peace conference was now lost.

Washington, thereupon, unofficially postponed the convening of a conference. It was left to the Australian Foreign Minister, Evatt, to continue hammering at the necessity of peace talks for Japan — but for the time being also his efforts would prove in vain.

Molotov, unexpectedly, made still another move for peace. On November 18, 1947, he officially proposed that the Foreign Ministers of the Big Four meet in a special conference, preferably in China, to prepare a draft for a Japanese peace treaty. This time, the Chinese Government appeared to be less anxious to please the Russians; it declined the Soviet invitation. Heavy fighting between the Chinese Communists and the Nationalists had broken out in North China. The unmistakable Soviet assistance given the Chinese Reds in their advance in China had apparently changed Chiang Kai-Shek's previous attitude of siding with Stalin on the question of the Japanese peace talks; the Generalissimo, more than ever before, needed American help; he could not afford to antagonize Washington any longer. By the end of December 1947, the United Kingdom also declared that it opposed Molotov's plan; consequently the Russian suggestion remained unsuccessful.

Bevin, on the other hand, again stressed the necessity for a conference of the 11 Far Eastern Commission nations. Washington, however, remained silent, and so this British move also led to nothing.

The result of the several endeavors undertaken in 1947 to convene a peace conference for Japan was indicated by an indefinite promise of President Truman on January 9, 1948, in his annual message to Congress, that the United States would continue its efforts in connection with the Japanese, German and Austrian peace treaties. The wave of hope for an early Japanese peace treaty, which characterized 1947, had subsided. The international developments in 1948, combined with the fact that presidential elections were due in the United States, did not favor any earnest attempt to revive the plans of peace with Nippon, and the question of the Japanese peace treaty was definitely in abeyance during 1948.

9. *SCAP Urges Japan to Remedy Economic Situation*

It will be remembered that the action for peace with Japan had been initiated in order to solve the economic problems facing that country. As peace became an illusion, the question of a remedy for the economic situation became even more urgent.

The American food imports, which started early in 1946, and the lifting of a few occupation controls in the spring of that same year had scarcely improved the situation. The economic plight of Japan remained alarming. As has been indicated above, the first steps to be taken were the enforcement of stringent controls and drastic measures by the Japanese themselves. Under the circumstances then prevailing, it would have been advisable for the Japanese Government to take over, if only temporarily, Japan's basic industries in order to mobilize the resources of the country in a centralized effort toward rehabilitation. As of the middle of 1946, the Occupation had tried to influence the Japanese Government to take steps for improving the economic situation. The Japanese, however, failed to introduce the necessary measures. They either lacked the will to do so, or their Government did not have the capacity and the power to cope with the situation. Notwithstanding the fact that its position seemed rather strong as a result of its backing by the people through the April 1946 elections, it took no steps to retard the rapidly approaching inflation.

Moreover, by the end of 1946 the Yoshida Government, then in power, had lost much of its support. Several of its latest actions had caused severe resentment in labor circles. The rising tension culminated in the threat of a general strike, scheduled to begin on February 1, 1947. The strike itself was called off, through the intervention of the Supreme Commander, who considered it contrary to the aims of the Occupation. The authority of the Yoshida Government, however, could not be restored. The occupation authorities insisted that general elections should be held to give the Japanese an opportunity to form a more representative government. These elections took place in April 1947. The result was the establishment of the first socialist post-surrender cabinet in Japan; Katayama was the new Prime Minister.

MacArthur, however, had not waited for the outcome of the elections. On March 22, 1947, five days after his famous peace appeal, he issued a stern warning to the Japanese Government, emphasizing that it had to readjust the entire economic policy of Japan and that, if drastic and effective steps were not taken by the Japanese themselves, further assistance from the Allies could not be expected. He ordered the Japanese Government to institute an Economic Stabilization Board for centralizing the economic measures to be taken. Katayama, succeeding Yoshida as Prime Minister, set out to implement MacArthur's ideas. Immediately upon assuming office, he issued a six-point economic rehabilitation program. At the same time, the Japanese did not fail to stress their dependence on foreign help and assistance. Katayama's Foreign Minister, Ashida, strongly advocated the reopening of Japan to foreign trade and the free investment of foreign capital; he also emphasized the necessity of finding a practical solution for the reparations question.

The Katayama Government enjoyed the outspoken sympathy of SCAP, and it seemed to have the firm support of the people. Notwithstanding these facts, however, the circumstances under which it was formed precluded, from the outset, the drastic action necessary to remedy the situation. Although he did what he could, Katayama failed to enforce the essential measures advocated by General MacArthur.

His Cabinet launched one rehabilitation program after another. In the middle of June 1947, an eleven-point economic emergency program was announced, followed at the end of June by a seven-point plan to promote a national movement for economic reconstruction. These plans were not successful. The Katayama Government lacked the push and power to implement its plans. The food situation became increasingly critical. An attempt temporarily to nationalize the coal industry, which would have greatly helped to increase coal production and to improve food distribution, was frustrated by the opposition parties. Prices rose sharply. Considerable amounts of food were available in the rural areas, but they failed to reach the population centers. The collecting of the food, its transportation to the cities and its distribution had been completely disrupted or had fallen into the hands of black marketeers and political bosses. In the middle of July 1947, Katayama announced what he called a last ditch fight to curb the disastrous rise in food prices. At the end of July, his Cabinet adopted a program of so-called essential measures to establish order in the economic circulation, to obtain a minimum living standard for the people and to promote foreign trade.

The Katayama Government, however, had already been forced to compromise on too many issues to be successful. All its attempts failed to provide the food necessary to remedy the deteriorating food situation. Unrest spread in the Tokyo and Kansai areas. SCAP had to release huge food supplies from America to halt the mounting threat of disorder. Katayama's desperate efforts to control critical materials, the black market and the inflation present a melancholy example of the frustrated endeavors of a government compromising in order to retain its position.

10. *Economic Situation Improves Slightly as Result of SCAP's Interference; Occupation Policy Gradually Changes*

Fortunately for Japan the economic situation showed some improvement as a result of SCAP's interference. In addition to the extending of fishing areas and the freeing of Japan's overseas trade, the Supreme Commander, on February 20, 1947, allowed the Japanese Government to increase its cotton spinning capacity to 4,000,000 spindles in order to stimulate the manufacture of export goods. In April 1947 permission was granted for the reconstruction of the Japanese rayon industry. In May, the first post-surrender shipment of Australian wool entered Japan, and in June the Allies announced formally that Japan would be allowed to participate in world trade within two months. In August 1947 private commercial relations were reassumed, and 400 private foreign trade representatives were allowed to enter the country. These developments reflected a change of policy in Washington regarding the approach towards the economic situation of the former enemy countries, Germany and Japan. The Assistant Secretary of State, Dean Acheson, in a public announcement on May 8, 1947, expressed the views of the State Department in this connection by saying: "The United States is prepared to take up the reconstruction of Japan and Germany independently, without waiting for an agreement of the four Great Powers".

This declaration set the pace for a new policy toward Japan. As the deliberations between the Allies to achieve a peace for Japan dragged on, the United States realized that it had to reckon with a prolonged occupation. Washington was not prepared, however, to continue footing Japan's huge food bill. Consequently, it decided to deviate from the post-surrender policy directive, which restricted its economic activities in Japan to the prevention of widespread unrest and disease, and it embarked on a program of economic reconstruction in order to enable the Japanese to gain the foreign exchange necessary for buying food abroad. The Far Eastern Commission, under pressure of the United States, reluctantly endorsed this change in attitude. It eliminated some of the uncertainties hanging over Japan by announcing that the level of the economic life to be allowed to the Japanese in their postwar reconstruction would be based on the standard of living of the pre-expansionist years 1930–34. The question of the reparation payments was reconsidered in this light. In April 1947, the United States delegate in the Far Eastern Commission submitted a final plan for settling the reparations problem. When it became evident that the Commission could not come to a decision in this important matter, Washington announced a unilateral solution. It decided on an advanced transfer reparation program, covering roughly 30 percent of the anticipated reparations. A keen observer could already predict that only this program would be executed, and that the remainder of the reparations would never be forthcoming. A further indication as to the future of the reparation program was given by Mr. Clifford Strike, who visited Japan twice in the course of 1947. He was sent to Tokyo by the U.S. War Department to study the economic situation and the reparation program. In February 1947, he made his first visit. Even at that early date he recommended much more lenient reparations than previously suggested by Ambassador Pauly. After his second visit in July 1947, Strike urged an immediate repeal of Pauly's plan. Although a long time passed before his recommendations were officially adopted as policy decisions, the outlook for Japan regarding future reparation payments brightened considerably.

An additional impetus to Japan's economic revival was given by the decision of the Far Eastern Commission in connection with the huge gold stock, held in custody by the Allied authorities in Tokyo. The value of this stock, estimated at $137,000,000, was put at the disposal of SCAP to be used in financing the rehabilitation of the Japanese export industry. MacArthur created a fund, from which loans up to yen 500,000,000 were made available for reconstruction purposes. At the same time the United States allocated $100,000,000, to be formed into a revolving fund, for financing a cotton credit for Japan.

As a result of these measures the Japanese crisis gradually relaxed, although not through the fumbling efforts of the Japanese Government. As early as September 1947, MacArthur could declare: "Japan has been gradually recovering her shattered economy; there is no more danger of vehement economic collapse". The basic shortcomings in the economic situation, however, had not been remedied. This would remain impossible without the full cooperation of all Japanese concerned, which, as will be described in the next chapter, was not forthcoming for the time being.

The changed attitude of Washington toward Japan met with criticism from several Allied countries. China announced its opposition to the American policy of fostering Japan's strength. The Soviet Union attacked the United States policy during the United Nations session of October 1947. The Russian Foreign Minister stated that the restoration of the industrial power of the former enemy country was contrary to the aims and objectives of the Potsdam Declaration. The unmistakable change in the attitude of the United States toward Japan would eventually lead to opposition by the other Allied nations, which feared a loss of their own prestige in the Far East.

11. *Summary of Events*

At this important moment in the history of the Occupation, when by the end of 1947 the first significant change in the occupation policy occurred, it may be useful to summarize the developments of the previous years.

It will be remembered that the first period of the Occupation had been reformative and corrective in character. The outline of a new, regenerated Japan had been traced, and measures had been taken to erect a legal and social framework for a democratized Nippon.

At the beginning of 1946, however, the consequences of the seriously deteriorating economy resulted in a definite breakdown of the food supply; the country faced famine, unrest and disease. These circumstances threatened to endanger the ultimate objectives of the Occupation. Consequently, the United States, as the main executive of the Occupation, felt compelled to remedy the situation by the allocation of food to its former enemy. This, however, imposed a heavy burden on the American taxpayer; it looked as if Japan would become more and more dependent on the United States. But the Americans could hardly be expected to encourage such a development. A revival of the Japanese export trade, and consequently a restoration of its industries, was therefore initiated, in order to allow Japan to gain the foreign exchange necessary to pay its food bill abroad.

With militarism subdued "for a hundred years to come", and with the framework of a new Japan erected, the granting of a restricted peace, combined with continued Allied supervision, presented itself as a logical solution. Moreover, it was recognized that an economic revival would hardly be possible in a continually occupied Japan. The idea "Peace for Japan" was introduced, and for a variety of political reasons it became the slogan of 1947. Hopes were raised in Japan and the rest of the world for an early peace settlement, but relations between the former Allies had deteriorated to such an extent that even the convening of a conference to discuss a Japanese peace treaty became a hopeless undertaking. The main obstacle was the attitude of the Soviet Union. An untimely and opportunistic initiative of Australia caused additional difficulties. Fearing a "white men's line-up", China sided with Russia, insisting on a veto at the conference table. Peace for Japan, evidently, was unobtainable.

The United States faced the consequences. It embarked on a program of economic rehabilitation and reconstruction in Japan. Initially the reason was to lighten the burden on the American taxpayer and to prevent Japan's becoming an encumbrance to the United States.

Strategical and political considerations, however, would soon enter the field of international planning and later would become a predominant influence. The rising tension between the Soviet Union and the Western world would definitely affect and frequently determine the American policy in Japan. As early as 1947 the transition in the U.S. appreciation of Japan from the position of a defeated enemy into an indispensable ally was already discernible. In the coming year this new American attitude toward Nippon would become abundantly clear.

CHAPTER V

THE OCCUPATION IN DANGER

In 1948 the United States embarks on a program of economic reconstruction for Japan, paralleled by changes in the political and social fields. The failure of the Japanese to cooperate, however, prompts Washington to order more drastic economic measures in Japan. As satisfactory results are not forthcoming and as the Far Eastern situation worsens, some circles in the United States consider complete military withdrawal from Japan. The U.S. Secretary of War, Royall, revealing this fact, rudely awakens the Japanese people to the danger from the outside world.

1. *Preview of 1948 Developments*

During the extraordinarily hot summer of 1948, laziness and apathy pervaded the Japanese people. The violent typhoons and the serious earthquakes which were to disturb the peace of the early autumn days had not yet awakened them. They seemed to have no inclination to work, no incentive to undertake anything new. A reasonable amount of food was again available on the markets. Easy money could be made quickly through the black market and other illegal transactions. There was a widespread feeling of indifference everywhere in the country. Moreover, the Japanese had become convinced that if circumstances became particularly bad the Occupation would again step in and remedy the situation through grants of food and other necessities of life. Why work and toil for daily bread if the United States would supply the necessary food? Wy not let the Occupation worry their heads about the future of Japan? The Japanese, who did not really understand the Americans and their motives, frequently wondered about the activities of the Occupation. But one thing seemed sure — the United States was going to take care of Japan and the Japanese, and in some way or other the United States even seemed to need the Japanese people, who believed that the best attitude was to extract as many advantages as possible from these circumstances and to profit to the utmost from American benevolence. Yet they felt intuitively that soon enough political and economic "typhoons" and "earthquakes" would come and destroy their pleasant dreams.

In the meantime the Americans labored on. Especially the top-level officials had little relaxation; an eight-hour day, seven days a week, kept them going. The huge task of reforming and reshaping Japan into a new and democratic nation had to be accomplished. And lately the economic reconstruction of Japan had been added to the duties of the Occupation. There was no time for laziness and letting down. On the contrary, increasing problems called for more serious efforts. The American sincerity and ardor contrasted sharply with the laziness and opportunism of the Japanese. No wonder the Americans gradually grew irritated and impatient with Japanese indolence and indifference; they felt the time had come to show the Japanese that if they did not care to work for themselves, the United States would no longer desire to help them and their country. Tempers flared up, and an occasional sharp outbreak indicated how strongly the Americans felt on the matter.

The developments during 1948 can be divided into three distinct, although closely connected and overlapping, periods. The first one was characterized by increased American assistance to Japan's economy. During the second period the discouraging Japanese reaction to this American effort demonstrated itself. The third period was marked by a growing American irritation at the indifference of the Japanese. This resulted in MacArthur's stern directive, issued on December 19, 1948, warning the Japanese Government to take immediate measures for a thorough housecleaning or face the alternative of having the Occupation choose its own methods to effect a drastic change in the economic field. A more serious consequence of the American irritation and disillusionment with the Japanese people was to be revealed in a statement by the U.S. Secretary of War, Royall, early in 1949, indicating that the United States were considering a complete military withdrawal from Japan.

2. *United States Embarks in Program of Economic Reconstruction in Japan*

The change in the U.S. policy with regard to Japan, from a

corrective and reformative attitude toward a policy of economic reconstruction as described in Chapter IV, had greatly advanced by the beginning of 1948.

It has been pointed out before that the Assistant Secretary of State, Dean Acheson, had indicated America's intention as early as May 1947. At that time Acheson had revealed an American plan for the reconstruction of Germany and Japan, labeling these countries the "workshops of Europe and Asia".

This idea had further been developed during 1947. The change was officially announced in the Far Eastern Commission on January 22, 1948, as a new American policy for Japan. "Japan", declared General McCoy, the American representative in this Commission, "should be made selfsupporting as soon as possible, with a reasonable living standard, so that she will not be too heavy a burden on the American taxpayer".

It is important to note that in those days the foremost reason underlying the U.S. decision to reconstruct Japan — and by so doing enable her to earn her own living — was the desire to reduce the amount of American help necessary to sustain Japan, and thus ease the burden on the American budget. Considerations of a more strategical or political character would only later enter the picture.

Whatever the reasons were for the change in the American policy, the growing economic crisis in Japan and the American decision to remedy the situation inevitably resulted in changes in the attitude of the occupation authorities. Until recently, SCAP's intervention in the field of industrial production and finance had been only nominal. Now circumstances forced the Occupation to take a stand on problems of foreign trade, foreign exchange, reparations, levels of production and the degree of American financial assistance. SCAP introduced an enormous program for the revival of Japan's trade and industries.

In order to execute this program, the measures taken in 1947 were greatly expanded. In the previous chapter some of these measures, namely the rehabilitation of the textile and rayon industries and the creation of the $ 500,000,000 fund for industrial loans, combined with the institution of the $ 100,000,000 revolving fund for cotton credits, have already been mentioned. In 1948 a further expansion of the textile industry was planned. As the export of manufactured textile goods had

always been one of the main sources of foreign income for
Japan, much attention was payed to its rehabilitation. In
January 1948, a technical mission of three prominent members
of the American Cotton Manufacturers' Association visited
Tokyo to advise the Supreme Commander on the problems
of Japan's textile sales abroad. In May, private banking circles
in the United States granted an extra loan of $ 60,000,000 for
further inducement to the textile industry.

At the end of January 1948, Japan's foreign trade was again
stimulated by the lifting of the quota restricting the entrance
of foreign business representatives. In the course of the year,
private trade, although still in restricted form, was resumed
with Australia, Indonesia, India, Thailand and some other
countries in Southeast Asia, on a government to government
basis.

The Far Eastern Commission, though reluctantly, followed
the new trend. At the beginning of January 1948, it allowed
Japan to revive its iron and steel production based on the
1933–35 level, and at the end of the year, on December 7, 1948,
the Commission announced that Japan's foreign trade could
virtually be restored to its peace time volume, subject to SCAP's
approval. In cases where the Far Eastern Commission failed to
reach a decision, the United States acted unilaterally.

One of the most indicative and illustrative measures taken in
consequence of the new American policy was the formal
abandonment of the plans to decentralize Japanese industry.

These plans had been embodied in a document, known as
FEC-230.

In order to understand the significance of this document, its
long history has to be traced. In February 1945, the U.S.
Government had constituted the Far East Sub-Committee of
the State-War-Navy-Coordinating Committee to prepare a
draft for a general policy relating to Japan. The Sub-Committee
aimed at a constructive solution of the problems arising from
the occupation of a broken and ravaged country and from the
implantation of democracy in an oriental, totalitarian-ruled
people. Its recommendations were largely the work of the
Under-Secretary of State, Joseph C. Grew, former U.S. Ambassador to Tokyo, who, assisted by some capable experts on
Japan, actually drafted the policy.

The suggestions were adopted by the U.S. Government in August 1945 as the basis for its post-surrender policy for Japan.

Grew's plans, however, had been opposed by another group of Far Eastern experts, who advocated a rather extreme policy toward Japan. They favored the abolition of the Japanese monarchy, the complete dissolution of large Japanese enterprises and a thorough and deep-reaching purge of business executives.

After Secretary of State Byrnes became head of the State Department, this latter group gained considerably in influence and set out to implement its ideas on the Japanese occupation. Grew and his subordinates resigned or were forced out of the State Department. The new policy-makers succeeded in inserting additional clauses in the post-surrender policy before the document was officially forwarded to MacArthur on September 6, 1945. These clauses instructed MacArthur to favor more drastic economic changes than originally envisaged by Secretary Grew.

The U.S. Government submitted these policy provisions to the Far Eastern Commission in Washington, which adhered to them on May 12, 1947. The challenged clauses on economic reformations were named FEC-230. This document clearly revealed the intentions of those who wanted to break down the Japanese industrial potential and to pulverize Japan's business. It aimed at a widespread distribution of income and of the ownership of the means of production and trade. It prescribed an extensive purge in the economic field, and it directed the Supreme Commander to implement a program for the complete dissolution of the larger industrial and banking combinations in Japan.

The contents of FEC-230 remained unknown to many responsible officials for a long time. Not until the end of the summer of 1947 were the consequences of its policy fully realized at Washington top level. At that time an American industrialist, who had visited Tokyo in connection with the expansion of Japan's textile industries, revealed the full implications of this paper to Defense Secretary Forrestal and to Commerce Secretary Harriman in Washington. It was then decided that FEC-230 had to be revised.

The resulting change indeed marked a turning point in the

economic policy of the Occupation; a beginning was made to plan the revival of Japan's industrial potential.

Unfortunately, however, much harm had already been done. The more extreme group of policy-makers had successfully installed some of its followers in SCAP's headquarters. Those people had tried to implement the FEC-230 policy as quickly as possible. Through the authority of the Occupation they had forced the Japanese Diet to pass an elaborate decentralization law and to carry out the economic purge.

Not until autumn 1948 was it possible to stop this course of events and to amend and moderate the dangerous directive. From now on the drastic policy of FEC-230, which could easily have reduced Japan's economy to chaos, was gradually reversed, and by the end of 1948 a moderate and constructive method of dealing with the economic problems of Japan had been adopted.

A relatively long time was required, however, for the occupation authorities to change their attitude completely. To begin with, MacArthur himself was not the man to admit mistakes made in Tokyo. Secondly, such a significant change in attitude by the Occupation as this swing from an extreme interpretation of FEC-230 toward a moderate reformative and constructive program could only be made gradually and slowly. Much time, energy and persuasion were needed to coordinate the work between Washington and Tokyo in regard to the implementation of this revised American policy for Japan. Several high-level conferences were held. The State Department, in February 1948, dispatched its Chief Planner, Mr. George Kennan, to Tokyo to explain the changed attitude of Washington. During March, the Under-Secretary of the Army, Mr. Draper, was sent to Japan, accompanied by a high-level economic and industrial advisory group; this group, under the chairmanship of Percy J. Johnson, was composed of prominent American businessmen, including Paul Hoffman, future Economic Cooperation Administrator of Europe.

This was not the first time that an official economic mission from the United States visited Japan to study its economic problems. It will be recalled that, in 1946, Ambassador Pauly had made a general survey in connection with reparation payments. In the autumn of 1946 a group of technicians, headed by Mr. Clifford S. Strike, had made a more thorough study of this problem. Strike had come to Japan for the second time in June 1947, accompanied by a group of experts from the Overseas Consultant Incorporation; they had cautioned against reparation payments and had emphasized that failure to restore the economic plight of Japan would result in a continued burden on the American taxpayer.

Mr. Draper, during his 1948 visit, came to the same conclusion. After the completion of his mission he declared that the United States should make a strenuous effort to rebuild Japan's economy to a high productive level. He warned against extracting further reparations from Japan. Unofficially, he indicated that he believed economic problems in Tokyo were being handled somewhat naively. He sounded a warning against the presence of some over-zealous and purely theoretical reformers on SCAP's economic staff.

Draper's point of view was vigorously supported by Percy Johnson's influential group, which urged in its official report that the United States should in its own interest assist in the industrial recovery of Japan. According to Johnson, this recovery should become the primary object of the Occupation. It should aim at establishing a self-supporting economy on a peaceful basis. Next to industrial recovery, Johnson emphasized the importance of increasing Japan's merchant navy and warmly sponsored the American program for allocating the necessary funds to aid Japan's recovery. Many of his recommendations were accepted. On May 20, 1948, $ 150,000,000 were appropriated by the United States Government for the economic rehabilitation of Japan and thereby any doubt as to Washington's intentions was removed; the United States had clearly and definitely changed its policy toward Japan; it had embarked on a large-scale program of economic rehabilitation of the former enemy country.

3. *Reversal of Economic Policy Paralleled in Political and Social Fields*

These fundamental changes in the economic aspects of the occupation policy, however, could not be implemented without influencing the political and social reformations instituted by the occupation authorities. It was unavoidable that the great economic changes would affect the developments in other fields.

As early as January 1947, the then Under-Secretary of War, Kenneth Royal, had already warned the American public of these consequences. Said Mr. Royal: "In 1945, the main American interest had been to prevent any revival of Japan's militarism. The well-being and the strength of Japan had been entirely secondary. Now, however, new conditions have made a change in this policy necessary and have forced the need for the revival of Japan's economy. An inevitable period of conflict between the original concept of broad deconcentration and the new purpose of building a self-supporting nation had to be expected. At some stage, extreme deconcentration of industry, while further impairing the ability to make war, may at the same time destroy the manufacturing efficiency of Japan's industry and may therefore postpone the day when Japan can become self-supporting. Another borderline situation between demilitarization and economic recovery is presented in the case of personnel. The men who were the most active in building up and running Japan's war machine — military and industrial — were often the ablest and most successful leaders of that country, and their services would in many instances contribute to the economic recovery of Japan".

Mr. Royall's indications had been crystal clear. The program of thorough military, economic and spiritual demilitarization and democratization of Japan had to stop short of the point where it would unduly interfere with the efficiency of Japan's trade and industries.

MacArthur faced the difficult task of effecting this policy. He had to keep the purge of prominent economic and industrial leaders under control; he had to prevent a too extreme decentralization of Japanese industries and business. He had to curb the liberties of the Japanese labor unions in so far as their newly won privileges threatened to impose too heavy a burden on the Japanese economy. In general, MacArthur had to moderate several of the reformations originally undertaken to crush Japan's war-making economic potential. Some of the reforms had overshot their targets, particularly those connected with strictly economic matters. A drastic change had to be made with those reforms which tended to disrupt Japan's economic life and to encourage leftist forces. MacArthur, in order to initiate the new policy, took two steps.

First, SCAP made known that the power of the Zaibatsu had been virtually abolished. This was a face-saving formula to cover the change in American attitude toward the decentralization of Japan's big enterprises and toward the purge of their leading men. By propagating that the purge had been accomplished successfully and that the Zaibatsu were dissolved, the Supreme Commander could inconspiciously stop the further execution of the deconcentration directives. He did not need to announce a change in policy with regard to this matter, and thus he avoided the criticism which such an announcement would undoubtedly have evoked abroad.

Secondly, MacArthur imposed several restrictions on the somewhat too progressive Japanese labor movement, which since its establishment had indulged in countless strikes and repeated demands for wage increases. When in the middle of July 1948, a large strike of public service workers threatened to dislocate the Japanese economy and to upset normal living conditions in the country, MacArthur ordered the Japanese Government to take steps to curb the rights of persons employed by government organizations and by public utilities. He instructed the Japanese to revise the National Public Service Law. Strikes of public service workers were to be prohibited as being contrary to the welfare of the country. Serious protests resulted from SCAP's action. The National Communications Union and the Government Railway Workers Union gave vent to violent objections. Even MacArthur's own Chief of the Labor Section resigned. In spite of this, MacArthur did not hesitate. He ignored the resistance from the Japanese, and he overrode the opposition in his own headquarters. Although the Japanese Government only reluctantly complied with SCAP's wishes, MacArthur succeeded in enforcing a revised National Public Service Law. It was obvious that MacArthur himself, counseled by several prominent officials and industrialists from the United States, had been convinced that a change in the occupation policy was necessary to prevent chaos and to avoid a complete disruption of the economic structure of Japan. MacArthur acted accordingly, as was borne out by the measures taken. In view of the fact that public service workers in Japan constitute a relatively larger group than in any other country, SCAP's persistence in enforcing restrictions in the Public Service Law was an unmistakable indication of the stiffening attitude of the Occupation. SCAP was resolved to take a firm stand toward a possible abuse by the Japanese labor movement of its newly won privileges.

In concurrence with this change in occupation policy, the Supreme Commander, in the middle of December 1948, unofficially advised the workers in the coal and electrical industries, the Japanese seamen, the fiber workers and private railway personnel that strikes were detrimental to the industrial production of their country and therefore were regarded unfavorably. The rehabilitation of Japan's economy was evidently given priority over the rights of the workers, even taking precedence, for the time being, over the political and social reforms.

4. *Japanese Fail to Join Americans in Reconstruction; Mounting Inflation Results*

Unfortunately, the Japanese response to the American appeal for the revival of the Japanese economy was, as has been said in the preview to this chapter, far from satisfactory.

First of all, the originally conflicting viewpoints between Washington and Tokyo on the change in occupation policy, and the difficulties in getting this new policy implemented, had adversely influenced the Japanese people and Government. The Japanese doubted the intentions of the United States and viewed the change with mistrust.

More serious, however, was the fact that many Japanese with considerable influence in the Government were inclined to take a very opportunistic point of view with regard to America's efforts for the rehabilitation of their country. They considered it advantageous for Japan to accept American money and materials, but at the same time, they considered it wise to proceed slowly with the implementation of the American plans. A large group of Japanese, led by reactionary politicians and influential profiteers, were bitterly opposed to any plan aimed at a healthier economy; they hoped to continue exploiting the existing situation to their own advantage. The

Japanese Government, unfortunately, failed to take a firm stand in this matter. On the contrary, in the course of 1948 even the Government itself fell victim to the swiftly spreading wave of corruption in the country.

The tendency towards large-scale corruption had set in as early as the end of the hostilities in the middle of August 1945. At that time the Japanese Government had released millions and millions of yen in cash and in surplus army stocks to military personnel, bureaucrats, capitalists and political party bosses. Afterwards, these goods found their way into the hands of black-marketeers and political racketeers. This mishandling of funds and military supplies was one of the main factors to cause the serious inflation which swept Japan in the post-surrender years, further upsetting its wartorne economy.

The actual cause of this inflation obviously lay much deeper than the August 1945 swindle. It was, in fact, the natural outcome of the wartime disturbances in the Japanese economy. Industrial production had been wholly inadequate, imports of raw materials had been insufficient, wage control had been lacking and price control had been inefficient. Government expenditures continuously exceeding the revenues had resulted in a sharp increase in the issue of Bank of Japan notes. Well-timed, thorough and methodical countermeasures could probably have stopped the inflation and might have prevented a continued deterioration of the economic situation. This opportunity was lost, however, as a result of the early reluctance of SCAP to intervene in economic questions and as a result of the incompetence of the Japanese Government. American efforts to remedy the food shortages and to boost imports of raw materials were impaired by the Japanese. Instead of helping in the reconstruction of their country, they stimulated the black-market, and consequently, instead of preventing it, increased the inflation.

The implications were serious. Only the farmers profited temporarily from the soaring prices. Japanese industrial laborers, however, had to fight constantly to increase their wages and to keep in step with the rising prices of daily consumer goods. Official price control assumed the character of a mere delaying action. Industrial activity, the key to the revival of Japan's vital export trade, became the chief victim of the inflation. There was an urgent need for working capital to overhaul and modernize the industrial equipment. Normally industry would have turned to the private banks for loans or other forms of advancing money in order to finance the rehabilitation of its workshops. Government restrictions on the activities of the commercial banks and the unstable financial position of these banks made it, however, impossible for industrialists to obtain the necessary loans from private sources. Consequently, industry had to rely for its urgently needed loans on the official Japanese Reconstruction Finance Bank. The increasing demands forced this bank to borrow heavily from the only remaining source, the Bank of Japan. The undesirable result of this was that the Government's influence over Japan's industrial apparatus was unduly strengthened.

The danger was greatly increased by the fact that industry was unable to repay its debts. The Reconstruction Finance Bank loans remained outstanding, and the Bank of Japan was never refunded. Inflationary costs caused the loans to be monetized by the Bank of Japan, and consequently more and more money was brought into circulation. Inflation caused further inflation. And the Bank of Japan, balancing on top of the steadily worsening financial structure, was powerless against this vicious circle.

The situation was aggravated by a general aversion to work. War-weariness and apathy, already apparent in the previous years, held many Japanese in their grip. Moreover, in several cases the necessary leadership and the technical knowledge for the revival of Japan's industrial activities were lacking; many leaders of industry and finance had been purged, and they were almost impossible to replace.

In addition to these disturbing circumstances, the granting of previously unknown liberties and privileges to the working classes, the sudden change of old patterns, and the introduction of new rules created unrest and instability throughout Japan. The rigid discipline of the prewar years, yes, even of generations and generations before, had been relaxed overnight. The unquestionable authority of the Emperor had been relinquished. Freedom and democracy had taken the place of the strict regimentation of the Japanese people by their government. Unfortunately, however, only the rights and the privileges of the newly introduced concept of life had been accepted; the concomitant duties were hardly realized. The Japanese indulged in an orgy of profiteering and greatly abused their newly won liberties. The notorious Showa Denka scandal, which filled the newspapers in 1948, was one of the most tangible proofs of how far the malignant influences had infected the Japanese people. Even the Government was deeply involved in all kinds of frauds and in the mishandling of funds. Several high Japanese authorities, including Prime Minister Ashida, were accused of having accepted large sums of money as bribes.

5. *Japanese Convinced United States Will Sustain Their Country*

In view of the foregoing one may rightly ask: What reason did the Japanese people have to be so sure that, independently of what they themselves did for the betterment of the economic circumstances in their country, a continous stream of American money and assistance would be forthcoming?

The fact was that the Japanese were convinced that in view of the increasingly dangerous international situation, resulting from the growing tension between Washington and Moscow, the Americans needed Japan and the Japanese.

The United States itself had given rise to this supposition. As early as March 1948, the United Press in Washington, quoting a high government official, had issued a report that America was prepared to aid Japan socially and economically in an effort to make her an eastern rampart against communism. MacArthur, in some of his public statements, had expressed the same idea. The majority of the Japanese people concluded that this fear of communism would be reason enough for the United States to continue pouring money into Japan. The Japanese could wait and see and, in the meantime, profit from the situation.

The international developments of 1947 had given the Japanese reasons enough to believe that they were right in their appreciation of the American attitude. As early as March 1947, when the President of the United States had announced his famous Truman Doctrine, many Japanese had sensed a foreboding of a change in the punitive attitude of the Occupation. They had understood that the presidential plans for sustaining

the economy of the free nations of the world, in order to prevent
them from being further endangered by the inroads of communism, would most probably include Japan. They calculated that
Japan would be among the countries which would profit from
this new American policy; consequently, their attitude had
gradually become more confident, more hopeful, but alas —
not more cooperative.

Sooner than they expected, however, the Japanese were to
discover that America's patience was not so unlimited as they
had thought, and that the assumption that the United States
needed Japan, and consequently would continue to sustain its
economy, whatever happened, was not so firmly established a
policy as they had presumed it to be. The following pages will
disclose that first Washington tried to remedy the situation by
issuing a stern warning, and when that failed, even considered
a withdrawal from Japan.

6. *MacArthur's Nine-Point Economic Stabilization Program*

Early in October 1948 the Ashida Government had to resign
because of the Showa Denka scandal. Mr. Yoshida, the leader
of the Conservative Liberal Party, was chosen to form a new
Government. It would be Yoshida's second postwar cabinet.
His position, however, was only slightly stronger than that of
his predecessor. Moreover, the new cabinet lacked both the
time and the power to remedy the situation. A wave of strikes,
on top of notorious scandals, rocked the country. The danger of
chaos and of widespread disturbances lurked around every
corner.

As the situation in Japan deteriorated, Washington became
more and more alarmed. Furthermore, it had become tired of
Japan's apathy and profiteering. It felt that large sums of
American money and much American energy were being spent
without definite achievements. It realized that many Japanese
people were of the opinion that profiting from the American
help was very pleasant, but that they themselves should exert as
little effort as possible in sustaining their economy. Washington
recognized that the time had come to alter radically this
highly unsatisfactory situation.

On December 18, 1948, the U.S. Government sent a forceful

directive to MacArthur, requesting that the Supreme Commander instruct the Japanese to take effective measures to check the economic deterioration. Washington ordered the immediate initiation of a nine-point emergency program, designed to stabilize Japan's economy.

On December 19, 1948, MacArthur forwarded these instructions to Prime Minister Yoshida. SCAP did not mince his words. If the previous warnings to the Japanese Government had been merely cautions, this one contained a threat. The Supreme Commander warned the Japanese that if the announced stabilization program failed to show quick results, the Occupation would take radical and direct measures. The nature of the measures was not disclosed, but it was clear that America's patience had run out and that a definite change could be expected. The program itself was comprehensive and significant. "Stop inflation, balance your budget, halt tax evasion, limit your credit facilities, stabilize wages and prices, and tighten your foreign exchange control", said MacArthur's message. The Supreme Commander insisted on an improvement of the rationing system, a betterment of food conditions and an increase in industrial production. In short, SCAP's instructions prescribed a stiffening of controls and a restriction of freedoms. He warned the Japanese that a period of severe austerity was ahead. Japan would have to surrender some of the privileges and immunities, inherent in a free society, in order to prevent improvident political conflicts, futile labor strikes and destructive ideological disturbances.

Two characteristics may be discerned in MacArthur's nine-point economic stabilization directive. First, it may be noted that the instruction came straight from Washington instead of emanating from the Tokyo Headquarters. Following the visits of Draper and other industrial missions, Washington had decided to take a more direct hand in shaping the economic future of occupied Japan. This decision of Washington became very clear when some months later a special emissary, Joseph M. Dodge, a prominent Detroit banker, was sent to Tokyo to supervise the rehabilitation of the Japanese economy. Dodge was given virtually dictatorial powers in the economic field. As Special Financial Adviser to SCAP, he got a free hand in straightening out the economic difficulties of the Occupation.

A second significant feature of the December directive was the drastic tone and the definite terms in which MacArthur's letter to Prime Minister Yoshida was couched. It was clear that, at the insistence of Washington, the attitude of the Occupation had become adamant. The period of American benevolence in democratizing Japan, sometimes called "a brave social experiment deserving more opportune times", was apparently at an end. The Japanese — and the Occupation as well — had to be brought back to sober realities.

7. *Japanese Reactions Unsatisfactory; Discouraging Election Results Follow*

The Japanese reaction was noteworthy. Within seven hours Yoshida's reply was received by MacArthur. The Prime Minister said that he fully endorsed the American program; together with SCAP he was of the opinion that "the speedy economic rehabilitation of his country had become the common objective of Japan and of the Allied Powers, particularly the United States". Yoshida assured the Supreme Commander that the matter would be seriously considered by the Japanese Government. Unfortunately, however, one of the points of Yoshida's election program had been a promise to foster economic recovery by releasing controls; MacArthur's instructions, on the contrary, urged a stiffening of controls. With new elections facing his Government by the end of January 1949, Yoshida did not dare to take drastic action. Contrary to his expressed agreement no actual steps were taken; the program remained in "respectful study". Yoshida's political opponents, on the other hand, considered his announced compliance with SCAP's instructions a welcome opportunity to attack his policy. The opposition parties demanded the immediate resignation of Yoshida's government.

On January 23, 1949, Japan went to the polls. Yoshida's government scored a definite victory, notwithstanding the manifold economic difficulties. This would prove fortunate in the future, for Yoshida would show himself a great statesman and a remarkably successful politician in bringing his country back to advantageous cooperation with the Occupation and finally to the San Francisco Peace Treaty. Early in 1949, however, these promising developments were still hidden in the mist of the future. The outcome of the elections seemed anything but satisfactory from the standpoint of the Occupation and its mission to democratize Japan. The middle-of-the-road-parties, particularly the Social Democratic Party of Katayama, the 1947 Christian post-war Premier of Japan, suffered a serious setback. Katayama himself failed to be returned to the Diet. Only those parties which stood further from the American conception of democracy made definite gains. The Japanese electorate chose a conservative majority, but at the same time notably increased the communist representation.

The situation in Japan looked anything but promising. The reactions of the Japanese people towards the Occupation reforms were difficult to evaluate. Japan's economy was only improving very gradually; her industrial recovery was alarmingly slow and the Japanese did not seem inclined to do very much about it themselves. Politically the situation was not reassuring either; both the return of the conservatives and the communist gains gave rise to anxiety. MacArthur's work, so hopefully begun, seemed to be turning into a failure. Obviously, the stern warning given Japan had not produced the anticipated results.

What was Japan thinking? What political developments could be expected in the former enemy country? Were all the favorable reports about the progress in democratizing Japan untrue? Had those reports been based on wrong impressions, or on lip service of the Japanese people? Where was Japan going? What was the best attitude for the United States to adopt in view of all these uncertainties?

8. *America's Policy at the Crossroads*

These manifold problems caused serious concern to the American leaders in both Washington and Tokyo; they realized that a solution had to be found but they were painfully aware of the enormous difficulties involved.

Two extreme theories for coping with the Japanese problem were developed. One was based on a very skeptical viewpoint with regard to the international position of the United States in general, and its position in Japan in particular. It favored a military withdrawal from Japan. The sponsors of this theory did not believe in the feasibility of defending Japan in case of war; they advocated that the United States should limit its western line of defense to the west coast of America and a few salients, such as Hawaii. No military commitment should be entered into so far as Japan was concerned. That country could be aided economically — on condition that the Japanese themselves showed sufficient interest in the economic restoration of their country; in this manner Japan would be given a chance to prevent communism from taking over the country; but that would be all.

The opposite school considered Japan an indispensable bastion of democracy in the Far East, which should be defended at all costs.

9. *International Developments Cast Their Shadows on Japanese Situation.*

In order to adequately appraise these two diametrically opposed points of view with regard to Japan, it is necessary to glance once more at the developments on the international scene, where enormous changes had taken place since we last considered them.

The tension between the Western world and the Soviet Union had constantly increased. In the beginning of 1948 the situation in Western Europe and in the Middle East had become definitely alarming. Arabs and Jews fought in Palestine. Large scale strikes, instigated by the Communists, swept Italy and France. Czechoslovakia, still considered a bridge between the democratic West and the communistic East, was threatened by a powerful communist minority. The problem of Germany's future caused incessant friction between the Soviet Union and the Western Powers. At the end of February 1948 the position became more serious still. Communist leader Gottwald seized the Czechoslovakian Government with the unquestionable assistance and consent of Moscow; the Foreign Minister, Jan Masaryk, whose sympathies for the Western world were well-known, committed suicide. Memories of Hitler's seizing of Czechoslovakia, and of the Munich Conference heightened the general feeling of alarm. Rumors of an imminent war pervaded

John Foster Dulles
Architect of the Japanese Treaty

Tokyo 1945

Tokyo 1950

Europe. In a countermove, five Western European countries, the United Kingdom, France, Holland, Belgium and Luxemburg, founded the Western Union at Brussels. Their aim was to form a Western European bloc against the ruthless attempts of Russia to dominate the continent. This development only seemed to increase the threat of war. Moscow answered by cutting off the Allied sector of Berlin from West Germany, blocking all rail and road communications between the town and the West German border. Thus, on March 30, 1948, the Berlin blockade began. In the beginning of April a Soviet move in northern Scandinavia caused fresh alarm. In Britain the people shivered at the thought of fleeing again to their wartime air-raid shelters, and a feeling of anxiety at the specter of a new war spread through the Western democracies.

The clearly demonstrated communist danger on the cold war front in Europe had had a profound influence on American foreign policy in general. In 1947, the United States had embarked on a program of restraining communist aggression in the world. Truman and Marshall had become convinced that the security of the United State called for a great effort to bolster the resistance of those nations which were immediately threatened by aggression. As a result of this policy, the United States assumed heavy commitments in Europe. The famous Marshall Plan, launched in 1947, had gradually got underway; millions of dollars had been allocated to strengthen Europe's economic defenses. In Greece and Turkey direct military assistance had been provided by the United States. Large-scale preventive measures were taken in America itself, where President Truman had called for universal military training, for temporary conscription and for a huge increase in the military budget.

In addition the security of the American continent as a whole had been strengthened. In the beginning of April 1948, the representatives of the United States and the South American republics met in Bogota to discuss the further coordination of Pan-American defense plans. At the time of their meeting there was serious trouble in the Columbian capital, and communist riots sounded a sinister warning to the participants of the conference, who had only to look at what was happening in Europe in order to be convinced of the generally alarming world situation. It seemed that the American measures to stop the spread of

7

communism had only stressed the Soviet determination to further its agressive policies.

Moreover, although the anticipated Western defense preparations against the rising wave of Soviet Communism had only started, the costs and the efforts expended by the United States in bolstering the free world had already reached considerable proportions. No wonder that in the beginning of 1948 the policy-makers in Washington raised the question of how far it would be possible to enforce their policy of containing communism all over the world.

Obviously, these considerations greatly influenced the American point of view with regard to the occupation of Japan; inevitably the question arose whether it would still be worth-while and justifiable to pour additional millions into Japan and to keep the largest part of the then existing U.S. Army in these far off islands.

This problem increased in significance as, in the course of 1948, the Asian situation also worsened, and Communism threatened to swallow the entire Far East.

These latter developments, of course, were of more immediate concern to the authorities in Tokyo and to those in Washington in charge of Japanese affairs, and had an even more direct bearing upon their considerations and decisions than the events which were taking place in Europe. Let us therefore study what happened throughout Asia after World War II in order to understand the implications of the Japanese question.

For a clear comprehension of the events in Asia after World War II, and their influence on the Japanese question, it is necessary to realize that they were dominated by a communist offensive, most successfully launched in China.

The immediate post-war U.S. endeavors to reconcile the Chinese Nationalists and Mao Tse-tung's Communists, culminating in General Marshall's mission from the end of 1945 to the beginning of 1947, had been in vain. In a last appeal to stop the imminent civil war, which threatened to devastate the unhappy country, the American Ambassador to China, Leighton Stuart, on February 20, 1948, urged the Chinese people to refrain from choosing the extreme left or the extreme right; he counseled them to overhaul their Kuo Min-tang Government and to unite the country. His warnings, however, were ignored, and nothing was done to prevent China's falling a prey to communism.

Mao's offensive, launched in force at the end of 1947, rapidly gained momentum. Early in March 1948 Mukden was captured by the communist troops. A successful offensive in Manchuria followed, and in the late spring of 1948 Chiang Kai-shek's forces had to evacuate Yenan. In September 1948, the North China People's Government was officially established.

The United States, in the meantime, in adherence to its policy of containment, continued to aid the Nationalist Chinese Government, notwithstanding the discouraging experiences of General Marshall. In April 1948, $460,000,000 were allocated to Nationalist China. On the other hand, in view of the successive failures of Chiang's Government, the question arose as to China's worth as an ally and an advance base in the Far East. General Wedemeyer, one of America's great experts on China, voiced the opinion that the money would be wasted if China was not given more support, support in fact of a military nature. He strongly urged America to extend its aid to Chiang Kai-shek so as to include weapons and other military assistance. Marshall, in the meantime appointed Secretary of State, was very reluctant to follow Wedemeyer's recommendations. He had firsthand knowledge of inefficiency and corruption in Kuo Min-tang circles. In his opinion the United States would, moreover, be spreading its forces too thin if it became involved in the Asiatic struggle at a time when all efforts were required to contain Soviet Communism in the West. He considered the defense of Europe the most important part of the American security scheme.

In the global struggle between the free world and the communist camp, however, the developments in Asia were of primary importance. One could not ignore the fact that events in China were playing directly into the hands of Stalin. Some observers advanced the theory that Mao Tse-tung's regime represented only a strictly Chinese version of the Communist doctrine, and that Mao was as far alienated from Stalin as was Tito. Others understood that the problem of China was of a much wider scope and could not be stated in the single, over-simplified question of pro or contra Soviet Russia. Both groups, however, failed to face the immediate consequences and were apt to forget that Stalin, for the time being, was greatly profiting from the developments in China.

In 1948 the situation in the Far East, viewed from the Western standpoint, went from bad to worse. Mao's march southward continued. Changchun, a keypoint in the Manchurian corridor to China, was captured in the middle of October 1948. At the beginning of November, Red Chinese troops threatened the ancient city of Peking. The United States evacuated its consular personnel, and the U.S. Marines occupied Tsingtao as the last escape port for American citizens from the northern part of China. Martial law was declared all over the country. Madame Chiang Kai-shek flew to the United States to plead for American help. The first lady of China, however, was received with marked indifference, compared with the frenzied enthusiasm displayed at her visit to Washington during World War II. The situation was now entirely different. The United States had become extremely reluctant to grant further aid to the Generalissimo. It looked as if nothing could stop the trend of events in Asia.

In view of the foregoing it will be clear that in those days many political and military leaders in the United States were deeply concerned about the fate of the Far East, and in particular about their biggest post-war investment in that part of the world — the Occupation of Japan.

Developments in the following months did not help to lessen their anxiety. The communist flood swept further down over China. In the beginning of December 1948, Peking was captured. Then the Kuo Min-tang Government announced that it was willing to talk peace with the Communists. But the selfconfident Chinese Communists asked a virtually unconditional surrender from the Nationalist Government and there was little hope for an agreement between Chiang Kai-shek and Mao Tse-tung. As the United Nations convened at the General Assembly meeting in Flushing Meadows in April 1949, to discuss peace for the world, the talks between the Nationalist and Communist Chinese broke down. Full-scale war flared up again in China. The Communists launched a new offensive on a 600-mile-wide front along the muddy waters of the Yangtze River. On April 24, 1949, Mao Tse-tung's forces swarmed across the Yangtze, and in the course of the year the remnants of the Kuo Min-tang fled to Formosa. The red dragon was ready to swallow the rest of China, and in fact, threatened the whole of East Asia.

In the meantime the Americans had gone to the polls and had re-elected Truman as their President. Secretary of State Marshall resigned for reasons of ill health, and Dean Acheson took his place. He was confronted with one of the most difficult tasks ever faced by any Secretary of State in the history of the United States. It was for him to decide the policy toward Asia. While the cold war seemed to be taking a turn for the better in the West since the 1948 spring crisis, it looked as if a crushing defeat loomed in the Far East for want of a stable American policy. The implications of a communist victory in Asia could be of incalculable significance for the world and could turn the tide of history. It was clear that the United States had to reconsider its basic policy in the Far East.

The big questions facing the United States were: Could and should America stay in the Far East, and if so, where and how?

It will be clear that the answers to these questions would have the most far reaching consequences with regard to the American position in Japan, and would decide the fate of the Occupation and, in fact, the future of Nippon.

10. *Japanese Unaware of Danger*

The Japanese, however, were not cognizant of this sword of Damocles, swaying above their heads. Some Japanese had viewed the events in China with discomfiture, but the general public in Japan did not realize the implications of the developments on the Asiatic mainland. They felt quiet and safe with the American Occupation taking care of their interests and their country.

The Occupation itself had fostered these feelings. The United States, repeatedly, had made it known that one of the reasons for America to extend help to Japan was to support that country against the threat of communism. Elaborate plans had been discussed, and several measures had been taken in that direction. There were rumors of an Asiatic Marshall Plan, under which Japan would become the supplier for the industrialization of the greater part of Asia, and at the same time be given a chance to become economically self-supporting, as well as politically independent. In short, there were strong indications that some people in the United States considered guaranteeing Japan's security and rebuilding it as a bastion of democracy in the Far East, thereby creating a strong and dependable ally in Asia as a substitute for China.

As indicated above, a large group of influential people in America were, however, opposed to these plans. Those who believed that the United States had to withdraw from Asia, and to concentrate on Europe, as well as those who had lost their confidence in the Japanese, were obviously not in favor of keeping a large and costly defense force in this faraway outpost of the Far East. By the end of 1948 this group had gained considerable support. One of the strongest opponents to the plan of reinforcing Japan as a bulwark for democracy in the Far East was the U.S. Secretary of War, Royall. It was again Royall who was to make clear to the Japanese that the guarantee of their defense by the United States was less sure than they had anticipated, and who thus would rudely awaken them from their illusory dreams.

11. *Royall Reveals that America Doubts Wisdom of Staying in Japan*

On February 11, 1949, Royall, accompanied by General Wedemeyer and by the Special Financial Adviser to SCAP, Mr. Dodge, arrived in Japan. This group had far greater authority than previous emissaries from the United States. Hence, the opinion prevailed that this mission had been sent to the Far East to study the political, military and economic position of Japan in view of the changed circumstances in Asia, and that it was the task of Royall to recommend a future policy for the Occupation. His words and actions would be observed with special attention.

One might ask: what thoughts prevailed in Royall's mind as he toured Japan at the time that country was one of America's most remote outposts in the cold war?

It is quite possible that when reviewing the U.S. occupation forces, lined up on the Palace Plaza in Tokyo, memories of the catastrophic developments during the first months of World War II flashed through his mind. Here again was a relatively small group of Americans, probably destined to defend faraway islands against an overwhelming attack. What guarantees were there that these rather green recruits, with their relatively simple equipment, could accomplish their mission? Were they not destined to become the victims of a new Bataan?

It must be admitted that such considerations, if at least they were ever entertained, could certainly have been stimulated by the fact that the American Army in Japan, in the beginning of 1949, was not an impressive group of soldiers. The old war veterans of the Pacific had gone home; new recruits had been sent to Japan. Their occupation duties did not help to shape them into tough combat soldiers; on the contrary, the occupation troops were somewhat easygoing and indolent. Lt. General W. H. Walker, the vigorous new Commanding General of the U.S. Eighth Army, had only just started his new training program. Under his leadership this Army would, in time, regain its fighting qualities, but in February 1949, Walker's hand was not yet discernible. As Secretary Royall saw it, Japan seemed a poor security risk.

Whether these observations convinced the Secretary of War that it was unwise to commit the United States to an all-out defense of Japan, will remain a secret. Undoubtedly, Mr. Royall was far from pleased at the thought of the military and, in particular, of the economic consequences of an over-all American defense plan for the far-flung Pacific. He must have disliked the consequences of an American commitment covering the thousands of Pacific islands, rimmed by Japan, Formosa and the Philippines, and probably including some outposts on the Asiatic mainland.

Anyhow, whatever his real thoughts were, Royall, at an unofficial press conference in Tokyo, confidentially told correspondents that in his opinion the U.S. armed forces had better pull out of Japan. "Japan", according to the Secretary of the Army, "had to be written off in the event of a war with Russia". In support of this he revealed that several prominent American strategists considered the whole Far East more of a liability than an asset. He said that the major interest of the United States lay in Western Europe. He clearly advocated a withdrawal of America's defense line to the west coast of the United States.

12. *Royall's Statement Awakens Japanese*

Somehow the contents of these confidential remarks found its way into the newspapers. The story, once revealed, was flashed around the world and immediately became front-page news. Official denials followed; they were, however, unconvincing. Many people knew that the military strategists of the United States were studying the problem of Japan's usefulness as a U.S. base in the Far East and Secretary Royall, through his revelations in Tokyo, had disclosed that serious doubt existed as to whether the defense of Nippon would be worth the sacrifice or whether such a defense would be practicable in case of war.

Reactions in Japan were violent. The Japanese were deeply shocked. For the first time since the occupation army had entered Japan, the weak position of their country became unmistakably clear to them. They realized that the security of Japan depended exclusively on the presence of the U.S. occupation forces. Japan itself was completely disarmed. The evergrowing Red menace in Asia suddenly became a grim reality, creating a sense of alarm among the Japanese. They had been awakened overnight. Their complacency was gone. Abruptly and unexpectedly they were faced by the dangers from the outside world. As circumstances developed it became clear that Royall's hint of a possible American withdrawal from Japan was to become one of the greatest dangers which have threatened the successful accomplishment of the Occupation. Royall's words sowed serious doubts in the hearts of the Japanese, doubts about America's intentions and its power to guard and protect the results of the Occupation, doubts which made the Japanese mistrustful of any future American plan with regard to their country.

CHAPTER VI

AMERICA'S PEACE PLAN BACKFIRES

The Soviet Union, looking for a way to thwart America's reconstruction policy in Japan, launches a peace offensive as a means of obstruction. The other Allied nations, exploiting their strong position as indispensable cooperators in America's piecemeal peace policy, also demand a speedy peace conference. America, faced with stagnation in reconstructing Japan and with the possibility of serious discontent in Japan, chooses a plan for a separate peace treaty. This proposal, however, backfires; the Japanese do not favor such a peace.

1. Little Soviet Reaction to Occupation during First Years

In order to understand the developments after Royall's visit, some knowledge of the Soviet attitude toward the Occupation is required. The Kremlin's actions would greatly influence the Japanese scene during 1949 and the following years.

After the Moscow Conference in December 1945, the Russians did not display much interest in Japan, at least not openly. They maintained, nevertheless, a large mission in Tokyo as the staff of the Soviet Representative to the Allied Council. The 200 to 300 members of this staff constituted an exceptionally large personnel for a diplomatic mission; the United Kingdom Liaison Mission, the second largest in Tokyo, counted only 60 persons. The Russians obviously were engaged in subversive activities and propaganda. At the same time they closely followed the developments of the Occupation and the reactions of the Japanese thereto. Officially, however, they limited their activities to protest actions in the Allied Council, principally on occasions that the Supreme Commander showed an inclination to slow down or to mitigate the process of reformation in Japan.

So long as the Occupation was instrumental in tearing down the former structure of Japan, so long as it was working for the liberalization of Japan's political, social and economic life, the Kremlin had good reasons to behave so prudently; during the first years the Occupation had been working in a direction more or less favorable to Moscow's aims. Notwithstanding the fact that MacArthur obviously was opposed to the introduction of any leftist ideas into Japan, the entire trend of the Occupation policy had been to effectuate a swing from the extreme right toward the left. A totalitarian government had been replaced by a democratic system under which all restrictions on political activities had been abolished. Communist leaders had been freed, the Communist Party had been revived and communist propaganda had been allowed. The organization of labor — always an attractive field for communist activities — had been initiated and encouraged. The purge of prominent industrial and social leaders and of die-hard conservatives in the bureaucracy and in politics had also been helpful in furthering Soviet plans. Even the deconcentration of Japanese industry, the inflation in the Japanese economy and the deterioration of Japanese morals were welcomed by the Kremlin as instrumental in weakening the position and the potential of the most reliable forces in the country, and as such favoring the ultimate realization of the aims of the Soviet Union.

2. As U.S. Policy Changes Toward Reconstruction, U.S.S.R. Activities Increase

When, however, in the course of 1948 the United States evidenced a reversal of policy to a more conservative approach and openly endorsed a speedy reconstruction of Japan, Moscow, deciding that the time had come to change Russian tactics, embarked on a program of severe criticism and unrestrained obstruction of the U.S. policy in Japan.

The first serious clash between the Russians and the Americans, resulting from the new Soviet attitude, took place August 24, 1948, when the Russian representative in the Allied Council lodged an emphatic protest against MacArthur's instructions with regard to the enforcement of the National Public Service Law. The reasons which prompted the Supreme Commander to order the enactment of this law, restricting the rights of government workers, have been described in the previous chapter. The Russian representative requested that the SCAP-sponsored ordinance be withdrawn immediately. Moscow could not tolerate, stated General Derevyanko, the enforcement of restrictions upon any employees, government or non-govern-ment. The Russians, the General declared, were most anxious to protect the newly won freedom of the Japanese workers. Moscow obviously favored the occurrence of large-scale strikes, in the hope that these would thwart the American program of economic rehabilitation.

A particularly welcome occasion for Soviet criticism of the American reconstruction plans for Japan was offered by MacArthur's nine-point economic stabilization plan of Decem-ber 18, 1948. As we have seen this plan was unfavorably received by the majority of the Japanese. Their disapproval of MacArthur's intension formed fertile ground for Soviet action. Moscow hoped to show the Japanese that the communists had a better understanding of their wishes and needs than did the Americans. On January 28, 1949, the Soviet member of the Far Eastern Commission registered a vigorous protest against the American-sponsored economic stabilization program.

The more the United States revealed of its intentions to rehabilitate Japan's economy and to rebuild the country, the stronger the Soviet reactions became. Gradually the Russians demonstrated an open hostility toward the Occupation. The Russian representatives, who had maintained quite amicable social relations with several occupation authorities in Tokyo, changed their attitude. They withdrew into practically total aloofness. General Derevyanko, returning from home leave in the late autumn of 1948, failed to call on MacArthur and even failed to inform SCAP that he had resumed his duties.

Simultaneously, the Soviets launched an attack on the Japanese Government accusing it of following the Occupation in its reactionary course. In the spring of 1949 the Russian representative on the Allied Council filed a protest in connec-tion with Yoshida's policy. He repudiated this policy as too reactionary, and contrary to both the Potsdam Declaration and the Far Eastern Commission directives. The American Chair-man of the Council, skillful debater William J. Sebald, did not trouble to answer the Soviet complaint, considering the remarks of the Russian pure propaganda. He, in his turn, accused the Soviet Union of purposely delaying the repatriation of Japanese prisoners of war from Manchuria. This clash between the representatives of the United States and the Soviet

Union was the beginning of a prolonged battle between the two nations in the Allied Council; reciprocal accusations were the order of the day. Both the United States and the Soviet Union claimed that they were the guardians of the Japanese people's interests. The Soviet representative pretended to defend the rights and the liberties of the Japanese workmen; the United States fought for the repatriation of the Japanese prisoners of war, accusing the Soviet Union of retarding the return of several hundred thousands of Japanese who were still in custody in Manchuria.

In the Far Eastern Commission, the Soviet Union followed the same course of action. There, however, even more than in the Allied Council, the Russians took care to ensure that their criticism of the Occupation and of the American policy toward Japan did not antagonize the Japanese people. The Russians realized that the Japanese profited from the American assistance and that the Japanese people, in general, welcomed the American attempt to rebuild their country. Russia could not oppose those actions without the risk of spoiling her chances to cultivate their good will. Moscow was careful not to seem to lag behind the United States in showing interest in the rehabilitation of the Japanese nation. Those considerations even led to an instruction to the Russian representative in the Far Eastern Commission, ordering him to propose the lifting of the restrictions on the development of Japanese industry. Panyushkin, the Soviet Ambassador at the Commission, submitted this Soviet plan on September 23, 1948. In addition to the revival of peaceful industries, the Russian plan contained provisions prohibiting any war industry and a suggestion to establish an International Joint Control Board to supervise the development of Japan's industry. The Far Eastern Commission, however, rejected the Russian proposal.

3. *Reactions to Royall's Statement Offer Opportunity for More Active Soviet Obstruction*

In the course of 1948 it must have become clear to Moscow that by means of protests and similar actions it could not further thwart the American reconstruction of Japan and antagonize the Japanese toward the United States.

Stalin, therefore, looked for other ways.

The statement in January 1949 by Secretary Royall to the effect that some circles in Washington were considering the advisability of a military withdrawal from Japan, and the Japanese reactions to this statement had been studied in Moscow with great interest. The shrewd political instinct of the Russians told them that there was a chance to realize their wishes.

The Kremlin carefully followed further developments.

The reaction to Royall's remarks had not been confined to Japan. His statement had caused world-wide anxiety, which had prompted President Truman to declare, in the middle of February 1949, that the U.S. policy toward Japan had not been changed. This declaration, however, failed to convince the world. Nor did the fact that Mr. Royall himself ordered his deputy, Mr. Draper, to deny his remarks, change the impression made by his statement. The Japanese, in particular, were very skeptical about these denials. Even the emphatic contradiction of the substance of the press reports about Royall's indiscretion, published by SCAP in April 1949, or the declaration of General Bradley, the U.S. Chief of Staff, issued at the beginning of May 1949, that Japan and Okinawa formed the foremost U.S. defense line in the Pacific, did not convince the Japanese. After all, they reasoned, Secretary Royall would not have made his remarks had they not contained much truth. Was not the rejection of MacArthur's request for more armed forces for Japan — in view of the growing menace of Chinese communism — a significant indication that the U.S. authorities were divided over the problem of Japan's defense? Why had MacArthur, on May 11, 1949, in an interview with the British correspondent, Ward Price, declared that he considered Japan "the Switzerland of the Far East", emphasizing a status of complete neutrality and of absence of armed forces for the country? Was it not a public secret that the over-all strategy in the Pacific was under serious consideration and that the military planning staff in Washington was studying the value of Japan as an American base in case of war? Moreover, United States officials had repeatedly stressed that the main interest of their country lay in Europe, where it was already heavily committed in bolstering the defence of the Continent. Newspaper stories indicated that in order to secure a Rhine frontier, America would have to concentrate such large forces in Europe that it would no longer be able to defend Japan or to hold the rest of the Far East in the event of war. Many factors made the Japanese people believe that Royall's indiscretions were based on facts.

Notwithstanding the official denials, therefore, the Japanese nation did not regain its confidence in the United States. The Japanese people had been awakened overnight to the dangers threatening their country from the outside. The Japanese had been made to realize that the United States was not the dependable guardian of Japanese liberty and freedom that they had hoped. The Japanese suddenly became seriously concerned about their national security, and nothing could lull them to sleep again.

The reaction to Royall's statement was not only one of fear and anxiety, but also one of dismay, resentment and mistrust. Those Japanese who had previously been most friendly to America felt particularly betrayed. Why, they reasoned, should they continue to cooperate with the United States, if after all they would probably be the victims of Russian revenge? Many Japanese wondered if it would not be better to explore the possibility of an amicable deal with the Russians. Unfortunately, Royall's statement had given much support to those who had been preaching the decadence of capitalist America and the inevitability of a world-wide communist victory.

A carefull study of these facts in Moscow must have confirmed the Russian assumption that Royall's indiscretion and the unexpectedly strong reactions to his words would present ample opportunity to obstruct the work of the Occupation in Japan.

4. *Kremlin Decides Proposal for Peace Best Way to Exploit Situation*

The Russians thought that the best way to exploit the situation was to suggest a peace conference for Japan. At such a conference, they felt, the Americans would have to lay their cards on the table. Either the United States would act according to Royall's words and comply with the Russian suggestion to withdraw all military forces from Japan, or the Americans would be hesitant to strip Japan altogether and would postpone the conference.

In the case of the United States being agreeable to leave the Japanese islands unprotected — or under a theoretical guarantee of the United Nations — the Soviets would gain a free hand in Japan. This, however, seemed too much to expect; the Kremlin was doubtful whether Washington would give up Japan so easily.

Even if the United States should hesitate to do so, the Russian chances were still very favorable. The Soviets could further rouse the Japanese feelings of uncertainty and mistrust. The Kremlin was convinced that its peacemove would in any event open up the possibility of creating serious trouble for the Occupation and that it would completely thwart the constructive work of the United States in Japan.

The developments on the international plane in those days, as well as the Far Eastern policy of the United States at that time, gave no reasons to presume that the United States would — as eventually happened — counteract the Soviet plans by a firm commitment to defend the Japanese islands — a commitment entered upon at the special request and with the full cooperation of the Japanese. On the contrary, in the spring of 1949 there were no such indications, and the future of Japan looked quite gloomy in view of the sinister plans of the Kremlin.

Their tactics decided, the Soviets looked for an opportune moment to launch their peace offensive. The question of a peace treaty for Japan had been evaded throughout 1948. Only a few insignificant references had been made to it. Secretary Marshall, during the session of the General Assembly of the United Nations in the fall of 1948, had emphasized the need for an early and just peace for Germany and Japan. At that same conference, the New Zealand Minister of Foreign Affairs, Smith Holland, had expressed the hope that an early Japanese peace conference be convened in which the smaller nations would participate. On the occasion of the anniversary of the Soviet Revolution on November 6, 1948, Molotov, the Russian Foreign Minister, had stressed the fact that the Soviet Union favored an early peace for the former Axis countries. These pronouncements, however, had been made for public consumption only. Simultaneously, several governments had exchanged diplomatic notes, emphasizing their desire for an early peace with Japan. The actual reason for this correspondence had been to discover the opinions of the other parties. In fact, there was no serious intention of convening a peace conference for Japan. The responsible statesmen of the world realized that peace for Japan at that time was a forlorn hope. The prevailing international circumstances made it impossible to find a practical solution for the problems inherent in any Japanese peace arrangement. This situation made the Russian plans for creating trouble even more dangerous.

5. *The Russian Peace Offensive*

The Kremlin decided to go ahead. It chose the Paris Conference of the Foreign Ministers of the Big Four Powers to start its campaign.

On May 23, 1949, Vishinsky submitted his completely unexpected proposal of peace for Japan. The Soviet representative suggested that a date be fixed for a meeting of the Council of the Foreign Ministers, to be attended also by Nationalist China — in order to work out a draft for a Japanese peace treaty.

The immediate reactions of the Western Powers to the Russian suggestion were negative.

Washington, in particular, was anything but pleased with Vishinsky's plan. It saw no point in convening a conference in which the Soviet Union would participate. It realized that Moscow would never consent to a peace treaty allowing U.S. forces to remain in Japan after it came into force. This, however, had gradually become a condition which many authorities in Washington considered an essential prerequisite to a peace arrangement with Japan. The theory of Secretary Royall, suggesting an abandonment of Japan, was losing the support it had had in America. It was realized that the liquidation of the American defense force in Japan would result in a power vacuum, which communism would try to fill as soon as the opportunity presented itself. In many circles — including the State Department — the opinion that the consequences of such a development were contrary to the interests of the United States, gained field.

As 1949 progressed the Americans became increasingly

convinced that retaining Japan as a bulwark in the defense of the Pacific was in the interests of the United States and of the free world. Moreover, the United States was seeking a substitute for China as a dependable ally in the Far East. During World War II and immediately afterwards, America had hoped that China would emerge as a strong and stabilizing Power in Asia, closely affiliated with the Western Powers for maintaining a free and democratic world, and at the same time offering a fertile field for economic cooperation. The rise of communism in China, however, had shattered those hopes. The United States looked for another country in Asia to fulfil the role originally allotted to China, and Japan was the obvious choice. This evidently would necessitate a change in policy toward the former enemy country. Although a considerable time would be required for the consequences of this policy to be fully appreciated and accepted, the policy itself gained more and more supporters. In view of these considerations Washington felt that to discuss a Japanese peace treaty with the Kremlin at the Paris Conference of the Foreign Ministers of the Big Four would be inopportune and useless.

The British and the French Foreign Ministers shared the opinion of their American colleague. The Western representatives, utilizing the fact that questions concerning Japan were not included on the agenda of the Paris meeting, refused to discuss the matter. As the Soviet representative could not force the issue, no official talks on Japan's peace were held during the conference.

6. America Realizes Russian Initiative Cannot be Ignored

The rebuff at Paris, however, did not mean the end of the Soviet peace endeavor. Soon it would become evident that the Kremlin's estimate of the situation that, although the United States rejected the Russian plan, it would nevertheless still have to face the difficulties created by the Soviet move, had not been wrong. America, trying to ignore the Russian initiative completely, discovered to its great dismay that it could not. Two circumstances forced Washington to reconsider the Soviet peace suggestion: (1) pressure from the other Allies and (2) reactions from the Japanese.

8

The pressure from the other Allies to convene a peace conference as soon as possible came first from the British Commonwealth. The Foreign Office undoubtedly realized the difficulties of a peace conference, attended by the Soviet Union, and it was certainly not willing to support a Russian initiative for Four Power talks on a Japanese peace arrangement. But a peace conference, attended by all the Far Eastern Commission members, remained an attractive plan in British eyes. Moreover, London had to reckon with the wishes of the other Commonwealth nations, of which Australia in particular continued to stress the necessity of an early peace treaty with Japan.

The pressure of the British Commonwealth at this moment was rather unfortunate. It practically forced the United States to suggest the convening of a peace conference, although the State Departement knew that it could not realize such a plan. As on a previous occasion in the history of the Occupation the British Commonwealth would force the United States to choose a course of action which Washington definitely did not anticipate; and again it would be Australia, which — undoubtedly against her will — would seriously embarrass her American ally.

Already during the Paris Conference this development had been discernible. The Australian Minister for External Affairs, Evatt, who at that time was the Chairman of the U.N. General Assembly, had strongly sponsored the Russian action for a speedy Japanese peace conference, suggesting that the question of a peace for Japan could best be dealt with by the United Nations.

One of the reasons for the Australian action was that they were afraid that the continuance of the Occupation would result in a permanent control by the United States of Japanese commercial interests. These fears were shared by the other British Commonwealth countries, which felt themselves excluded from the Japanese market. The British Commonwealth hoped that the conclusion of an early peace with Japan would open up vast possibilities for British commercial expansion in the Far East.

The reactions of the Japanese people to the renewed peace proposals, as voiced by Vishinsky and favored by the British Commonwealth, in particular Australia, increased the difficulties for the United States. In Japan the hope for a speedy conclusion of the "forgotten peace" was revived. To neglect these feelings would certainly create serious dissatisfaction among the Japanese. America could not risk antagonizing the Japanese further, and it was clearly contrary to the American interests that the Soviets should figure as the main sponsors of a Japanese peace treaty. This would afford the communists too easy a chance of gaining the goodwill of the Japanese people; there was reason enough for the United States to fear that the communists would exploit the Japanese feelings.

When on June 9, 1949, some weeks after Vishinsky's proposal, the Red China Government also suggested that a Big Four Conference be convened to draft a Japanese peace treaty, Washington realized that it obviously had to do something to keep the initiative. The pressure of the British Commonwealth, indirectly supported by Moscow and Peking, forced the United States to take a step which it would have preferred to avoid.

Consequently, the U.S. Secretary of State, Acheson, at the end of June 1949, declared at a press conference that the United States was going ahead with preparations for the Japanese peace conference. Acheson stressed, however, that the peace treaty for Japan should be drafted by all 11 nations of the Far Eastern Commission, a condition which up to then had been unacceptable to the Russians.

Thus, Acheson's statement was, in fact, nothing but lip service; a suggestion for the holding of peace talks to be attended by the 11 Far Eastern Commission nations, being definitely contrary to Soviet wishes, had very little chance of materializing.

These circumstances, however, did not alter the fact that the State Department was anything but pleased with the several peace proposals. On the one hand, Washington realized the drawbacks involved in even trying to convene a conference; on the other hand, if no peace-signing was attempted, it faced the grave consequences of Allied counteraction and Japanese disillusion.

7. Piecemeal Peace Policy Forces United States to Comply with Allied Wishes

What was this Allied counteraction which the U.S. Government feared, and why did the other Allies — in particular the British Commonwealth — hold such a strong political position? The answer is that by their recent policy of a gradual return of certain sovereign rights and responsibilities to the Japanese and of rebuilding the economic potential of Japan — the so-called piecemeal peace policy — the United States had made themselves rather dependent on Allied cooperation.

To understand the position, one must remember that already some time before the United States had effected a change in policy toward Japan. The economic rehabilitation of the former enemy country had been followed by even more progressive measures. As said above, this new policy was called the "piecemeal peace policy".

Under this policy, America gradually granted Japan practically all the rights and privileges of an independent government, without actually restoring to Japan her status of a sovereign nation. MacArthur, in his address on May 31, 1949, emphasized this development by saying: "The character of the Occupation has gradually changed from the stern rigidity of a military occupation to the friendly guidance of a protective Power".

The piecemeal peace policy dated back as far as October 1948, from the time that the American State and Army Departments had formulated a change in U.S. policy toward Japan. As outlined in previous chapters, the original purpose of this change was to relieve the American taxpayer of the burden resulting from the huge expenses involved in maintaining Japan under the Occupation. When the Americans decided to bolster Japan's position further in view of the mounting communist threat in Asia, the piecemeal peace policy had been expanded, aiming at giving the Japanese a gradually increasing measure of political and economic self-sufficiency. This policy had been chosen as next best to a peace treaty which, as has been explained, seemed further off in 1948 than ever.

The new policy emphasized that American control on Japan would be reduced as far as compatible with safeguarding the objectives of the Occupation. The Army had to be relieved of the responsibility for Japanese civil affairs and, in particular, for the Japanese economy. Japan would be permitted to organize a 150,000-man national police force, well-armed and well-trained. The Japanese Government would even be given some latitude in amending laws which had originally been enacted on the orders of the occupation authorities. As the execution of this policy got underway, the Japanese became more and more inclined to consider this emancipation process a right, instead of a privilege. The Occupation had more or less stimulated this state of mind. MacArthur had promised the Japanese people "progressive latitude in stewardship of their affairs". The Japanese attitude made it practically necessary for the United States to continue along the road of liberalization of the Occupation, and of retarding the American interference in Japanese affairs. If not, it risked losing the good will of the Japanese people.

For the implementation of this policy, however, the United States ultimately needed the consent and the cooperation of the other Allies. First, the Far Eastern Commission had to sanction several of the liberalization measures. Secondly, the Allied Powers had to cooperate in order to develop Japan's international trade and shipping, to free her fishing industry and to restore her international relations.

As a first step in this direction, the United States had requested the Far Eastern Commission, in the beginning of 1949, to pass a directive allowing Japan to participate, with due restrictions, in international activities. The U.S. representative in this Commission emphasized the desirability of granting Japan the right to direct her own affairs, as far as compatible with safeguarding the aims of the Occupation. In a move further to stimulate Japan's recovery, the United States on May 12, 1949, announced that it would extract no more reparations from Japan under the interim removal program, and that as of October 11, 1949, Japan's peaceful industries would be allowed to develop without restriction.

The United States, however, could not continue this unilateral action. Soon she would arrive at the point where the direct and active cooperation of the other Allied nations was mandatory.

This cooperation, unfortunately, was not forthcoming. The

British Commonwealth particularly was not willing to follow the United States along the road of this new policy. Early in September 1949, the Australian Prime Minister stated that no further rapprochement between Australia and Japan would be contemplated before a peace treaty had been signed. Australia was obviously taking advantage of the fact that the United States needed her cooperation for the piecemeal peace program in order to further its own aim, which was a peace for Japan. The other Commonwealth nations sided with Australia in her attitude toward the Japanese question. Thus, the situation developed into a veritable dilemma for the United States.

8. *Difficulties for United States Increase as a Result of Chinese Crisis*

Washington's problem regarding the Japanese peace was aggravated still further by another development in the international field — the fact that communism had apparently come to stay in China.

In October 1949 the Communist People's Republic of China had been proclaimed in Peking, with Mao Tse-tung as the Chairman of the Central People's Government. The city of Changsha, the capital of Hunan, had been taken by the Communists, and in the middle of October the fall of Canton was imminent. The Chinese Communists landed on the island of Amoy. Simultaneously they launched an offensive toward Chungking, the wartime capital of Chiang Kai-shek. The position of the Red Chinese regime seemed to be secure, and the eventual collapse of the remainder of the Nationalist forces in South China and the capture of their stronghold of Formosa a foregone conclusion.

On October 2, 1949, the Soviet Union recognized Red China. At the same time, India's leader, Nehru, made clear that he also was ready to recognize the Peking Government. Moreover, there were strong indications that Britain, in order to safeguard her commercial and financial interests in China, and to assure her hold on Hongkong, was seriously contemplating doing the same. The U.S. State Department was also studying this problem. There were powerful influences in the State Department favoring the recognition of Mao Tse-tung. Officially, however, the United States was still aiding Chiang Kai-shek. The authorities in Washington failed to decide which policy to follow. The majority of the American people, moreover, were opposed to dealings with the Chinese Communists. This attitude was emphasized when, by the end of October 1949, the Red Chinese jailed Mr. Angus Ward, the U.S. Consul-General in Mukden. The Ward incident became one of the most serious stumbling blocks for any U.S. policy favoring recognition of Peking.

This situation did not facilitate America's decision with regard to the Japanese question; it only complicated the issue.

If Washington decided to convene a peace conference, it had to reckon with the Russian demand for Red Chinese participation, and as circumstances developed, the United States could further expect that India and Britain would sponsor the Soviet request. Thus America would be faced at the conference by a communist participation with the strength of two veto's, and with Britain — also holding a veto — sympathetically inclined toward at least one of the Communist Powers — Red China. Furthermore, the United States had to recognize the fact that India, the foremost South Asian member of the Far Eastern Commission, would side with London and probably Peking. This, obviously, would be a completely unacceptable position for the United States. The State Department, foreseeing these developments, became less and less enthusiastic about peace talks for Japan.

9. *Allied Pressure, at First Successfully Sidetracked by Washington, Becomes too Strong to Resist*

The above mentioned considerations convinced the American Secretary of State, Acheson, that it was in the interest of the United States to counter the mounting British pressure for the convening of a Japanese peace treaty conference, although this was not in accordance with his public announcement of June 1949.

In his first attempt to hold up a peace conference Secretary Acheson was successful. When in September 1949 the British Foreign Secretary, Bevin, attending a Western Powers conference at Washington, personally urged the advisability of holding peace talks for Japan, Acheson convinced him that such talks had to wait until the Allies had made a decision about Red China. Although Acheson had to consent to Bevin's wishes to issue a joint communique for public consumption declaring that a peace treaty for Japan was long overdue and that serious steps would be taken to hasten its conclusion, the British Foreign Secretary, behind closed doors, agreed that the time was not yet ripe to formulate a peace policy for Japan.

Soon, however, Bevin would have to yield to pressure from other Commonwealth members and from business circles in the United Kingdom.

Japan's future was, undoubtedly, of great importance to British commerce in the Far East. As mentioned before, anxiety existed in Commonwealth circles about the preponderant American position in Japan. The Commonwealth countries feared — and in fact had some reason to suppose — that the United States did not for the time being contemplate changing its position in Japan; America seemed convinced that its piecemeal peace policy, under which the United States would retain influence in Japan, would best serve the interests of the United States. Australia particularly did not like this aspect. Canberra had repeatedly asked London to sponsor Australia in its protests against America's attitude and to urge the United States toward a more active policy in preparing a Japanese peace conference. Economic circles in the United Kingdom joined Canberra in bringing pressure to bear on the British Foreign Office. These circles shared Australia's anxiety about the economic developments in Japan. Bevin, who in view of the political situation in his own country, preferred not to be accused of pro-American leanings, and who himself expected economic advantages for Britain from a return to normal circumstances in Japan, informed Acheson that he had changed his point of view, and that he had to insist on a speedy convening of a peace conference.

In view of the fact that America could only expect mounting opposition from her Allies to her Japan policy, and as no other way seemed to be open, it looked as if the United States would have to yield to the Allied pressure and convene a conference with all its perilous consequences.

10. *Separate Peace Introduced to Solve Dilemma*

By now the wavering attitude of the State Department with regard to the developments in the Far East in general, and to the position of Red China in particular, had revenged itself. No clear-cut and definite policy had been established in Washington to guide the United States in its search for a solution to its dilemma. The necessity of having to hold a peace conference for Japan, attended by Russia, and with India and probably other Commonwealth countries insisting on the participation of Red China, was indeed a gloomy prospect.

MacArthur in particular, who was a fierce opponent of any move to recognize Mao's Government and who greatly deplored the vacillating disposition of what he called the "ignorant home front as far as Asiatic developments are concerned", dreaded the alarming outlook of a Red-dominated Japan peace conference.

It was MacArthur who cut the Gordian knot. The Supreme Commander changed the somewhat lukewarm attitude he had assumed with regard to the recent peace conference endeavors and decided to support publicly the sponsors of a speedy conclusion of a peace treaty for Japan. Basically, the Supreme Commander had for the past two years favored and advocated the idea of peace for Japan. In view of the complicated international circumstances, however, MacArthur had consented to the piecemeal peace policy. Recent developments showed that this compromise had become ineffective. Other ways had to be chosen with regard to the future of Japan.

Upon the instigation of MacArthur a new course of action for the United States was embarked upon. Although it is highly unlikely that the Supreme Commander had not been in very close contact with Washington on this matter, it was SCAP who, indirectly, informed the world about the new plan of action. On November 5, 1949, an Associated Press release, featured in Manila, expressed as the official opinion of MacArthur that a Japanese peace should be concluded as soon as possible. The report quoted MacArthur as saying that, in his opinion, China and Russia could be present when the victorious World War II Allies laid down the terms for defeated Japan's re-entry into world affairs, but only if they agreed to

Britain's and America's plans. It was intended that these plans would already be well developed before the actual peace conference started.

With this proposal the path along which — in the future — the Japanese peace deliberations would proceed had been established. The Supreme Commander had laid the foundations for the so-called "separate peace", which would be the eventual solution of the Japanese peace dilemma. But a long and rugged road had to be traveled before that goal would be reached. At first MacArthur's suggestions seemed too ambitious, too farsighted. Serious obstacles and bitter disillusions were to mark the first steps of this journey. Only later, in the middle of 1950, would the going become more smooth and the outcome more promising.

The authenticity of the Manila dispatch was above doubt. At the time the article appeared in the papers, SCAP's public relations officer happened to be in the Philippines on a short visit.

The press release quoted MacArthur as having definite plans for Japan once the peace treaty had been concluded. The Supreme Commander, according to the Manilla dispatch, was of the opinion that Japan should be encouraged by her former enemies to guarantee her security in communist-menaced Asia by entering into a pact safeguarding her independence. Three alternate plans were given. First, Japan's entrance into the United Nations, with that organization guaranteeing her territorial integrity. Second, and considered most likely, a pact granting to America air, navy and army bases on long-range terms. A third alternative could, according to the news release, include British Commonwealth participation in the defense of Japan. Special emphasis was given to the second solution, which would provide for the continued stationing of U.S. armed forces in and around Japan as a security screen against aggressive aims of other countries.

The State Department, which undoubtedly had previously approved the publication of these plans, immediately sponsored the contents of the Manila dispatch. Two days after MacArthur's Manila statement, a seven-point peace proposal was issued by Washington. The press headlines of November 8 and 9 informed the world that the United States would go ahead with its plans for a peace treaty for Japan, and at the same time that the United States intended to make arrangements under which U.S. armed forces would continue to be stationed in Japan for many years after the end of the Allied Occupation. Full autonomy was to be granted to Japan within six months after the signing of the treaty. It was revealed that Secretary Acheson was already sounding Bevin and Schuman as to whether and where the Japanese peace treaty conference should be held.

11. *Reactions to Separate Peace Plan*

The announcement of such definite plans for the speedy conclusion of a peace treaty for Japan evoked widespread repercussions in the world. The United States had definitely pushed the peace problem of Japan into the limelight. Peace for Japan became, overnight, one of the most urgent and important issues in international politics.

At the same time the expectations of the Japanese people were raised to great heights. The Japanese press immediately published the American promises in full. The Japanese, who until then had been somewhat skeptical about the possibilities and the prospects of a speedy peace, hoped that now at last the return to normal international relations was about to be realized; soon it would become clear to them, however, that a separate peace had consequences which Japan did not consider acceptable.

Australia did not want to lag behind those who were pressing for a speedy peace for Japan. The Australian Minister for External Affairs, Evatt, remembering his success with the Canberra Conference of 1947, persuaded Britain and New Zealand to convene a second Canberra Conference, to be held in November 1949, in order to review the Commonwealth attitude toward a Japanese peace treaty. Before the actual convening of this conference, however, the Canberra Government publicly stated that so far as Australia was concerned, no peace for Japan would be possible without Russian participation. Australia also criticized any plan to keep American forces in Japan after the peace treaty. The contents of the Australian dispatches, moreover, made it clear that the Australians were, in general, opposed to the recent change in the American attitude toward Japan and to the inclination of the Occupation to favor the conservative influences in that country. Canberra accused Washington that by its new approach it was making Japan overvulnerable from the left. According to Canberra, the weapon fit to counterbalance communism in Japan was a much more liberal government than the one now sponsored by the Occupation. The Australian Government hoped that a peace for Japan would strengthen such liberal forces.

During the Canberra Conference, Australia successfully convinced Britain that a peace treaty for Japan without Russian participation was not advisable. In the middle of November 1949, the British Under-Secretary of Foreign Affairs made it known that Britian believed a final peace treaty for Japan should be settled by all the Far Eastern Commission nations, including the Soviet Union. On the other hand, Britain and New Zealand succeeded in somewhat calming Australia. They dissuaded that country from taking too definite and hasty steps in connection with the settlement of the many outstanding Far Eastern problems. In particular the presence of Britain's foremost expert on the Far East, Ambassador at Large Sir Esler Dening, had a wholesome influence on the Canberra Conference. The Australian Government was persuaded that in view of the unsettled position of the Commonwealth toward Red China, an ultimate decision on the Japanese peace treaty had to be delayed until a clearer estimation of the Far Eastern situation could be obtained. The decision to sponsor the convening of a Japanese peace conference was postponed until a future meeting of British Commonwealth Foreign Ministers could be held. This conference took place at Ceylon early in 1950.

As might be expected, Moscow welcomed the renewed endeavors of the Western democracies to hold a peace conference for Japan. It hoped to take the greatest possible advantage of this situation. The Soviets, after the rise of the Peking Government, felt themselves in a particularly strong position in the Far East. In the beginning of November 1949, the Kremlin instructed Malenkov, a member of the Russian Polit Bureau, and the Secretary of the Russian Communist Party, to announce to the world the five basic aims of the Russian foreign policy. Together with collaboration with the Big

Powers, the reduction of armaments, a ban on atomic weapons, and the development of economic relations among all countries of the world, Malenkov listed the enforcement of the Potsdam Declaration and the conclusion of a peace treaty with Japan as the most important items on the Soviet list of desirable international developments.

Malenkov's statement was of course advocated by the Russian representative in the Allied Council for Japan. This representative declared on November 15, 1949, that Moscow favored the speedy convening of a peace conference; he emphasized that under certain circumstances there would be no objections from the Russian side to the participation of all the Far Eastern Commission countries in such a conference. This last remark — indicating a change in the Kremlin's attitude — could only be seen as an encouraging gesture toward Australia. Both Canberra and London had stated previously that Russia's attendance at the conference was an indisputable prerequisite. This had been a particularly welcome pronouncement for Moscow. Russia did not fail to take careful note of the attitude of the British Commonwealth, and it no longer considered it opportune to insist on its former standpoint of a Big Four Conference. By this move it planned to upset America's Far Eastern policy. Soon it would become evident how shrewdly Moscow had estimated the situation. Once again the United States was about to face new and serious difficulties with her peace plans for Japan.

12. America's Peace Plan Backfires

As has been stated previously, the United States planned to arrange a peace treaty under which the U.S. forces would remain in Japan for an unlimited period of time in order to guarantee Japan's security. The treaty was to be drafted in close cooperation with the Commonwealth nations and other Western Allies, and only afterwards would it be submitted to the Soviet Union and China on a take-or-leave basis. Whether Red or Nationalist China would eventually participate had not been decided. But Washington reckoned with the possibility that it would be Red China. Furthermore, Washington envisaged the possibility that the communist nations would refuse to sign the treaty, in which case America planned to make it a separate peace treaty between Japan and the free world. By accepting such a treaty Japan would commit herself irrevocably to the democratic camp, and would antagonize Russia, as well as the new Power in Asia — Red China. The success of such a treaty was obviously dependent upon the enthusiasm with which the Japanese people would accept such an arrangement. Yet, the United States failed to enlist the cooperation of the Japanese. This circumstance would prove to be the great stumbling-block to achieving a solution on the peace problem.

Why did America's peace plan backfire?

There was only one, be it a very important reason. Contrary to exceptation, the Japanese people were not favorably inclined toward a separate peace treaty for their country.

Strangely enough the United States had been wrongly informed as to the attitude of the Japanese. Undoubtedly, the United States had hoped that, after all the benevolent assistance extended to the Japanese people under the Occupation, Japan would only be too glad to take the American side and to declare herself a faithful member of the community of free and democratic nations, opposed to any rapprochement with Russia or with Red China. The Japanese reactions in the autumn of 1949, however, showed that these expectations were erroneous.

The Japanese attitude should not have been such a complete surprise for Washington. For months before, there had been strong indications that the Japanese people were keeping an open eye toward the new regime in China. This had been clearly borne out by the reactions to Secretary Royall's statement in the beginning of 1949. The general attitude of Japan's leading statesmen and politicians during the previous year might have given the State Department another hint in that direction. It was remarkable with what care prominent Japanese, including Prime Minister Yoshida, had avoided making any public statement detrimental to Peking or Moscow. Their attitude should have betrayed certain tactics. These straws in the wind, however, seemed not to have been discerned by the American observers in Japan. Even Yoshida's reactions to the Manila declaration of November 5, 1949, were overlooked, — although they had been very explicit. In an administrative policy speech on November 2, 1949, the Prime Minister, commenting on the Manila press release, emphasized his nation's earnest desire for an early peace treaty. Simultaneously he declared, however, that a completely unarmed state would be the best guarantee for Japan's national security. He stressed that the renouncement of war meant that Japan would not arm either after the peace treaty or at any time in the future. Yoshida added that in view of the feverish interest of the Japanese people in the peace treaty, such a treaty, even with a few Allied Powers, might be better than nothing. The Prime Minister, on the other hand, emphasized that Japan would only be ready to conclude such a treaty on the condition that it would lead to a peace arrangement with all countries concerned.

13. Japanese People Refuse Cooperation

Yoshida's speech was followed by a flow of statements, press releases and commentaries. The majority of the Japanese appeared opposed to accepting the consequences of a separate peace. The Japanese people hesitated to join the Western bloc. Japan longed for peace but was not willing nor inclined to accept a separate peace, combined with an American security agreement. It was now abundantly clear that the Japanese people were, in fact, sitting on the fence in the ideological battle between the Western democracies and the Soviet bloc.

The question arises why the Japanese people were so hesitant to join the Western democracies. Had they not been convinced, by their own crushing defeat, of the might of America? Had they not profited greatly from the benevolent attitude of the victorious nations? Were these two reasons not strong enough to convince them of the wisdom of choosing the democratic side in the controversial world situation?

Unfortunately, it had become evident they were not.

The Americans, regarding the Japanese attitude as ungrateful in the extreme, were greatly disappointed. They considered the Japanese reluctance as an indication that the great work done by General MacArthur and his staff had been a failure and that the Occupation, in its endeavor to reform, to rehabilitate and to reconstruct Japan, had made a serious mistake.

The tragic truth, however, was that the Occupation was not in the least to blame for this unexpected development. On the contrary, this deplorable hesitation of the Japanese people was caused by circumstances which were in no way connected with the Occupation. The fact was that, until now, Japan had been guarded and sheltered by the Occupation from the strife and the threats of the outer world. Not that this outer world had not touched Japan; serious spiritual and moral tension had resulted from the international developments in Asia and the rest of the world. But on the whole, the Japanese people had felt themselves safe behind the armed might of the occupation forces. When, however, through Royall's statement it became clear that this security screen could be withdrawn at a moment's notice, the Japanese were greatly concerned. Evidently the time had come for the Japanese to re-enter the dangers and the controversies of the outer world, but the Japanese people hesitated to make the inevitable choice. They were completely unprepared for such a decision, and they were deeply shocked by the prospect of having to make it.

At the same time the Japanese feared that the security measures offered by the United States under a separate peace agreement would probably not be dependable. What guarantee could the United States give that it actually would and could defend Japan in case of war? The Japanese people had lost much of their confidence in the might and power of the United States.

CHAPTER VII

DILEMMA OF THE SEPARATE PEACE

Economic and political reasons underlie Japan's hesitation with regard to a separate peace. In particular the rise of communism in East Asia and the American reaction to it create fear and doubt in the minds of the Japanese people, feelings which are aggravated by Soviet action. The continued pressure for a peace treaty for Japan, however, forces the United States to take action. Washington chooses John Foster Dulles to solve the dilemma.

1. *Two Reasons for Japan's Hesitation toward Separate Peace*

In order to comprehend fully the significance of Japan's reluctance to favour a separate peace treaty, a further study of the underlying factors, some of which have been mentioned at the end of the previous chapter, seems necessary. Generally speaking, the reasons for Japan's hesitation might be divided into two groups: (1) economic and (2) political. Both were based on the apprehension that by signing a separate peace treaty Japan would commit herself to the democratic world and would alienate the communist Asiatic bloc. Japan feared to face this consequence.

Economically, Japan realized that a voluntary adherence to the free world might lead communist-dominated Asia to sever its trade relations with Japan. The Japanese were not sure that the democracies would compensate Japan for the loss of her China trade by sponsoring Japan's trade with other parts of the world. Consequently, the Japanese were very reluctant to expose themselves to the possibility of being cut off, economically, from the Asiatic mainland. Thus arose opposition to a separate peace arrangement.

Politically, the reasons for Japan's hesitation to sign a separate peace treaty were more comprehensive and more difficult to understand. Japan, as an Asiatic country has had long and close ties with China, and she has an instinctive desire to preserve those ties. The Japanese, however, are a realistic people; when the good of their own country depends on choosing the West

9

instead of Asia, they will do so, providing that this choice is profitable. This condition, however, was not guaranteed in the eyes of the Japanese. On the contrary, recent developments in Asia had caused the Japanese to doubt the future of the Western — or more specifically, the American — position with regard to the Far East. As has been said before, Japan had lost its confidence in the United States. The Japanese were not sure that America was resolved to defend Japan under all circumstances, and Japan even wondered if America commanded the necessary forces to realize such a defense in the event of war.

The above-mentioned considerations made Japan definitely reluctant to commit herself to the Western democracies.

For a better understanding of the considerations and the attitude of the Japanese people toward a separate peace, both the economic and the political or, in other words, the psychological reasons underlying their convictions, will be further explored.

2. Economic Reasons

In order to appreciate the economic reasons causing the Japanese to fear antagonizing Asia as a result of too close ties with the West, it is again necessary to review the economic developments in occupied Japan.

As has been described in a previous chapter, the Occupation, during the first months, had not given much consideration to the day by day economic situation in Japan. The main emphasis had been on its demilitarization and on reformative measures in all fields. The increasing food shortage had resulted in the import of food from the United States, and the lack of consumer goods had drawn attention to the advisability of reviving some of the utility industries. As, however, the continuing shortages in Japan had threatened to impose an ever-increasing burden on the American taxpayer, the United States had decided on the economic reconstruction of the former enemy country. Under the direction and with the help of the occupation authorities, industries had been rehabilitated, raw materials had been imported and steps had been taken to revive Japan's export trade.

Parallel with these developments the United States had

gradually changed its policy with regard to the amount of reparations to be paid by Japan. Immediately after the armistice considerable reparation payments had been planned. These plans had been based on a report of the American Ambassador Pauly, issued in February 1946. Pauly's report had been of a very general character. In order to formulate a more detailed reparation program, which would take into consideration the economic future of Japan as stipulated in the Potsdam Declaration and in the post-surrender policy directives, the U.S. Government, in the autumn of the same year, sent a group of technicians to Japan, under the direction of Clifford S. Strike. His mission was charged with the task of making a new and more elaborate survey of the reparations possibilities. Mr. Strike came to the conclusion that the question was so complicated that it should be dealt with by a larger and more varied group of experts. He warned against hasty decisions, based upon a superficial study of the reparation problem. This could, in his opinion, only lead to economic chaos in Japan.

Pursuant to his recommendations, he was again sent to Japan in June 1947, this time accompanied by a large and competent group of technical experts from the Overseas Consultants Incorporation. This group came to the conclusion that only a relatively small amount of reparation payments — consisting mainly of primary war industries — could be exacted from Japan if that country was to be given a fair chance of becoming economically self-sufficient. Mr. Strike warned against the danger to the American taxpayer resulting from continually sustaining Japan. If the Japanese economy was not rehabilitated as soon as possible, this burden could not be lightened for years to come. Hence, the speedy reconstruction of Japan was a direct American interest.

Shortly afterwards a commission, headed by the U.S. Under-Secretary of the Army, William J. Draper, came to Japan to investigate this matter further. Draper's report, endorsing the recommendations of Mr. Strike, concluded that an industrialized Japan was of economic, political and strategical interest to the United States. Draper emphasized that an economically independent Japan would relieve the United States of a yearly burden of approximately $500,000,000. He, moreover, stressed the importance of an industrialized Japan as the workshop of Asia. As such, that country could become an important initiator for improving the standard of living in the Far East, one of the basic aims of American policy for that part of the world.

These recommendations were carried out, and during the latter half of 1947 a gradual change in the American attitude toward its former enemy became discernible. Washington had come to the conclusion that an economic revival of Japan would be in the interest of the United States; consequently, America embarked on a program of rehabilitating Japan's trade and industries.

Obviously, such a policy was very favorable for Japan. It would have been logical for the Japanese people to respond wholeheartedly to the American rehabilitation program and for them to join the Americans in rebuilding their country as soon as possible. In Chapter V it has been explained that this cooperation was lacking. This had induced the U.S. Government, disillusioned by the passive response of the Japanese and irritated by their lack of interest, to instruct MacArthur to sound a firm warning to the Japanese, stressing that earnest and speedy endeavors were expected in order to revive the Japanese economy. Furthermore, Washington had requested Joseph M. Dodge, a well-known financial expert, to go to Japan to take the necessary steps for implementing its economic rehabilitation program. Mr. Dodge, arriving in Japan in February 1949, diagnosed Japan's economic ills as springing from excessive government spending, inordinate extension of bank credits and uneconomical methods of production. On the basis of these observations he proclaimed the so-called Dodge Line, an extensive austerity program aimed at putting the Japanese economy on a sounder financial basis. He called for the curbing of inflation, the stabilization of prices and wages, boosts in production, reduction of manufacturing costs, cuts in domestic consumption and enlargement of the export volume. Simultaneously, Dodge instituted the U.S. Counterpart Fund for Japan, which guaranteed a more responsible way of spending the U.S. aid funds.

The Japanese Government followed up Mr. Dodge's recommendations dutifully though sometimes grudgingly, with substantial success. Inflation was stopped, and by the middle of

1949 the index of consumer goods prices had gradually declined. The circulation of bank notes was brought back from yen 386,000,000,000 at the end of 1948 to approximately yen 300,000,000,000 in the middle of 1949. The tax system was revised with the help of an American expert, Dr. Shoup. Prices were stabilized, government expenses were trimmed and a balanced budget was reached for 1949–50.

Furthermore, the rationalization of industry had been given fresh impetus through the elimination of overemployment and through increased efficiency in plant operation; substantial progress had been made in the reduction of production costs. In addition, there was a renewed will to work; the Japanese people — by natural inclination an industrious nation — were impressed by the serious efforts of the Occupation to rehabilitate their economy and were spurred on by MacArthur's and Dodge's stern warnings; they gradually lost their apathy and aversion to work and they set themselves to co-operate with the Americans in the economic rehabilitation of their country.

As was to be expected, the above-mentioned measures led to a certain shortage of funds, and even to a deflationary trend. But notwithstanding this disadvantage, a notable revival in the Japanese economy had been achieved. The export total for 1949 reached 60 percent of the import, which was a great improvement over previous years, when only 38 percent of the import had been balanced by the export.

At the same time the United States continued to extend unilateral economic help to Japan. On May 12, 1949, Washington announced that it would not exact further reparations from Japan under the interim removal program and that it would allow the development of Japan's peaceful industries without any limitation, as of October 1 of that year. At the end of June 1949, the Supreme Commander gave Japan's exporters and manufacturers access to foreign currency. In the middle of October 1949, the occupation authorities announced that as of December 1 the export trade from Japan would be put on a private basis, and as of January 1, 1950, the import trade would be freed in the same way.

In the meantime, scores of Japanese technicians were sent to foreign countries, particularly to the United States, to be briefed on the newest technical improvements in industry.

Many U.S. experts visited Japan to assist in the rehabilitation of the Japanese economy. Coal production and electric power generation were increased enormously and the shipbuilding industry, which had been completely stopped in 1945, was thriving again in 1949 with a backlog of roughly 400,000 gross tons for new construction.

Under SCAP's supervision and responsibility a large number of trade and financial agreements were concluded with many foreign countries, chiefly with Southeast Asia, South America, Africa and the Sterling Area. Mr. Logan, known for his successes in arranging trade agreements for occupied Germany, had been invited to visit Japan. He arrived in October 1949 and advised SCAP's Headquarters on the revival of Japan's foreign trade. His recommendations greatly stimulated the trade between Japan and the outside world.

By the end of 1949 the economic situation of Japan had definitely improved. Now that the Japanese themselves were at last actively participating in the rehabilitation of their country's economy, the steps taken by Mr. Dodge, MacArthur's financial adviser, had led to tangible results. The Director-General of the Japanese Stabilization Board declared, in the beginning of October 1949, that the inflational spiral had ended. In November, Mr. Ikeda, the Japanese Minister of Finance, stated before the Diet that Japan's economy had been placed on the road to stability.

Notwithstanding these very encouraging developments, however, the situation at the end of 1949 was still far from satisfactory. The necessary imports still exceeded the provenues of the export by 40 percent. A deficit of roughly $400,000,000 continued to burden the U.S. budget. Japan's industrial capacity was still far behind pre-war standards. Only very strenuous efforts by the Japanese people and far-reaching measures to increase Japan's export trade could eventually lead to economic self-sufficiency.

Most Japanese industrial and financial leaders considered the restoration of Japan's trade with the Asiatic mainland as indispensable for the economic independence of their country.

The Japanese pre-war trade pattern had rested on three bastions, China, the America's and the Sterling Area. The China trade had represented roughly a quarter of the total imports and exports. Furthermore, Japan's economy was closely and intricately interwoven with China's, both traditionally and geographically. Hardly a Japanese therefore believed in an economically self-sufficient Japan without its historical trade with China. This was emphasized by the fact that Japan was not confident about the opening of markets in other parts of the world. The Japanese feared that the creation of new markets would take too long to bridge the gap, and that Japanese economic expansion southward would meet with considerable antagonism from the peoples of Southeast Asia, as well as from those Western countries which depended to a large extent on trade with those parts of the world. The Japanese suspected that the West, notwithstanding its promises of compensation, would be neither able nor willing to live up to its good intentions.

Hence, it is understandable that the Japanese, now their interest in the economic welfare of their country had been re-awakened, were reluctant to give their adherence to a policy which would be detrimental to the revival of the trade with the Asiatic mainland, a trade which was considered indispensable to Japan as a source of revenue.

This, however, seemed to be one of the consequences of a separate peace treaty with the West.

Japan was not willing to risk this consequence and, therefore, it did not favor a separate peace treaty.

3. *Political Reasons*

Notwithstanding the great importance of the economic considerations underlying Japan's reluctance to side with the Western democracies, they were overshadowed by objections of a more political and psychological character.

The Japanese felt that their adherence to a separate peace treaty with the West would imply that Japan was willing to side with the democratic world against the communist nations. By so doing, Japan would alienate the communist-dominated mainland of Asia and dissociate herself from a large and important part of the world with which she previously had been closely connected — racially, geographically and historically.

Moreover, Japan realized that a separate peace would

necessitate the continued stationing of U.S. armed forces on her territory after the treaty was signed, which in one respect would emphasize Japan's adherence to the Western bloc. In another, it would most certainly antagonize the Sino-Soviet combination. This would have been an acceptable consequence for the majority of the Japanese people if they had been sure that the presence of the U.S. forces really constituted a guarantee for Japan's security. Unfortunately, however, the Japanese were not sure of this. Therefore, Japan seriously doubted whether a choice in favor of the West would be best for Japan. What was the future of the Western Powers in the Far East? Would the United States yield to communist pressure in Asia? These and many similar questions occupied the Japanese people.

It might well be considered strange, in view of the overwhelming defeat the Japanese had suffered at the hands of the United States during World War II, and in view of the great assistance granted Japan by the Occupation during the postwar period, that such thoughts prevailed in the Japanese mind. It must be admitted, however, that the international developments since 1945 had given the Japanese reason to doubt the intentions and the potential strength of the democratic nations. Only a study of these developments, and a realization of the decline of America's position from a mighty and invincible Power at the end of World War II to a nation with a wavering and incomprehensible Far Eastern policy will give the necessary background to understand these feelings and considerations on the part of the Japanese.

4. *Decline of U.S. Position in Far East Causes Doubts*

Until 1945 the people of Asia had accepted the fact that the ultimate power in the world resided in the West. The developments of World War II, however, had sown some doubt in the minds of the Asiatics. They were no longer convinced that Western power was almighty. Moreover, not only had doubt been conceived, but serious resentment had developed against the predominant position of the white men all over Asia. In the wake of the war an explosive revolt of formidable proportions had swept through the entire Far East and caused tremendous national, political and social upheavals. All forces freed by this revolution were directed toward freeing Asia and toward increasing its potential powers.

The West, particularly the United States, failed to grasp the true character and magnitude of this revolution. It did not understand that World War II had destroyed most of the traditional patterns in the philosophical and sociological fields and had undermined the century-old beliefs and religions of Asia. A feeling of nihilistic opportunism prevailed. The Asiatic people were searching for a new ideology — a new common belief in the possibilities of life. The West had overlooked the fact that the revolt in Asia was primarily of a spiritual character. It had failed to make any offer to Asia on human and social terms. The fact that the West did not appeal to the Asiatic people in a language they could understand and in a way they could comprehend must be considered an error so great that the whole course of the relationship between Asia and the Western world has been impaired for hundreds of years to come. The West, during 1946–47, lost its biggest chance of making a constructive contribution to the East, particularly in the sociological and philosophical fields.

The United States probably made the most serious mistake of all the Western countries. The Americans, in the eyes of the Asiatics, had come to Asia as friends and partners, not as rulers. The Asiatic peoples had looked up to them with great admiration, confidence and hope. The Americans, they hoped, would help create a new world in which Asians would play an equal role. Unfortunately, nothing like that happened, with the exception of the American effort in Japan. But great though this effort undoubtedly was, it was by no means sufficient to satisfy the people of Asia. Once the dream was gone, the feeling of frustration was acute. The Asiatics failed to understand the real American intentions in Asia. The disappointment in the United States and the confusion about its attitude toward Asia were followed by mistrust and hostility. America had failed to provide the political, social and philosophical leadership necessary to prevent Asia from shifting to the left.

It would have been perfectly possible for the United States — and for the Western world in general — to have led the Asiatic revolt. No doctrinal reasons dictated that the Asiatics should lean toward communism. But the unwillingness of the Western democracies to assume social responsibilities in Asia in the post-war years drove the Asiatic revolt involuntarily into the arms of the Soviets. By repudiating the burden of social responsibility, the West had declined the broad horizons and the possibilities of political leadership; the consequences would be catastrophic.

5. *Communist Influence Growing; United States Influence Declining*

Where the United States failed, the Soviet Union stepped in. The Kremlin, for long years, had made a thorough study of Far Eastern problems. Although it had made many mistakes, it had nevertheless discovered some basic truths. It had learned that Asia had to be regarded as a whole; hence, it had made its appeal to Asia as a whole. Moscow understood what actually stirred the soul of the Asiatic peoples. Stalin, convinced that only that which is rising and developing is invincible, knew that he had to choose the rising tide of nationalism in Asia in order to achieve his aim. He also knew how to direct this tide, how to channel its forces and how to integrate his policy with the new developments in Asia and their deep undertones. Stalin's conception of strategy and tactics is highly flexible. Despite his comparatively rigid doctrinal framework, his policy is elastic and opportunistic. He clearly discerned that resignation was no longer a typical emotion of Asia, and that this resignation had given way to a real sense of anger against the acceptance of misery and poverty as the normal condition of life.

Stalin, as has been said, knew how to use these emotions for his own ends. He had discovered that the desire for national liberation and renovation was the most powerful force behind the Asiatic revolt. His scheme appealed to the deepest and innermost feelings of the Asiatic people. Stalin showed them a new and fascinating road, even a short cut, to the realization of their dreams. In general, he did not endeavor to create satellites in Asia. His method was a more subtle, a more shrewd one. Stalin wished to have at his disposal dependable allies, willing to accept the undisputed leadership of the Kremlin. Accordingly, Moscow had to become the guiding star of a new world. Stirring their longings for racial emancipation and national independence the Russian leader incited the peoples of the Far East to world revolution. He held out communism for the Asiatics as a sacred symbol, somehow identified with the popular clamor for unrestricted self-government, but also for a better standard of living; Stalin knew how to evoke ideological ardor, but at the same time, he realized the significance of his promises for economic support.

It is outside the scope of this book to make a more elaborate study of Stalin's approach. The above may suffice to manifest the force of the Soviet appeal.

It is, however, of importance to realize how many of Stalin's promises and appeals found a confirmation in Russian history and a firm basis in the development of the Soviet Union during recent years. Had not Stalin created a powerful and victorious nation which defeated the highly mechanized German armies? Had not Stalin successfully industrialized the potentially rich, but until recently backward country of Russia? Had not Stalin succeeded in making his country a political force second to none in the world, the equal of such giants as the historically powerful British Commonwealth and the United States, with its newly born might? Is it not understandable, therefore, that Asia looked with respect and even admiration toward the Kremlin? Is it not clear how Moscow's appeal to the Far East met with overwhelming response from the uncritical masses of Asiatics, including many Japanese? Obviously this shrewd and bold Soviet policy turned the Asian revolt into a Red storm, which swept over the entire Far East and threatened to engulf the whole continent.

6. Communism Sweeps over Asia

The results of the Soviet policy by the end of 1949 and the beginning of 1950 were indeed breath-taking.

In order to illustrate the rising tide of this mighty Red flood, to appreciate the magnitude of this historical development, a more elaborate study has to be made of the situation along the Red front in Asia at that time. Such a study will reveal more clearly its tremendous impetus, will display more vividly its alarming character; a realization of the facts will explain the greatness of the shock to the Japanese people when they awakened to the dangers threatening their country.

A survey of the 1949 cold war in Asia has to begin in *Afghanistan*. At the end of that year unmistakable indications revealed that this country felt itself betrayed by the United States and by Britain, and that it was turning to Russia for friendship.

Also *India*, its eastern neighbor, showed an outspoken inclination toward the left. An attitude of neutrality on the part of Nehru was the best that could be hoped for, even though the United States had exerted itself to win the favor of the Indian Prime Minister, and had that same year rolled out the red carpet for Nehru on the occasion of his visit to Washington. India, in December 1949, was one of the first countries to recognize the Peking Government. Moreover, the smoldering conflict between India and Pakistan emphasized the insecurity of this subcontinent and prevented any long-term planning for its badly needed economic stabilization.

After India, the attention automatically switches to *Tibet*. In the beginning of 1950 the Chinese Communists announced the liberation of Tibet as one of the glorious combat tasks of the Chinese People's Army. In the middle of 1950 the fate of the "roof of the world" seemed to be sealed. More serious however, than this threat to the country of the Dalai Lama, was, from a Western point of view, the communist menace in *Burma*. This rice bowl of Asia, after achieving its independence, had been plunged into bloody internal strife. At the end of 1949, there were clear signs of Red Chinese aid to the Burmese Communists in their endeavor to "liberate" the country. *Thailand*, high on the list of Peking's aggressive plans, was also in a particularly vulnerable position. Her importance to the democratic world as a rice producer and a strategically located country is obvious. The Western world, however, had failed to inspire the Thailand Government with much confidence. Notwithstanding the fact that this country was anti-communist, it was very conscious of the mighty force of neighboring Red China, against which it would have no chance of survival. Bangkok, in those days, wondered whether a deal with Peking would not be for the best.

A review of the communist front in Southeast Asia at the end of 1949 would not be complete without considering Asia's tinderbox, *French Indo-China*. If one could speak of a real battlefront anywhere in the Far East, it was in this former French colony, where the Moscow-recognized regime of Ho Chi-ming was fighting a bloody war against French-sponsored Emperor Bao Dai. Indo-China, the conquest of which would place the Red forces in a position to overwhelm the rest of Southeast Asia, was seriously endangered by the communist threat.

British Malaya, since the end of 1945, had been continuously plagued with communist-instigated riots. Tens of thousands of British troops had been engaged for years in a so-called anti-bandit campaign, which was nothing but a battle against the communists threatening to overthrow the British rule in that country. A somewhat different situation prevailed in *Indonesia*, which, by the end of 1949, was dangerously wavering in the Red storm. It was not yet clear in which direction the new Indonesian Republic would go, but the government in power was engaged in a rather unpopular and hesitating campaign against communist-inspired rebel forces. And finally the *Philippine Islands* were constantly in danger through the activities of the communist Hukbalahaps, who had plunged the country into chaos and bloodshed.

This brief estimate of the situation prevailing in the peripheric countries of Southeast Asia reveals an alarming picture of general unrest and strife, which were undoubtedly stirred up by the communists. Those countries, however, had still escaped communist domination. In *China*, on the other hand, the trend of events had taken a much more ominous turn. The communist forces of Mao Tse-tung had swept over that huge country and its 400,000,000 people. The Chinese Communists, riding on a wave of nationalism and of disillusionment at Chiang Kai-shek's handling of the great inheritance of Sun Yat-sen, had conquered China in less than a year. The Chinese people seemed to stand united behind their new leaders. In China, more clearly than in any other country of the Far East, the communist appeal to revolt against corruption, misery and poverty had demonstrated how strong was its grip and how irresistible its challenge. Some people flattered themselves with the hope that the Chinese revolution was nothing but a peasant insurrection, which had no ties with Marxistic

Communism. Mao Tse-tung, in the middle of 1949, shattered all their hopes by declaring: "We belong to the anti-imperialistic front, headed by the Soviet Union, and we can only look for genuine and friendly aid to that front, and not to the Western imperialists".

Notwithstanding the fact that historical Russo-Chinese antagonism will, in the future, probably prove to have deeper roots than any agreement between temporary rulers, the Mao-Stalin partnership has had to be accepted as a fact in Far Eastern politics. The co-operation between the Chinese and the Soviets, formally agreed upon during the two months' conference between the leaders of the Red world in the winter of 1949, was, moreover, a relationship of equal partners. When on February 14, 1950, the Thirty-Years Pact of Friendship, Cooperation and Mutual Assistance between the Soviet Union and the People's Republic of China was made public, there could be no misunderstanding about China's position. China was not a satellite of Moscow, but a mighty ally in the communist struggle against the West. Peking and Moscow had found in each other a brotherhood of identical interests and ideologies. Besides gaining a victory of incalculable value for its position in Asia, communism, by uniting the two largest countries of the world into a gigantic bloc, had scored a further stupendous success, for which the Western democracies had, as yet, no answer. The solidarity of the Chinese and the Russians was to influence not only the future of those great Powers, but also the history of all mankind.

This study of the effects of Soviet policy and of the mounting Soviet influence in Asia during the post-war years makes clear the enormous changes that had occurred in the Far East and the dangers which darkened the Asiatic horizon.

It was therefore perfectly understandable that the Japanese people looked with great apprehension toward the development on the Asiatic mainland. After all, the only protection Japan could hope for had to come from the United States. Japan itself had been stripped of all armed forces and war industry, the Japanese were completely dependent on America's willingness and power to defend the country.

7. America's Reactions Unfavorable; Washington, however, Considers Change to Firmer Policy.

Had America's reaction towards the Asiatic developments given the Japanese reason to expect that the United States was willing and in a position to defend Japan?

By the events, described in the preceding pages and also in Chapter V, the contrary had been proved. Royall's words had shatterred what confidence was left. The wavering and incomprehensible Far Eastern policy of the United States in the post-war years was bearing its bitter fruit. This policy had been inconsistent indeed. While on the one hand the United States had encouraged and helped progressive movements in Asia, it had, on the other hand, supported reactionary leaders clinging to ideologies and circumstances of the past. The publication of the American White Paper on China in the beginning of August 1949 may be cited as a striking example of confused United States foreign policy. This paper contained serious criticism of the Red Chinese Government; it accused Peking of fostering foreign domination of China by Soviet Communism. At the same time, however, the White Paper seriously criticized Chiang Kai-shek's Government. This document was more than a record of unsuccessful American foreign policy in the Far East; it revealed America's failure to understand the political and social developments in that part of the world.

Fortunately, though, the course of events had, at last, awakened Washington to the dangers threakening the United States' position in Asia. In the course of 1949 the leaders of the United States seemed to realize that a firmer attitude was necessary. Probably Secretary of State Acheson's greatest contribution to America's foreign policy is that he realized this necessity, and that he set out to formulate a new, more practicable and consistent policy.

Until 1949 the actions of the United States in the international field had been guided by the principles of the so-called *policy of containment*. Under this policy the United States had set out to stop communism wherever and whenever it threatened to engulf another nation. This had led to the impractical dispersal of forces in the military, as well as in the economic and financial sphere. So far as Asia was concerned, the policy

had failed. It was based on a miscalculation of American
military and economic power and, consequently, its execution
had become a military and political impossibility.

Acheson, in the course of 1949, began to work out a new
policy, the so-called *policy of the situation of strength*. Only where
strategically necessary and justifiable, would the resistance
against communism be actively sponsored and encouraged.
This would allow of a more economic use of the forces at the
disposal of the United States. The available economic, financial
and military potential of the Western democracies could be
concentrated at vital points in the defense structure of the
democratic world, rather than being spread over the entire
globe. For example: England would have to be defended;
Tibet could be considered as expendable. Finland's position
could be envisaged as non-essential to the defense of Europe;
the negative attitude towards Spain, on the other hand, had to
be revised.

However, the formulation and implementation of a new
policy takes time, especially in a democratic country like the
United States. The new attitude of the State Department,
moreover, was not readily understood, neither by the people
of the United States, nor by the people abroad — and certainly
not in Asia.

In order to remedy this situation, Secretary Acheson, in the
middle of 1949, organized a Foreign Policy Board, under the
chairmanship of Ambassador Philip C. Jessup. It was the task of
this Board to formulate and elaborate Acheson's new political
ideas. It had therefore to review the entire East Asian situation
and to make recommendations on future American policy
accordingly.

The first actions of this Board were not very successful.
During the last months of 1949, its Chairman toured the Far
East. Jessup's public statements in the course of his trip were
far from reassuring and his appearance failed to inspire any
confidence. During a conference of American Far Eastern
diplomats at Bangkok, presided over by Jessup, some of the
participants even went so far as to declare that they doubted
whether there was still time for the United States to forestall
communism in Asia. Such statements were hardly encouraging.

Moreover, Acheson's own handling of his new policy

failed to convince the Asiatics. Notwithstanding his statement
that the impregnable line of American defense in the Pacific
was to include Japan, Okinawa and the Philippines, Acheson
did not indicate in what manner he intended to carry out his
plans. He created considerable disillusionment by his declaration on January 10, 1950, that so far as the nations outside
the announced defense area were concerned, the United States
was not in a position to do more than give some financial and
moral help. This did not sound very hopeful and was small
help in bolstering the morale of the threatened Asiatics.
Furthermore, the confusion about the situation in China, which
at that time practically paralyzed U.S. foreign policy in the
Far East, added to the general feeling of unrest and the uncertainty about America's intentions.

Acheson's plans, undoubtedly, had great merits. But a long
time would be required for the new attitude of America in the
Far East to become clear and for the United States, by a firm
and uncompromising policy, to inspire new hope in Asia.

With Red China's strength still growing and America's
attitude undecided, the communist threat toward the free
countries of Asia increased. Communist waves washed the
shores of Japan. A guarantee that they would be checked could
not be given.

No wonder that the Japanese people viewed the future with
grave concern. No wonder they felt alarmed at the prospect
of entering the cauldron of international politics.

This, on the other hand, did not alter the fact that Japan was
longing for peace. But it was very reluctant to accept a peace
on the American conditions. As has been said before, Royall,
by his revelations in the beginning of 1949, had sown doubts
in the Japanese mind; the developments in Asia, as described
above, had only nurtured those seeds of doubt and mistrust.
It is easy to understand why the Japanese people, by the end
of 1949, were scanning the horizon for an answer to their
problem: how to achieve peace without seriously endangering
the security of their country?

8. *Situation Exploited by U.S.S.R.*

The Soviet Union did everything in its power to increase these
feelings of anxiety and fear. The Sino-Soviet treaty of February

10

1950 contained a hidden threat to a Japan sponsored by the United States. It was significant that this treaty, concluded after long and difficult negotiations between the two foremost communist Powers, should so unambiguously express the intention of the Sino-Soviet bloc "to prevent jointly the rebirth of Japanese imperialism and the repetition of aggression on the part of Japan or any other State which would unite in any form with Japan in acts of aggression". Furthermore, Moscow and Peking pledged themselves "to work for the conclusion, in the shortest possible space of time, jointly with the other Powers allied during the second World War, of a peace treaty with Japan".

On the one hand, the Sino-Soviet combination clearly wanted to discourage any rearming of Japan with American help, and it warned against a separate United States-Japan treaty. On the other hand the communist nations indirectly invited Japan to enter into peaceful relations with the Communist world. On January 11, 1950, Moscow publicly stated that in her opinion Japan had to choose between a socialist democracy and an alliance with the imperialist West. In the case of her adherence to the "peace-loving democracies" — sponsored by the USSR and Red China — Japan would have a chance of becoming a great and independent country, working for world peace. If Japan should choose, however, an alliance with the "capitalistic nations" — under leadership of the United States of America — she would revert to the position of a "satellite", without "freedom and sovereignty", and "be used as a springboard for imperialistic adventures against the peoples of Asia!" This was clearly an invitation, or rather a threat, to join the Sino-Soviet combination. The Communists opened a possibility for Japan "to work for the conclusion of peace in the shortest possible time, jointly with the other Powers allied during the second World War". Moscow and Peking offered Japan an equal place in leftist Asia. In view of the recent developments in the Far East — the increasing power of communism, and the decline of the West — this offer had obvious attractions for Japan.

In addition to persuasion and to threats from without, Moscow embarked on a program of weakening Japan's resistance from within. The Kremlin, apparently dissatisfied with the activities and accomplishments of the Japanese Communist

Party during 1949, forced a reorientation in the leadership of the party. As will be remembered, the first part of 1949 had been characterized by serious and even sanguinary disturbances in Japan instigated by the Communists. These incidents were shrewdly timed to coincide with the communist victories in China and with the dismissal of great numbers of laborers in government and private enterprises in Japan. The riots were highlighted by the case of a runaway train at Mitaka which killed or injured many innocent people, by insurrections in Taira and Hiroshima, by threats to and intimidation of the authorities in several medium-seized towns, by the murder of President Shimoyama of the Japan National Railways and by the communist assault on the police station of Fukushima. Such events aroused deep anxiety in the country. The Japanese people were antagonized by these tactics and turned away from communism in increasing numbers. Although the January 1949 elections had still shown an increase in the communist following, further developments indicated a definite decline in party membership. As early as September 1949, General MacArthur could declare that "the threat of communism as a major issue in Japanese life is past, having fallen victim to its own excesses". A statement of the U.S. Chief of Staff, General Lawton J. Collins, issued during his October visit to Japan, to the effect that the occupation forces were to remain in Japan for the security of the country, helped to reassure those Japanese who had been frightened by the prospect of internal revolts.

As a result of these events the clever and comparatively independent leader of the Japanese Communist Party, Nosaka, became convinced that a more conciliatory attitude toward the Occupation — at least for the time being — would be more profitable. Moscow, however, was of another opinion and disapproved of Nosaka's tactics. Early in January 1950, the Soviets cracked down on the communist leader. They requested a penance from Nosaka in acknowledgment of his presumed mistakes, and they demanded a recognition of Moscow's indisputable leadership. Nosaka complied. Through a series of changes in organization the Japanese Communist Party was brought back under the direct supervision of the Kremlin; it reiterated its unswerving cooperation with Moscow for the overthrow of international monopolistic capitalism and for the establishment of a communist world community. The Japanese Communists joined Moscow in a program of resistance against a separate peace arrangement, against the rearmament of Japan and against the prolonged stationing of U.S. security forces in their country.

The aims and policies of the Kremlin were clear. On the one hand Moscow warned Japan not to declare itself for the democratic world. On the other hand it attempted Japan to join the communist bloc. By this, Moscow hoped to win Japan over to its side, or at least to prevent its becoming a member of the Western combination of democratic nations.

9. *Postponement of Peace Treaty Advisable in View of Japanese Reactions*

The foregoing shows what strong economical and political reasons impelled the Japanese people to postpone choosing between Washington and Moscow. Japan's hesitation was not only obvious; it was even understandable.

And so, notwithstanding the fact that the United States had granted the former enemy country many millions of dollars by way of aid, notwithstanding the incalculable amount of energy, talent, knowledge and enthusiasm which had been spent by the United States on the rehabilitation, reshaping, reformation and reconstruction of Japan, notwithstanding the gigantic work done by MacArthur and his staff — notwithstanding all these benefits from the United States — Japan was not willing to join the United States in its battle against world communism. On the contrary, the threat and the persuasion from the East were stronger than anything done by the West.

For the second time the question arose: Had all the endeavors of the Occupation been in vain? Had all the work and energy spent in Japan been for nothing? Was MacArthur's work a failure?

No wonder that these and other uncertainties embarrassed the men called upon to formulate a policy for Japan. It was generally known that the feelings of the people were anti-communist and definitely not pro-Russian. There was no natural inclination in Japan to join the Sino-Soviet communist combination, even though beleaguered by whispered promises from that side.

What then did the Japanese really want?

An answer to this question was given in a declaration of the Peace Problem Council for Japan, composed of 60 Japanese professors, politicians and other prominent representatives of Japan's public life. On January 15, 1950, this Council voiced the wishes of the common people as follows:

(a) The Japanese people, if allowed to express their frank desire, want an over-all peace.

(b) Japan's economic independence cannot be obtained through a separate peace.

(c) The Japanese people, in order to guarantee their post-war security, desire neutrality and inviolability as well as admission to the United Nations.

(d) The Japanese are opposed to offering military bases or to having military forces stationed in their country, from whatever other countries, and for whatever reasons.

This declaration expressed universal opinion.

These wishes obviously could not be fulfilled. The realization of these desiderata would only result in a power vacuum in Japan which would open wide the doors of the country to communism. This was contrary to American policy; the United States definitely was not willing to hand Japan to Stalin on a silver platter. Yet America realized the uselessness of forcing a peace treaty upon Japan which this country was not willing to accept. Consequently, the realization of Washington's peace plans, disclosed by the Manilla press release of November 5, 1949, and voiced by the State Department on November 8, 1949, had again to be delayed. On January 1, 1950, the United States notified the British Commonwealth that the draft for a peace treaty, as promised previously, would not be ready at the time of the convening of the British Commonwealth Colombo Conference in January 1950.

Clearly, Washington had failed to settle the peace problem for Japan. In fact, the problem seemed insoluble for the time being. As tension grew between the United States and Red China, heightened by the communist decision to seize the U.S. Consulate-General in Peking, the possibility of an American recognition of Mao's regime rapidly diminished, thus enlarging the difficulties of formulating long-term policy arrangements for the Far East. Peace for Japan seemed further away than before. In Washington a strong feeling prevailed that it was better to continue the Occupation as it was, so long as the Far East remained in such a turbulent state.

10. *Differences between State and Defense Department Complicates Issue*

The problem of drafting a peace treaty for Japan was further aggravated by differences of opinion between the American State Department and the Department of Defense.

In the autumn of 1949 it became clear that the State Department definitely did not want to give up Japan as a part of the American sphere of influence. In fact, it is doubtful whether any large group of people in Washington had ever favored the complete abandonment of Japan. On January 10, 1950, Acheson reaffirmed the American policy with regard to this question by declaring that the impregnable defense of the United States in the Pacific included Japan, Okinawa and the Philippines. Notwithstanding the many inconsistencies in the American foreign policy of those days, this announcement by the Secretary of State had to be considered as a definite commitment on the part of the American Government with regard to Japan.

That the Japanese, as we have seen before, did not believe this, was another matter. In line with this policy, however, the State Department, when, in November 1949, it had pronounced itself in favor of concluding a peace treaty with Japan, had simultaneously desired a unilateral agreement with the former enemy country in order to obtain military bases in Japan.

In late November 1949, this State Department plan was forwarded to the Department of Defense in Washington for comment. The U.S. Under-Secretary of War, Tracy S. Voorhees, in charge of occupied areas, opposed the State Department plans, and the Joint Chiefs of Staff agreed with Mr. Voorhees. The basic objection of the Pentagon was that the conclusion of a peace treaty would so weaken the United States' influence over Japan that the agreed objective — the holding of Japan within the non-communist world and the adequate provision for her defense — would be impossible to achieve. The military feared that under the circumstances as suggested by the State Department and within the limits of American military strength as imposed by Defense Secretary Johnson, Japan could not be defended against a major assault.

In order to investigate this problem further Secretary Voorhees went to Japan early in December 1949, accompanied by some of his most trusted military advisers. General Mac-Arthur, in explaining the Japanese situation to Mr. Voorhees, took the side of the State Department and reaffirmed that he was a stout supporter of an early peace treaty for Japan.

By the end of January 1950, the U.S. Joint Chiefs of Staff, Generals Bradley, Collins and Vandenberg, and Admiral Sherman, arrived in Tokyo to study the difficult security problem of the Japanese islands. They received the same advice from General MacArthur — an early peace treaty, combined with reasonable security arrangements. The Supreme Commander convinced the visiting authorities of the necessity of including a sovereign Japan in America's over-all defense scheme.

Back in Washington, however, the Joint Chiefs of Staff failed to formulate a practical solution for the several problems connected with Japan's security. On the one hand they realized that they could not give up Japan to the communists in case of war. Japan in the hands of the Soviets would constitute a most serious threat to the security of the United States. It would open to Stalin the possibility of creating air and sea forces, built in the workshops of Japan and operating from Japan's numerous bases. As such it would enable the Soviet leader to organize those components of his armed forces which he was lacking in the Pacific theatre. On the other hand, the Joint Chiefs of Staff were hesitant to commit their forces on an island chain, thousands of miles from the American mainland. They were particularly reluctant to base them in a country whose teeming population depended for its survival on large food imports and whose people, moreover, were not very willing to accept American protection. The American military authorities realized that they could not guarantee the Japanese people the necessary food supply nor the immunity of their country in case of war. They feared that their forces would be trapped in Japan, not only by the enemy, but also by hostile forces inside the country. With a view to this, plans were drawn up to station American forces on the islands around Japan, from where it would be possible to neutralize, and, if necessary, to pulverize the Japanese war industries, and thus to deny their use to friend and foe alike.

MacArthur and other men of influence were opposed to such a solution; they felt that this would mean the end of an important work, conceived and executed by the American Occupation of Japan. Fortunately, their opinion prevailed. On April 22, 1950, the U.S. Secretary of the Army, Gray, in his annual report to Congress emphasized the need of maintaining the security of Japan by stationing U.S. forces in that country, even after the conclusion of the peace treaty.

How this decision could be worked into a peace arrangement acceptable to the Japanese remained a problem.

11. *Several Allies Continue Pressing for Peace*

The Allied nations, in the meantime, continued to bring pressure to bear on Washington for the speedy conclusion of a peace treaty. As outlined before, the British Commonwealth, in particular, kept stressing the necessity of an early peace. London had declared itself an opponent to neutralization of Japan; it emphasized that the continued stationing of U.S. armed forces there would remain of paramount importance, even after the peace treaty had been effected; it failed, however, to indicate how the problems created by such an ambiguous policy should be solved.

The Philippine nation, which until recently had favored a punitive peace for Japan, appeared to have changed its attitude by the end of March 1950. In the Manila Chronicle of March 23, 1950, the President of the Philippine Republic, Quirino, stated that he hoped for a speedy peace for Japan, on the condition that the United States would be willing to guarantee the security of the Philippines.

Several other Far Eastern Commission countries favored the conclusion of a peace treaty for the former enemy country. The Soviet Union, for purely opportunistic reasons, showed itself one of the most staunch supporters of this idea. Early in March 1950 Moscow, repeating its previous suggestions, again launched a peace offensive, this time in the Tokyo press. It hinted that in combination with Peking, the Soviets might invite Tokyo to unilateral peace deliberations.

The United States was clearly pressed to consider a peace for Japan. The British Commonwealth Consultative Conference on Japan's peace treaty problems, convened in London on May 1, 1950, stressed this fact by urging Washington to pursue its most serious efforts in seeking a solution to its self-created Japanese dilemma.

12. *Developments inside Japan also Press for Speedy Peace*

In addition to international pressure there were other reasons which forced the United States to consider the negotation of a peace arrangement for Nippon. The delay in convening a Japanese peace treaty was endangering the Occupation itself. In the late spring and early summer of 1950, it became evident that large groups of the Japanese people harbored resentment against a continued occupation of their country. The Japanese became restless and irritated by the presence of foreign troops on their soil. The piecemeal peace program had developed to such an extent that the Japanese felt themselves, in practice, already independent and sovereign, but for the signing of the long expected peace treaty. MacArthur had encouraged these feelings. The United States had, time and again, promised Japan a swift return to the status of sovereign nation. Many Japanese did not understand Washington's hesitation. Japan had been promised peace; the Japanese people longed for peace; and now Washington seemed to delay the arrangement of a peace settlement.

The Soviet Union, furthering its policy of thwarting America's position in Japan, welcomed these Japanese feelings, and tried to exploit them for its own purposes. On March 2, 1950, the Soviet representative in the Allied Council urgently requested information on the proposed U.S. military program in Japan. He stated that this program was contrary to the Potsdam Declaration, and that it constituted an encroachment upon the freedom of the Japanese. MacArthur indignantly refuted these accusations, but a relatively large part of the Japanese press indirectly showed its sympathy with the Russian point of view.

The Japanese Communist Party also tried to stir up trouble and to create anti-occupation feelings. Communist-sponsored students, in the beginning of May 1950, created an incident at the Sendai University, when Dr. Eells, the Educational

Adviser to SCAP, lectured at that university on the "Freedom of Learning". Eells was forced to discontinue his talk. In the middle of May, a similar incident took place at the Hokkaido University. Furthermore, on May 30, 1950, a captain and two American soldiers were molested by communist demonstrators during a gathering on the Imperial Plaza. It was the first time that occupation personnel on official duty had been threatened by Japanese. Obviously, the communists were trying to discover how far the Occupation would go in its tolerant attitude toward the Japanese people, and whether or not these anti-occupation demonstrations would meet with their sympathy.

These events created an unfavorable though erroneous impression; many people asked themselves if there was really a strong feeling of resentment against the American Occupation.

The unfortunate result was that the majority of the population became less inclined than ever to favor a separate peace arrangement with its pro-American consequences.

It is important to note, however, that not all Japanese were opposed to a separate peace arrangement or were as reluctant to make a choice as most of their compatriots. A small group of responsible persons had, on the contrary, become more and more convinced that a separate peace treaty would, temporarily, be the best solution. In particular Prime Minister Yoshida and his advisers sponsored this idea. On January 25, 1950, in answer to questions by a communist member of the Diet, the Prime Minister stated that under the prevailing international circumstances the conclusion of a separate peace — and not of an over-all peace — was unavoidable for Japan. It was the first time that Yoshida had expressed himself so clearly in favor of a separate peace. When in the course of the following months the U.S. determination to defend Japan became clear, Yoshida's school gained followers. On June 1, the Prime Minister considered his position strong enough to issue, through the Japanese Ministry of Foreign Affairs, a White Paper, in which it was said that Japan was ready to conclude a peace treaty with any country willing to accord Japan her independence and equality. Yoshida, however, was far in advance of his countrymen; a most serious turn of events was necessary finally to persuade the Japanese people.

13. U.S. Appoints Special Envoy to Solve Peace Dilemma

As a result of these developments, Washington was convinced that the conclusion of some sort of a peace arrangement for Japan could now no longer be delayed. Yet it had to find a satisfactory solution for the differences between the State and Defense Departments and for the problems originating from the general Japanese attitude toward a separate peace.

For some time the Administration had been looking for a special, high-level adviser who could be charged with the staggering task of solving the Japanese peace problem. In the early spring of 1950, John Foster Dulles agreed to accept this difficult assignment. On April 6, 1950, the former Senator was appointed as Foreign Policy Adviser to the U.S. Secretary of State.

Dulles was now the man who was to find a solution for the Japanese deadlock.

After a thorough preparation in Washington, Mr. Dulles came to Japan early in June 1950. He had familiarized himself with Washington's plans, which were to give the Japanese practically complete sovereignty, under the supervision of a Civil Administrator for the Allied Powers — a solution parallel to the arrangement in Western Germany. This, obviously, did not mean the conclusion of a real and unrestricted peace, nor even of a separate peace treaty. Simultaneously, arrangements would be made under which the Allied forces, as a security guarantee against outside threats, would continue to stay in Japan. Dulles's visit was for the purpose of sounding General MacArthur and the Japanese on the implementation of this projet.

It must have been clear to Dulles, however, that this solution was anything but satisfactory. It was only a compromise; it did not satisfy the urgent Japanese wish for real peace and complete independence; it failed to comply with the desires of the Allies for the immediate conclusion of a full-fledged Japanese peace treaty; it hardly met the requirements of the U.S. military authorities and it did not solve the problem of the Japanese resistance against the continued presence of U.S. forces in their country.

Fortunately Dulles, more than anyone else, realized the

seriousness of these objections. During his stay in Tokyo it became evident that he favored another solution — a bold and imaginative one. He appeared convinced that the only way to retain the confidence of the Japanese people and to make them agreeable to and even desirous of the continued stationing of friendly armed forces in Japan, would be an unrestricted peace treaty. This treaty should be on the basis of complete equality, restoring full sovereignty and independence to Japan. Such a treaty, in the opinion of Dulles, had to be combined with a military agreement between Japan and certain friendly countries, the United States in the first place.

Dulles realized that his plan would meet with serious resistance, not only in America but also in other Allied countries. The time was not yet ripe to take this step.

An unexpected and dramatic event in the Far East, however, was to become the incentive which would impel the hesitating participants to accept this courageous and far-reaching solution of the Japanese peace problem; the North Korean invasion of Syngman Rhee's Republic was to break the deadlock of the Japanese security problem.

Chapter VIII

DULLES BUILDS PEACE

The United States, resolved to arrange a peace for Japan, charges Dulles to break the deadlock. After three visits to Japan and after talks in Manila, Canberra, London and Paris, Dulles finds a satisfactory formula. He overcomes the difficulties resulting from fears of renewed Japanese aggression, from the Korean war and the Chinese intervention, from MacArthur's dismissal and from Britain's China policy. Four times the peace endeavors seem likely to fail, but by the middle of 1951 Dulles's persistance is crowned by the issuing of combined U.S.A.-U.K. invitations for a Japanese peace conference.

1. Dulles's Mission and his Background

The United States faced a dilemma with regard to the Japanese peace treaty. On the one hand Washington, realizing that the Occupation was rapidly outgrowing its usefulness, wanted peace for Japan, and at the same time it wanted to retain Japan in the Western sphere of influence. Consequently, it had to guarantee Japan's security, which implied the stationing of U.S. armed forces in Japan, at least temporarily. Japan, on the other hand, was anxious to regain her independence and sovereignty through a peace arrangement, but hesitated to accept the U.S. security offer. It was reluctant to choose the side of the West.

As has been pointed out in the previous chapter, Washington, in view of the awkwardness of the situation, decided to appoint a foreign policy adviser to the U.S. Secretary of State, charged with the special task of solving the Japanese dilemma. John Foster Dulles was nominated on April 6, 1951.

Who was Dulles, and what made him the obvious person to choose for this difficult task?

John Foster Dulles, born in 1888, was the grandson of General John W. Foster, Secretary of State under President Harrison, who acted as mediator at the Shimonoseki peace conference at the end of the Japanese-Chinese war in 1895. Therefore, diplomacy was in the blood of the young Foster, and his grandfather stimulated its development by encouraging him

to study international law and by taking him to the Hague
Conference of 1907. Dulles accumulated considerable experience
in international affairs both as a private lawyer and as a member
of several official missions abroad. In 1919 he was sent to the
Versailles Peace Conference as a member of the reparations
commission. This experience particularly influenced his
future work on the Japanese peace treaty.

Dulles had been a great believer in his old college professor,
the late President Woodrow Wilson; he had seen him go to
the conference with high ideals and visionary hopes, which had
gradually evaporated under the pressure of the European Allies,
who displayed a spirit of strong vindictiveness, demanding
large reparations and seeking vengeance from Germany. In
Dulles's opinion this sowed the seeds for another war. The
ideals and the philosophy which were to guide his task of
Japanese peace-making were derived from these experiences.
His background and his convictions made him resolved that
the Japanese peace should be a prudent and a Christian peace.
He realized that vindictiveness would only bring misery and
poverty, which in turn would breed communism. Dulles
clearly saw that if Japan should accept communism, the results
would be disastrous for the West. The Japanese industrial
power, combined with the resources of the Asiatic mainland,
might enable the Soviet Union to fight, and perhaps win, an
interminable war. Dulles's principal aim therefore was to
retain Japan, by her own choice, for the Western democracies.

2. *Dulles's First Visit to Japan*

This simple and bold approach to the Japanese peace problem
was not commonly shared in the United States. In principle,
Washington agreed with Mr. Dulles. But so far as the manner
of implementing Dulles's peace plans was concerned, opinion
was divided.

The military authorities in particular hesitated. They were
reluctant to accept a peace arrangement which would not give
them iron-clad guarantees for the safety of the U.S. forces
stationed in Japan. A voluntary and genuine acceptance by
the Japanese people of the continued presence of American
security forces in Japan was, in their opinion, a "conditio sine

qua non" for a satisfactory peace arrangement. How to realize this condition, however, remained a problem.

The State Department had not formulated a definite plan. It awaited Mr. Dulles's recommendations. Both the Pentagon and the State Department were of the opinion that the problems could best be studied on the spot. Hence, two missions — one military and one political — left for Japan early in June 1951.

The military mission was headed by Louis Johnson, the U.S. Secretary of Defense, accompanied by the Chairman of the Joint Chiefs of Staff, General Bradley. They were to study the military implications of a peace arrangement, keeping strictly to the military field. At the time of their departure from Japan they were convinced that the occupation controls had to be lifted as far as feasible, and that the Japanese had to be allowed as complete a command as possible over their own affairs, especially over economic matters; they realized that the continuance of the Occupation would end all hope of making Japan a reliable friend in the Pacific. Yet, they clung to their opinion that the responsibility for the defense of that country had to remain with the Occupying Powers.

The second mission consisted of Mr. Dulles and his party. Dulles wanted to orientate himself on the spot with regard to the manifold questions arising from the conclusion of a peace treaty for Japan. He hoped to learn the opinion of the Supreme Commander and of the Japanese people on the subject.

Before leaving Washington, Dulles had handed President Truman a memorandum outlining his views. He had repeated that the first aim of any Japanese peace arrangement should be to bring Japan into the Western bloc, and he had stressed that the proposals to the Japanese should be made on a basis of full equality and recognition of their national aspirations. Dulles, however, was not sure to what extent President Truman would sympathize with his ideas.

Upon his arrival in Tokyo he discovered that General MacArthur, the Supreme Commander, agreed with him on the most essential points of his peace plan. MacArthur, convinced, as we have seen, of the need for an early peace treaty, emphasized the fact that a continuance of the Occupation would constitute a danger in itself. By 1950, according to the Supreme Commander, the Occupation had served its purpose.

MacArthur had stressed repeatedly the necessity of withdrawing the Occupation after a maximum of five years. In his opinion time was pressing and the Americans had to leave Japan before their presence was seriously resented by the Japanese. Moreover, the Supreme Commander supported Dulles's point of view that a treaty would have to guarantee the security of demilitarized Japan and as such have to ensure the continuance of American bases and the stationing of American forces in Japan. These controversial questions, in the opinion of MacArthur, should be considered against the background of Japanese — and world — security, rather than viewed from the stand-point of American security only. The Supreme Commander furthermore considered Japan's cooperation essential; the Japanese themselves would have to choose the side of the West; they would have to ask, voluntarily, for American help and protection during the period when their own security forces would be in process of organization and training.

This was precisely Dulles's opinion. On June 22, 1950, before the American Chamber of Commerce in Tokyo, he stated unequivocally that it was for the Japanese to decide on the desirability of an American security guarantee. Analyzing the problem facing the Japanese people, he remarked that the world of today was divided into two parts, the free and the captive. He pointed out that every nation had to make its choice, and that it was essential for a nation to choose the side of the free world by the free and manifest will of its own people. He stressed that as the conditions laid down in the surrender policy directive became fulfilled, Japan's destiny would be more and more in the hands of the Japanese people. Then Japan would have to choose the road she wanted to take.

Said Dulles: "Sooner or later the Japanese people will make their choice, and by so doing they will determine their future destiny. I am confident that when the hour of decision comes, the Japanese people will elect to become dependable members of the world that is free".

3. *Outbreak of Korean War Stimulates Japan's Decision to Join Free World*

Dulles himself did not realize how near that hour of decision actually was. On June 25, 1950, the North Korean armies overran the Republic of South Korea — an action which shocked the Japanese people severely. The North Korean attack was clearly and unmistakably Moscow-sponsored. It could be seen only as a prelude to communist aggression, aimed at Japan. History had shown that Korea had always been the stepping-stone, as it were, to Japan: in other words, any attempt by Asiatic countries to dominate Japan had commenced by conquering Korea. The Japanese people realized that a communist Korea, combined with Red-dominated Kuriles and Sakhalin, would present the constant danger of a communist invasion of their country from two sides. Indeed, Japan would be held in the grip of a gigantic communist nutcracker.

The world was stunned by the overt act of communist assault on Korea. But, although Washington was seriously alarmed, it was better prepared for such events than during the previous years. Acheson's policy of the situation of strength had gained scope and confidence. Here was a situation where bold action was necessary in order to stop communist expansion. The United States took such action. Washington, without hesitation, decided to help the endangered South Korean Republic.

That decision was not an easy one. By the end of June 1949, the United States had withdrawn their liberation forces from Korea, leaving only a small military mission behind. New troops therefore had to be sent over to implement Washington's policy of armed assistance to the Seoul Government. MacArthur's occupation forces — which were directed to join the Korean battle — were hardly prepared for a tough and bitter fight in the rugged Korean country. During the first weeks, and even during the first months of the conflict, the chances were definitely against the heavily outnumbered American and South Korean troops, fighting a delaying action in Korea. Gradually, however, the situation improved and the communist offensive was halted.

The courageous American attitude had set an inspiring example and swung the rest of the democratic world into swift action against the agressor. The firmness and determination with which the United States executed its decision to

11

counter the communist attack and with which it prepared
itself to throw back the invaders restored much of America's
prestige in the Far East. The Korean war shifted the course of
the turbulent current flowing through Asia. It swept away many
doubts and hesitations. It convinced the Japanese that the
United States was willing and capable of acting in case of
aggression and that the United States was resolved to retain
its position in the Far East. Furthermore, it made the Japanese
people conscious of their security problem and of the actual
dangers threatening their country. It blasted all hopes of
permanent neutrality. It solved for Japan the problem created
by their reluctance and hesitation to join the free world. The
Korean invasion, and the American reaction to it, decided for
Japan the problem of taking sides in the world conflict.

Japan chose the side of the democracies. On August 19,
1950, she announced her decision to the world. The Japanese
Ministry of Foreign Affairs, the Gaimusho, released a White
Paper, entitled "Our Position in the Korean Conflict". The paper
stated that in this phase of the world-wide struggle between
the two incompatible forces — communism and democracy —
no room for neutrality existed. In the cold war, said the Japanese
statement, we have to choose, to choose now and without hesitation, and our choice obviously lies with the free world.

4. *Faith in Japan Justified: Truman Authorizes Preliminary
   Peace Talks*

In the meantime, Japan had passed through some critical
months. When the war in Korea increased in range and fierce-
ness, MacArthur had been obliged to send practically all his
occupation troops to the battlefield to reinforce Lt. General
W. H. Walker's forces, which were fighting a last-ditch battle
for the Pusan beachhead. Japan had been completely stripped
of ground forces. By so doing MacArthur had shown great
confidence in the Japanese people; but he was convinced he
could trust them. The course of events justified his faith. Later
on, recalling those days during his address before Congress in
Washington in the spring of 1951, MacArthur said:

"That Japan may be counted upon to wield a profoundly
beneficial influence over the course of events in Asia is attested

by the magnificent manner in which the Japanese people have met the recent challenge of war, unrest and confusion surrounding them from the outside, and checked communism within their own frontiers, without the slightest slackening in their forward progress. I sent all four of our occupation divisions to the Korean battlefront without the slightest qualms as to the effect of the resulting power vacuum upon Japan. The results fully justified my faith".

Indeed, MacArthur could be proud of the spectacular and daring decision taken in the midsummer of 1950. At the time this decision had been anything but easy. Not only had the Supreme Commander had to count on the Japanese people — after five years of occupation — being loyal to the Occupation, but, by stripping Japan of all American forces, he had gambled heavily on Russia's hesitation to force an all-out world war. Intuitively, MacArthur felt that the Soviets did not want to risk a world conflict by attempting to invade Nippon.

He realised, however, that the danger of internal uprisings in Japan had to be reduced to a minimum. In this connection MacArthur, upon the outbreak of the Korean war, took far-reaching measures to increase the security of the country. On the day of the Korean invasion, the Akahata, the foremost communist newspaper in Japan, was suspended. This was followed by the liquidation of 550 minor communist newspapers throughout the country. On July 8, 1950, 14 days after the Korean invasion, the Supreme Commander authorized the establishment, training and arming of a Japanese National Police Reserve of 75,000 men. In addition, the Maritime Safety Board, a coast-guard in embryo, was expanded to 8,000 men.

One of the most dangerous hearts of communist activity in Japan was formed by the several leftist-inclined student organizations. The police, therefore, were instructed to raid the nationalist headquarters and the branch offices of the communist-dominated National Federation of Students' Self-Government Associations, one of the most active leftist organizations in the country. Furthermore, a warrant was issued for the arrest of Tokuda, the most prominent communist leader in Japan, and for eight of his lieutenants. These measures from SCAP were followed by purges of several Japanese governmental organizations. On July 31, 1950, the press and radio, by voluntary action of their own members, purged themselves of communist influences. At the end of August the electrical industry followed their example. In the beginning of September 1950, 12 leaders of the Japan Liaison Council of Labor Unions were purged from public services for engaging in a series of anti-occupation activities. Moreover, the Central Seamen Union voted for full cooperation with the U.N. police action in Korea. These actions, by the Japanese themselves, were most encouraging; apparently, they had decided that communism should be done away with in their country.

The Communists, on the other hand, were not willing to give in without battling for their position, and they chose the Japanese students to do their fighting. At the end of September thousands of students in Tokyo held a mass rally, opposing the proposed purge of Red professors. This action was followed, on October 5, 1950, by a parade of 2,500 leftist students of the Tokyo University. At the end of October the rallies led to a bloody clash between police and students at the Waseda University.

In the meantime the purges continued. Early in November the Ministry of International Trade and Industry screened its employees. The Tele-Communications Ministry, the National Railways and the Finance Ministry followed its example. As a last act of open violence, Japanese and Korean communists clashed with the police in the town of Shiga on December 5, 1950; but after this, the Communists had to revert to secret action. Communism in Japan had been driven underground.

These developments, however, were still unknown when MacArthur sent his troops to the Korean battlefield. In those midsummer days of 1950 nobody knew what the coming months would bring Japan and how the Japanese would react to the new situation. Fortunately Dulles, approving of MacArthur's decision to deplete Japan of practically all the occupation forces, did not lose sight of his mission. Sharing MacArthur's faith in the people of Japan, he urged the furthering of the Japanese peace plans and thus greatly strengthened the morale of the Japanese.

"The battle in Korea", said John Foster Dulles on June 30, 1950, speaking in San Francisco about his recent trip to Japan, "should not lead the free world to forget about Japan or to postpone the dealing with its problems. The very fact that the attack in Korea may be aimed at Japan, and designed to check positive and constructive action there, shows how important it is to take such action. We could indeed lose more in Japan than could be won in Korea".

MacArthur responded to Mr. Dulles's plea for a speedy peace treaty by stating on September 1, 1950, the fifth anniversary of VJ Day, that Japan was qualified to resume its membership in good standing among the free nations.

Washington agreed; Dulles's report on his visit to Japan, and the Japanese decision to join the free world had, apparently, overcome the reluctance of the military authorities and had convinced the American Government that it should proceed with the Japanese peace-making. On September 14, 1950, President Truman authorized the State Department to enter into preliminary discussions with interested nations for the purpose of concluding a peace treaty. Instead of ending the hopes for Japan's peace, as appeared likely, the Korean war had accelerated the American efforts in this direction. The North Korean aggression had recoiled on the Communists in so far as their action had been planned to thwart the American plans in Japan.

Technically, the Korean invasion helped to demonstrate that the possession of mere bases in Japan would not deter, and might even provoke, an aggressor. What was necessary was the full and voluntary cooperation on the part of the population in the defence of the democratic world and of their own country. This cooperation had now been pledged. Consequently, the American State and Defense Departments had been provided with a basis on which to seek a solution for the difficult security problem. They decided that for the time being the defense of Japan would be entrusted to an international, probably a U.N. army. Its main components would be U.S. and, eventually, Japanese forces. As the number and strength of the Japanese forces increased, the U.S. forces would be diminished, until Washington was satisfied that Japan was capable of defending herself. Washington envisaged the restoration of complete sovereignty to Japan and the signing of a military alliance with Japan on the basis of full equality. John Foster Dulles had achieved his first success on the road to a Japanese peace treaty.

Fate seemed to smile approvingly on these developments. It may have been more than mere coincidence that General MacArthur's forces rushed ashore at Inchon on September 15, the day after President Truman's decision for the holding of discussions on Japan's peace. The military appeared anxious not to remain behind the diplomats. As the triumphantly successful amphibious operation developed, which led to the recapture of Seoul and took place under the direct command of SCAP's Chief of Staff, Lt. General Edward M. Almond, and as communist forces were driven back over the 38th Parallel, victory in the Far East seemed certain both in the military and diplomatic fields. The initiative had passed from the hands of the Communists into the hands of the Free World, thanks to the bold decisions of Washington and the courageous leader: ship of MacArthur and Dulles.

5. *Seven-Point Peace Program Issued: Russian Reaction*

With the President's approval, Dulles set out to take the second step towards realizing a peace treaty for Japan. He drafted a seven-point program as a basis for his explanatory talks with the representatives of the Far Eastern Commission countries. According to this program the United States envisaged a treaty with Japan which would end the state of war with that country, restore Japan's sovereignty and bring Japan back into the society of free nations as a full member. Any nation at war with Japan, willing to make peace on the proposed basis, might be a party to the peace treaty. The program suggested that Japan should be admitted to the United Nations at the earliest opportunity. So far as geographic aspects were concerned, it was taken for granted that Japan would recognize the independence of Korea. For the Ryukyu and Bonin islands a United Nations trusteeship was proposed, with the United States as administering authority. The future of Formosa, the Pescadores, South Sakhalin and the Kuriles would be decided later by China, the Soviet Union, the United Kingdom, and the United States, and their decision would have to be accepted by Japan. As for the security of post-treaty Japan, pending satisfactory alternative security arrangements such as assumption by the United Nations of effective responsibility, there should be continued cooperative responsibility between Japan and the United States, and perhaps other countries, for maintaining international peace and security in the Japan area. Japan's eventual rearmament was envisaged as an inevitable condition, as was the continued stationing of U.S. forces in Nippon after the treaty. Dulles's suggestions, furthermore, claimed most favored nation treatment for Japan and advocated the waiving of all war claims, on the understanding that the Allied Powers would hold Japanese property in their own territory and that Japan would compensate the Allies for losses suffered in Japan during the war.

Dulles planned to sound the other Far Eastern Commission nations on these proposals during the fifth session of the U.N. General Assembly, which was to convene at Flushing Meadows, New York, in the middle of September 1950. He intended to make it clear from the beginning that the United States had decided to continue with the peace-making for Japan, regardless of the attitude of the other nations, several of which had been pressing for peace in any case.

The first conversations of Mr. Dulles at New York were encouraging. Most nations agreed on the desirability of arranging a peace treaty for Japan as soon as possible.

President Truman, in the middle of October 1950, sounded a hopeful note, by stating: "We are moving forward with preliminary negotiations for a peace treaty with Japan and we look with confidence to a new Japan, which will be both peaceful and prosperous".

Prime Minister Yoshida expressed the general feeling of hope and expectation of his nation by emphasizing that the Japanese looked forward to an early peace and to eventual membership in the United Nations.

Mr. Dulles's first endeavors for a conciliatory and just peace with Japan appeared successful. Soon, however, it would become clear that his path was not strewn with roses. Several serious difficulties loomed ahead.

The Soviet Union started the counter-offensive to Dulles's peace plans by ordering its representatives to attend again the meetings of the international organizations dealing with Japan — at which they had not been present for some time. On October 19, 1950, Russia ended its nine-month boycott of the

Far Eastern Commission by officially requesting the ousting of Nationalist China from this organization. On November 8 the Russian representative on the Allied Council reappeared at the weekly meeting of that organization, after an eight-month absence, but his attitude had not changed. Soon the Russian and the U.S. representatives clashed again — this time over certain measures taken by SCAP during the previous months, in implementing his piecemeal peace policy.

In October 1950 the first talks of Dulles with the Soviet representative in the United Nations, Jacob Malik, took place. It had not yet become clear which line Russia would follow with regard to the new peace proposals. The cordial atmosphere at the beginning of the talks even led to some speculation that the Soviet Union might be willing to take part in the discussions

On November 24, 1950, however, Mr. Malik, in reply to the American memorandum on the Japanese peace treaty, posed several controversial questions, asking for clarification of most of the suggestions made by Dulles in his seven-point proposal. Moscow invoked the agreement of January 1, 1942, obligating the Allies not to conclude a separate peace with the enemy nations. It reminded the United States that the Cairo Declaration had already dealt with the future of Formosa, the Pescadores, and Sakhalin, and it wondered on what grounds the United States was now proposing a different solution for the disposal of these territories. It disputed the American right to a trustee-ship of the Ryukyu and Bonin islands. Furthermore, the Kremlin fiercely attacked the American plans for retaining forces in Japan. It revealed its opposition to any Japanese rearmament, and unnecessarily requested information on the plans of the United States for guaranteeing a future peaceful economy for Japan. In short, it raised difficulties regarding all the essential points of Dulles's proposals, thus making it abundantly clear that Moscow was not willing to accept the American plans. In particular the American suggestions for safeguarding Japan's security and for rearming Japan were violently opposed by Russia — an opinion reflected in the Soviet press.

The opposition to Japan's rearmament coincided with the Kremlin's protest to Britain and France in connection with plans to rearm Western Germany. Rearmament of the

former enemy countries, said Moscow, was against the will of
the free and peace-loving people of the world. This theme had
been repeatedly stressed by the Communists — in particular at
the Soviet-sponsored Stockholm World Peace Conference,
organized in the fall of 1950. Obviously, Moscow feared the
rearmament of Japan and Germany and was trying to mobilize
world opinion against it.

Washington, however, did not waver. In an unusually
forthright note to the Soviet Union, dated December 28, 1950,
the State Department declared that it would go ahead with its
plans to grant peace to Japan, with or without Russia. The State
Department upheld Japan's right to arrange her own self-
defense and made clear to Moscow that it would adhere to the
essence of Dulles's seven-point peace proposals.

6. Chinese Reactions to Peace Proposal and Chinese Intervention in Korea Threaten Peace Plans

Dulles's peace plans were soon to be even more seriously
threatened. Red China, in the beginning of November 1950,
charged the United States with having started a war of aggression
in Korea. It must be admitted that from the Chinese point of
view this accusation seemed not unfounded. MacArthur's
friendly gestures towards the Formosan Government, stressed
by his over-publicized hand-kiss of Madame Chiang Kai-shek
on the occasion of the General's visit to Taipeh, at the end of
July 1951, had greatly aroused the suspicion of Peking. This
suspicion had been aggravated by the decision of the American
Administration to order the 7th Fleet of the U.S. Navy to
maintain the status quo in the South China Sea. Moreover,
MacArthur's November offensive towards the Yalu-river
looked like a real threat to Chinese interests. In view of the fact
that the United States action was supported from American
bases in Japan and that the Sino-Soviet agreement of January
1950 warned against aggression on the part of Japan, or any
other State which would unite with Japan in acts of aggression,
the Chinese accusation carried an ominous warning for Japan.

China's threat to the peace and security of Japan became
even more dangerous when hundreds of thousands of Chinese
soldiers joined the North Koreans in their winter counter-

offensive. Peking, accusing the United States of aggressive aims towards the Chinese homeland itself, had called upon volunteers to defend the sacred soil of China. By the end of November 1950, an estimated 200,000 Chinese crossed the Yalu-river and threw the U.N. forces back to the south, pursuing them over the snow-covered mountains and plains of Korea. The North Korean capital, Pyonyang, was recaptured by the Communists. American forces had to evacuate the port-city of Hamhung, and the U.N. front fell back south of the 38th Parallel. This overt Chinese intervention in the Korean war created an entirely new situation in the Far East. Chinese and American forces faced each other in a bitter and full-scale war in Korea.

A great and chilling fear ran through the world. Was the outbreak of a global war round the corner? Should the intervention in Korea be continued now that the Chinese had entered the conflict? The President of the United States considered the situation so grave that he declared a state of emergency in the country. Britain and the other West European countries in particular were seriously alarmed about the trend of events. The Americans, and in the first place MacArthur personally, were fiercely criticized for their conduct of the Korean operation, which, in the opinion of the Allies, had incited the Chinese to intervene in force. Fundamental differences of opinion between the United States and the United Kingdom over Far Eastern policy questions threatened to split the Western Alliance, endangering their cooperation under the Atlantic Pact. In the beginning of December 1950, the British Prime Minister decided to fly to Washington in order to prevent a complete breakdown in Anglo-American relations. Even though the Truman and Attlee discussions led to an agreement that no appeasement would be tolerated with regard to the Korean situation, and to a British promise that they would continue to do their duty in Korea, the Allied diplomatic front in the Far East had been further impaired.

The Chinese were not slow in taking the greatest possible advantage of those spectacular developments in the political field. They exploited the differences of opinion between the Western Powers to further their campaign against the American-sponsored Japanese peace plans. Foreign Minister Chou En-lai,

on December 1, 1950, made an three-point statement regarding
the U.S. proposal for a peace treaty with Japan. He vigorously
attacked the United States for it policy of undermining the
principle of unanimity of the Great Powers. He stressed the
right of the People's Republic of China to take part in peace
talks with Japan, and he claimed that the United States lacked
any legal ground for unilateral action in this matter. Simultaneously, the Chinese press threatened the Japanese people,
stating that their country was being used as a base for the
American aggression in Korea. This aggression, according
to Peking, was clearly aimed at China. There was no doubt
about the effect of the Chinese accusations. Alarm and speculation followed. People asked themselves anxiously what
China's intentions toward Japan would be and what the Soviet
attitude was in this respect. Were the Communist Powers
prepared to risk provoking a world war?

Notwithstanding these dangers and uncertainties, however,
the United States abided by its decisions regarding Japan.
On January 10, 1951, Acheson declared that the United States
was not seeking the views of Peking on the Japanese peace
treaty. The State Department, ignoring the Chinese threat so
far as the Japanese peace was concerned, continued with its
plans.

In Japan itself the Chinese intervention also caused considerable apprehension. As the Chinese soldiers swept like locusts
over Korea, threatening to cover the entire peninsula, a feeling
of imminent danger grew in Nippon. The Japanese were
afraid that World War III would break out at any moment.
They were not sure that the United States would be in a
position to defend Japan, in view of the American commitments
in Europe. The hidden threats of Chou En-lai, declaring that
China was the country which had suffered most from Japanese
aggression and that now the time might come for Japan to
suffer, added a note of special gloom to the Japanese feelings.

But not only the Japanese were perturbed. Although the
political leaders of the United States favored continuing their
plans for a Japanese peace arrangement, military circles in
Washington asked themselves whether it would be wise to
carry on. The Pentagon was not at all sure that it would not
have to evacuate the American forces from Korea and fall back

on Japan. Evidently, the swiftly developing world crisis had
changed the opinion of the military authorities with regard
to a settlement of the Japanese question. The goal was now
to build a defensive force in Nippon. The Pentagon, on the
other hand, had not entirely reversed its approval to grant the
Japanese almost full sovereignty. So far as the framing of the
actual peace treaty was concerned, however, it favored a
delay for the time being; the military authorities were of the
opinion that in view of the alarming Far Eastern situation some
other device should be found to meet the Japanese wishes for
greater independence. The chief impediment to peace, therefore,
appeared now to be neither the Russian answer nor the Peking
threat, but the objections voiced by the military authorities in
Washington. They insisted on maintaining their power of
command in Japan, in view of the Korean war.

7. *Dulles Overcomes Objections; Second Visit to Japan*

Mr. Dulles, however, managed to overcome even this serious
obstacle. His answer to the military authorities was that in
order to keep the dubious and temporary advantages of a
military occupation, they should not risk the future loss of
Japan politically. He emphasized that the peace promise to
Japan had to be kept; otherwise a strong tide against the United
States could be expected in that country. He was convinced that
if and when the Japanese were given unrestricted equality as
a sovereign nation, they would, of their own free will, wholeheartedly cooperate with the United States and the United
Nations. He said that the possibility of a defeat on the Korean
battlefield further necessitated the regularizing of relations
with Japan. This could be done by means of a short and simple
treaty, adhered to by all the nations willing to sign, but it had
to be a real peace treaty. Dulles won the day. The U.S. Joint
Chiefs of Staff agreed that the peace-making with Japan should
go on, notwithstanding the fact that severe setbacks of the U.N.
armed forces in Korea threatened to create a situation of
grave danger in the Far East.

With this home victory achieved and with the prospect of
peace for Japan brighter than ever before, Dulles prepared to
go to Japan for the second time, in order to hold explanatory
talks with the Japanese themselves.

Fate again was kind enough to help John Foster Dulles. His unlimited confidence in the Japanese people, displayed during the discussions with the military authorities in Washington, was not put to the severe test of a further deterioration of the situation in the Far East. Slowly the U.N. forces recovered from the severe November blow; the Chinese attack lost its momentum. General Collins, the U.S. Army Chief of Staff, in the middle of January 1951, assured the world that the U.N. army would stay in Korea and fight. This statement lessened the fear of a complete disaster and gave hope that a beachhead in Korea could be secured. It looked as if the dangers threatening Japan had become less acute. Nothing prevented Dulles from carrying out his plan to return to Japan for the purpose of familiarizing himself with Japanese opinions on the several aspects of a peace treaty.

8. *Japanese Attitude toward Peace*

The Japanese people had for some time been studying and formulating their desiderata for a peace arrangement.

What was the general opinion of the people regarding the peace treaty?

As has been stated before, the Japanese Ministry of Foreign Affairs had published a White Paper in the late summer of 1950 clarifying Japan's position with regard to the Korean hostilities. This statement, compiled under the direct supervision of Premier Yoshida, happened to contain the basic principles of the more conservative groups of Japanese toward the problems underlying any peace talks. Summarizing, the White Paper said that the Korean war revealed that the so-called peace movement, advocated by the Communists around the world, actually destroyed the real peace sought by the democracies. The Foreign Ministry recognized that the United Nations were fighting to defend the democratic peace. It stated that, notwithstanding the fact that an open clash between the two opposing forces had not yet taken place, the ideological war, unremittingly waged by the Communists, had already started in Japan. And it concluded that, with due consideration to the prevailing circumstances, no chance existed for maintaining neutrality between the two conflicting entities. The White Paper concluded that, consequently, there was no alternative left Japan but to join the group of democratic countries and to confederate with the United Nations. The White Paper abstained from expressing a definite opinion on one of the most controversial issues connected with a future peace for Japan — namely — the problem of Japan's rearmament.

So far the views of official Japan.

Let us now study those of the Japanese political parties.

The views, expressed in the White Paper, were also held by the Liberals, which formed the government party. In its peace program, which was accepted during its national convention at the end of January 1951, the *Liberal Party* advocated the early conclusion of a peace treaty with as many nations as possible. It accepted the necessity of a joint guarantee for Japan's security on the basis of her participation in the United Nations. It advocated the establishment and the reinforcement of police and maritime safety forces for defending Japan against any revolutionary activities and against the violation of peace and order. It requested the restoration of complete independence, the withdrawal of reparation demands, an open-door policy and the assurance of equal opportunity for Japanese immigrants overseas. So far as geographical questions were concerned, the Liberal Party advocated the reinstatement of island territories placed under Japanese jurisdiction after the Sino-Japanese war of 1894–95.

The wishes formulated by the *Democratic Party* were practically the same. As a party in opposition it was somewhat more explicit as to the geographical questions and requested permission to hold such territories as belonged to Japan racially and historically — the Kuriles, the Ryukyu islands, Oshima, etc. The Democratic Party, furthermore, was definitely outspoken with regard to the problem of Japan's future security. Contrary to the Liberal Party, which restricted itself to expressing hopes for a joint guarantee on the basis of Japan's admission to the United Nations — placing emphasis on the importance of patriotic spirit rather than on the strength of armed forces — the Democratic Party, under pressure from Dr. Hitoshi Ashida, the former Premier and one of the Party's leaders, openly emphasized the necessity of self-defense, giving assurance that rearmament would not necessarily violate the constitutional provisions.

The *Socialist Party* was fundamentally opposed to the views of the two conservative parties. The Socialists based their peace program on the so-called three principles of peace, which were drawn up in the autumn of 1950, and affirmed by the party's National Convention of January 22, 1951. The three prin ciples were:

(1) The party advocated the conclusion of a general peace treaty on the grounds that a separate peace would doubt-lessly impair Japan's relations with other nations and would thereby endanger Japan's right of neutrality. Under these circumstances the Socialists deemed it imperative that Japan should not, of its own accord, risk favoring a separate peace.

(2) Under currently effective constitutional provisions con-cerning Japan's neutrality, the party opposed the con-clusion of any military or political agreement permit-ting to a particular nation or group of nations the estab-lishment of strategic bases in Japanese territories, in view of the military obligation entailed by such an agreement, even in the case of its not having an aggressive character.

(3) On the conclusion of a peace treaty, Japan should be granted the right to maintain neutrality and territorial security. The Socialists hoped that Japan would be accepted into the United Nations and obtain therefrom a joint guarantee of security; but such a guarantee of security must be granted with due consideration of her constitutional provision that there be no obligation incumbent upon her to maintain her own armed forces.

Thus, the Socialists were clearly opposed to rearmament and were not willing to accept a security guarantee from the West in the form of the temporary stationing of armed forces in Japan. In fact, the crux of the matter lay much deeper; the Socialist Party did not want to make the choice between the Communist and the Free World, referred to by Dulles. It advo-cated strict neutrality. And it persisted in its attitude, notwithstanding the fact that the developments in Korea and the general trend of events in the world made its three principles for peace appear somewhat academic. As a consequence of its persistence, the Socialist Party lost many sympathizers and exposed itself to the dangers of a serious party schism between its right wing — which favored recognizing realities in international politics — and its left wing, supported by several labor unions — which leaned toward communism.

One of the problems most hotly debated by the Japanese was the question of the rearmament of their country. There was undoubtedly considerable opposition in Japan to rearmament. Late in December 1950 Prime Minister Yoshida had publicly stated that his Government did not consider it necessary for Japan to rearm at that time. Yoshida was very reluctant to express himself further on this point. The Prime Minister had good reasons for his careful attitude; on the one hand he wanted to postpone the financial burden of rearmament for Japan as long as possible; and on the other hand he feared the reactions abroad — particularly in the South Pacific countries — if Japan should express a wish for immediate rearmament.

The conservative opposition, however, free from government responsibility, stressed the need for rearmament. In particular Ashida strongly supported the point of view that Japan should "accept the consequences of joining the free world in their struggle against totalitarianism" and should rearm so far as was compatible with Japan's economic position.

General MacArthur, in his address to the Japanese people on January 1, 1951, had given new impetus to the debates on the rearmament problem. "Prevailing international lawlessness", said MacArthur, "might make the Japanese abandon their constitutional provision renouncing arms". MacArthur's recommendation to the Japanese people was: "to mount force to repel force".

Public opinion on this question, however, remained strongly divided, as did the Japanese views on the terms of a peace arrangement.

Premier Yoshida, in the late fall of 1950, had undertaken to effect a rapprochement on the peace treaty question between his Liberal Party and the Democrats. Yoshida's attempts failed. The endeavors of Yoshida's adviser, Shirazu, to reach a compro-

MacArthur's Headquarters in Tokyo

To Baron Lewe van Aduard.
with best wishes

From chiga Yoshida

Tokio.
Jan. 27.
1953.

Shigeru Yoshida
Japan's Indomitable Prime Minister

mise on the peace problems with the Social Democrats were
equally unsuccessful.

The same fate befell a movement to form a unified front of
the prominent political parties on a non-partisan basis. This
plan had been strongly advocated by Baron Shidehara, the
Speaker of the House of Representatives. Shidehara's own
Liberal Party, however, had not shown much enthusiasm for
this endeavor. The Democratic Party had stated that since the
movement aimed at including all political parties, the Socialists should also be invited to participate. Owing to this
prerequisite, Shidehara's plan was doomed to failure from the
outset. There was practically no common ground between the
Socialist Party and the more conservative parties with regard
to the problems of peace.

9. Dulles's Conferences with Japanese Satisfactory.

Upon the arrival in Japan of Mr. Dulles at the end of January
1951, no compromise had been reached by any of the political
parties. It was even difficult to discern a general trend of opinion
in Japan. The Japanese press in those days published a score
of articles, public opinion polls and interviews, in which all the
different aspects of peace and security were reviewed. The
opinions on the several problems diverged widely. Some
Japanese argued that no peace at all would be better than a
peace without China and Russia. Others clung to the attractive
idea of Japan — forever disarmed by its new constitution —
as a sort of Asiatic Switserland. Others again were opposed to the
secret dealings which they suspected were going on between
the Government and the Occupation authorities regarding
a peace arrangement; they openly criticized those dealings,
though normally decisions on national policy in Japan are not
made by public debate.

Leading Japanese circles sponsored and favored the discussions on the subject of peace. They evidently hoped to use
the several openly expressed opinions for bargaining purposes,
both internally and internationally. It was obvious that they
were preparing themselves to drive a hard bargain with the
Americans on the terms of the proposed peace arrangement.
Dulles himself had encouraged the Japanese to do so by stating,

12

upon his arrival in Tokyo on January 25, 1951: "We look upon Japan as a party to be consulted and not as a vanquished nation to be dictated to by the victors". Those words were music to Japanese ears. They would certainly avail themselves of that opportunity. In their opinion Japan, indeed, had the right to be consulted. The Japanese had become very conscious of the fact that the Western world needed Japan, and that Japan had gained a right to independence and sovereignty. This was not surprising; MacArthur had repeatedly stressed that point.

The general feeling of having nearly regained the status of sovereign nation had, moreover, been stimulated by the rapid progress made in America's piecemeal peace program. One of the most significant measures taken in this regard was the authorization, granted by the Supreme Commander at the end of August 1950, for the establishment abroad of Japanese branches and agencies of commercial firms, subject to the consent of the countries concerned. Of similar importance had been the permission, given by SCAP in the middle of September 1950, to establish Japanese Overseas Agencies for commercial and semi-consular activities in Stockholm, Paris, Rio de Janeiro, Sao Paulo, The Hague, New Delhi, Calcutta, Bombay, Karachi, Brussels and Montevideo. Of particular interest to the Japanese were, furthermore, the large-scale depurges of many top-level persons in the political, business, press, art and economic fields, who were granted amnesty from the postwar purge. In the middle of October more than 10,000 Japanese returned to public life, followed by more than 3,000 army and navy officers in the middle of November 1950.

The Japanese, unfortunately, overestimated their position. They became so aggressive in their reactions to Mr. Dulles's proposals and in their consideration of the peace problem in general that, on Januari 31, 1951, the American envoy had to emphasize that his mission was in Japan only for consultations, as differentiated from negotiations.

In the meantime, Dulles's talks went on. His schedule was crowded with conferences with Japanese leaders from all walks of life. He listened most attentively to the several desiderata of his Japanese visitors. But on the other hand he minced no words in clarifying the American viewpoint and expressing his own opinion. By his frank and common-sense approach,

Dulles won the confidence of the Japanese. He was even successful in reaching an agreement with them on the principles of a future peace arrangement for their country.

Before leaving Japan, Mr. Dulles, in an address to the America-Japan Society on February 2, 1951, summarized these principles and the basic philosophy underlying his mission. Emphasizing the point that the Japanese themselves had to strengthen their country against indirect and direct aggression, he said: "Japan, if it is disposed to protect itself, can, if it wishes, share collective protection against direct aggression. That, however, is not a choice which the United States is going to impose upon Japan, it is an invitation". These words indeed were indicative of the spirit of his peace mission. Japan had to be left completely free to decide her own course.

Mr. Dulles predicted, furthermore, that Japan could have a good economic future and could, by her conduct and example, open for herself new and historic opportunities for leadership in Asia. "We seek", he remarked, "a peace which will afford Japan an opportunity to raise her standard of living by the inventiveness and industry of her people, and an opportunity to achieve moral stature and respected leadership in Asia through the force of good example".

The solid foundation of justice and loyality, upon which Dulles planned to build his peace of trust and of opportunity, was clearly revealed.

Major politicians in Japan, the Socialists excepted, welcomed Mr. Dulles's speech. More unity had been achieved by the American envoy that could have been expected. Yoshida voiced his complete satisfaction with the mission's study of the peace treaty problems. So far as the Japanese aspect of his work was concerned, Dulles could proceed confidently on his road to peace.

10. *Dulles Visits Philippines and Australia*

Mr. Dulles, however, was not to return to the United States for the present. More problems were awaiting him. He faced the task of convincing some of the Allied nations most directly concerned of the soundness of his peace plans. He planned to visit the Philippines, Australia and New Zealand for some earnest and personal conferences with the responsible authorities. These countries had indicated that they intended to persist in their implacable attitude with regard to Japan; they requested reparations; they were against rearmament. Contrary to the United States, which felt that the world crisis called for an immediate return of Japanese sovereignty, and which wanted to raise the defeated country to the status of an effective ally, those countries were still severely prejudiced against Japan. They could not forget the Japanese race to power and the Japanese victories in World War II; neither could they forgive Japanese cruelty, nor the Philippino's the devastation wrought by the Japanese in their country.

In Manila, where requests for astronomical indemnity payments were voiced, Dulles was short and to the point. He told the people of the Philippines that the United States was determined not to repeat the errors of the Versailles treaty. Reparations, according to Dulles, were not merely a matter of justice, but rather one of economics. The United States was was not willing to aid Japan continuously, and America did not plan to shoulder the burden of contingent Japanese reparation obligations.

In Canberra Dulles was persuasive. He knew that MacArthur had convinced the Australian Prime Minister Menzies, during the latter's stay in Tokyo in August 1950, of the necessity of Japan's eventual rearmament. Nevertheless, he understood that Australian public opinion would hardly stomach a full-fledged and immediate rearmament program for Nippon; hence he stressed the fact that the Japanese people, in general, were opposed to rearmament. Dulles, however, aimed at a peace treaty without restrictions, even on rearmament. In order to overcome the objections of the Australians and New Zealanders to the future rearmament of Japan, and to make his Japanese peace proposals more acceptable for them, he suggested ending their apparent state of isolation in the Pacific through the conclusion of a security pact between the United States and the Australasian countries. Such a pact, containing provisions in case of aggression, would probably modify their fears of a revival of Japanese imperialism and would give them a sense of greater security in view of the Red menace threatening the Far East.

Dulles did not make any definite promises with regard to a security pact. But he stated that such an agreement would be favorably looked upon in Washington. He made it clear, however, that a full-fledged Pacific pact, as repeatedly advocated by Australian and New Zealand authorities, was quite another question. Such an all-embracing, multilateral pact was, in the opinion of the State Department, not feasible for the moment. The United States was reluctant to commit herself to such an over-all agreement. Washington was of the opinion that there was no basis for such a pact without such Asiatic countries as India and Indonesia participating. A Pacific pact, exclusively between white men's countries, would only enhance the controversies between East and West. Bilateral security agreements with Australasia, said Dulles, were however a different and most probably acceptable matter. The Australians and New Zealanders, apparently pleased with this prospect, seemed willing to join America in its peace endeavors for Japan.

Hence, Dulles set out to work on plans for a security agreement in the Pacific as a means of overcoming the opposition of some of the Allied nations toward his Japanese peace plans. By careful study of the question, a project of a broader political aspect took shape in his mind. The presidential envoy visualized a set of defensive agreements covering the Pacific. Not only could Japan be transformed into a bastion defending the interest of the free world in the Far East, but such a bastion could be strengthened further by a network of treaties and security arrangements among other Pacific countries and the United States of America. Avoiding the difficult question of a multilateral defense pact for the Pacific, a possibility presented itself of approaching the same objective, along other lines.

No wonder then that Dulles, returning to Washington on February 25, 1951, looked back upon his trip with great satisfaction. He had obtained a clear picture of the wishes and sentiments of the Japanese people; he was convinced that the majority of the Japanese were fully in accord with his peace proposals. He felt that he had done very well in Manila and Canberra. In general, he had successfully clarified the U.S. position in connection with the peace treaty, not only in Japan, but also abroad. There was hope that the Australasian countries would cooperate. President Truman, acknowledging Dulles's success, gave instructions on February 27, 1951, to make preparations for a Japanese peace treaty. John Foster Dulles, having obtained the official approval from Washington for his plans, could thus proceed with his historical task.

In order to assure the full support of the American nation Dulles reported on the progress of his work to the people of the United States. Speaking on a nation-wide radio program he endorsed MacArthur's 1951 New Year statement to the effect that the Japanese people had won the right of restoration to a position of equality and sovereignty in the family of free nations. He stressed that a collective security agreement would prevent the recurrence of Japan's militarism and would protect all Pacific nations against communist aggression. He said that he hoped the Japanese peace treaty would be concluded by the middle of the year, and he emphasized the fact that the United States had decided to proceed without Soviet participation, should the Kremlin disagree with the general formula accepted by other Allies.

11. *MacArthur's Dismissal Threatens Peace Plans; Dulles Again to Japan*

On March 3, 1951, following his address, Mr. Dulles handed his peace proposals, somewhat modified after his journey of orientation, to the 11 Far Eastern Commission nations for their study and comment. It looked as if peace for Japan would be realized without further difficulties. To a close observer, however, ominous signs were already discernible in both the international and national spheres — signs which boded grave danger for the success of Dulles's work.

Dulles was on the West coast when — on April 11, 1951 — the first of these perturbing events occurred. He had just delivered a speech at Whittier College near Los Angeles, in which he had elaborated on his peace proposals and stressed the determination of the United States to go ahead with the peace plan for Japan. His address had been a public explanation of the new treaty draft handed to the Far Eastern Commission countries in the previous month.

Then the news broke. The President of the United States

had relieved General MacArthur of all his commands in the Far East, including his position as Supreme Commander for the Allied Powers in Japan. The shock and amazement were universal. It is outside the scope of this book to study the details of the Truman-MacArthur controversy; their differences of opinion were connected with the Korean war, and not with Japan. MacArthur's dismissal was the climax of a series of clashes over Far Eastern policy questions during the previous six months, which had been raised purely in connection with the Korean war, the Chinese intervention and the attitude of the Allies on these matters. Suffice it to state the facts, without further comment, and to ascertain that the Truman-MacArthur meeting on Wake Island in the autumn of 1950 had aggravated and not moderated the conflict. The tension between the United States and its Allies, resulting from MacArthur's actions and public speeches, had strengthened the feelings in some circles in Washington that the General endangered a U.S. policy of unhampered cooperation and unity with its Atlantic Pact partners.

So far as Japan was concerned, the release of MacArthur seemed an incalculable loss. The General represented everything that the United States had stood for and accomplished in Japan. The Japanese knew that in MacArthur's hands their fate was safe and their future protected. Consequently, Washington was seriously concerned about the reactions in Japan to the General's replacement. Would the Japanese consider the recalling of MacArthur a sign that the United States, after all, had decided to turn away from the Far East in order to concentrate on Europe? Would communism gain in Japan? Would a considerable part of the Occupation's work be undone? What would be the effect of MacArthur's dismissal on Dulles's peace plans? These and other questions faced the American authorities immediately upon the President's decision.

The State Department decided that the best way to cope with the situation would be to request Dulles to go to Japan to assure the Japanese that no change in the American policy toward Japan was comtemplated. Dulles agreed to depart forthwith, but before leaving he wanted to orientate himself on the attitude of the American people. It could be expected that the Democratic electorate would — in general — sponsor the

Truman decision; the Republicans, however, would most certainly object to the dismissal of the Supreme Commander. It was a well-known fact that MacArthur — who had the sympathy of the Republicans — was a supporter of an early peace for Japan. Would his release cause the Republican Party to withdraw its support of the Administration's policy for a speedy peace treaty? It was in itself a miracle in those days, when the United States was so utterly divided on its Far Eastern policy, that unity of opinion on the Japanese problem could have been achieved. Would this harmony be destroyed by a change of opinion in Republican circles? Much would depend on MacArthur's own attitude. Fortunately enough the reaction, according to first indications, was reassuring. No change in policies with regard to Japan seemed contemplated by the opposition Party, or by MacArthur himself. During his flight to Japan, Dulles had the opportunity to emphasize the continuity of bipartisan cooperation with regard to his work; in a dramatic two-way radio conversation with the General over the Pacific, Dulles publicly stated this fact and, moreover, obtained MacArthur's blessing to go ahead with the work for a fair and just peace for Japan.

"Carry on with the peace", was the message Dulles received from the General. His release as Supreme Commander and his personal grief did not interfere with what he considered the interest of his country and of Japan. MacArthur, after his return to the States, continued to render his services to the cause of Japan. Mr. Dulles, in his address before the Governors' Conference at Gatlinburg on October 1, 1951, said: "With the President's knowledge and approval I continued regularly to consult with General MacArthur, and I was constantly strengthened by the pledge of his support".

The present, but to an even greater extent, the coming generations of the peoples of the free world will realize the gigantic work General MacArthur accomplished in furthering the cause of democracy, by his leadership of the war and of the Occupation of Japan. Only a man of his strength of character, his farsightedness and belief in the future of mankind could have erected such a monument of hope and inspiration for the people of this world.

In Japan, Dulles convinced the Japanese that no change in

the American peace policy was under consideration. He calmed all fears which might have been roused. In an address to the United Nations Association of Japan on April 23, Dulles assured his audience that the principles of a prompt peace, a just peace and a peace insured by collective power for Japan had solid bipartisan support of the United States. "The change in the Supreme Commander", said the American envoy, "has left U.S. policies untouched in so far as related to Japan".

MacArthur's departure actually did not influence the peace preparations. The well-timed visit of Dulles to Japan was a wise and highly successful move, offsetting much of the harm which otherwise might have followed the sudden replacement of the Supreme Commander. Furthermore, the highly capable successor of MacArthur, Lieutenant General Matthew B. Ridgway, quickly gained the confidence of the Japanese people and skillfully overcame the difficulties inherent in succeeding such an outstanding and world-famous figure as General of the Army Douglas MacArthur.

12. *Britain Proposes Red China's Presence at Peace Deliberations.*

Another and even more serious danger to Dulles's peace plans came from the side of the United Kingdom through its insistence on the participation of Red China in the peace-making.

In order to understand the difficulties caused by the British attitude, it must be remembered that the United Kingdom and the United States of America had followed a more and more widely divergent policy with regard to China.

The American attitude toward Red China had stiffened, when in November and December 1950 the Chinese intervened in force in Korea. At that time the American public became unmistakably opposed to any rapprochement with Peking.

The British, however, were of the opposite opinion. They pretended to believe that eventually the Mao-regime would turn away from Moscow, and that by following a policy of conciliation the West could lure Peking to the side of the democratic world. London therefore disapproved of the negative attitude of America toward China. In the late fall of 1950, Britain and the rest of Western Europe even evinced a feeling of reproach toward the United States in general and

MacArthur in particular for their attitude regarding China. They blamed the Americans for having more or less forced the Chinese into the war by their aggressive manner in Korea. Moreover, the Asian countries, headed by India, joined Europe in criticizing the United States for its Far Eastern policy.

The differences of opinion between the Americans and their Allies unfortunately led to a rather confused attitude with regard to the Chinese intervention in Korea. This became evident through the actions of the United Nations in New York. This organization had called upon Peking to come to Lake Success to answer charges of aggressive intervention in the Korean war. China answered that it did not recognize these charges, but that Peking itself had serious complaints with regard to American aggression in Formosa. It would therefore send its delegate, General Wu, to the United Nations for the purpose of voicing the Chinese complaints. The United Nations agreed to receive General Wu. The British even went so far as to wait for him in London and to accompany him to New York. The Foreign Office hoped that if the Chinese General was given a fair chance to talk matters over, the difficulties would clear up. According to British opinion, China was not so bad; on the contrary, America was the one to be blamed for a too aggressive policy.

The behavior of General Wu at Lake Success, however, was very disappointing. His attitude was most provocative. He seemed to have come to New York only to stress the fact that Peking was not willing to come to terms with the West. Furthermore, on the day of his arrival, November 20, 1950, the great Chinese offensive in Korea broke loose. The Red Chinese left New York with no agreement reached; they left behind an unacceptable Red Chinese proposal for peace in the Far East. The United Nations, however, were not inclined to give in. They decided to continue their endeavors to reach an armistice in Korea. They formulated a plan for a cease-fire in Korea, to be followed by immediate negotiations on all Far Eastern problems by the United States, the United Kingdom, the Soviet Union and Red China. Early in January 1951 these proposals were submitted to Peking, through the offices of the Secretary General of the United Nations. The plan failed completely. Washington, which had grown more and more impatient, requested the

United Nations to brand China as an aggressor. Several countries, particularly India, seriously objected. Nehru stated that to do so would only increase the conflict. In the meantime, Moscow and Peking, on their part, accused the United States of aggressive aims on the Asiatic mainland, and by strengthening the apprehension of the conflict spreading and by hinting at the implications of the Sino-Soviet Treaty of 1950, they succeeded in adding to the confusion and disunity which embroiled the free world.

The United States eventually persuaded the United Nations to officially disapprove Red China's policy. Moscow promptly reacted and accused the United Nations of being an American organization. It predicted the defeat of the United Nations, unless they accepted Communist China's peace offers. By spreading fear and by holding out offers of an arrangement through appeasement, the communist world hoped to extend and widen the rift between the Western Allies. The rather militant attitude in many American circles did not help to foster mutual understanding and to reduce the breach threatening the free world.

Naturally, these differences of opinion on the Chinese question between London and Washington were reflected in their relations with regard to Japan. In the first place MacArthur himself, at that time still firmly in power, was, as the U.N. Commander in Korea, not too happy about the British reactions to his conduct of the Korean campaign. This led to a gradual deterioration in the relationship between the Supreme Commander and the amiable Head of the United Kingdom Liaison Mission in Japan, Sir Alvary Gascoigne. Notwithstanding the coming peace treaty and the other problems connected with Japan's future London, in the beginning of February 1951, decided to recall its Ambassador from Tokyo and leave the Mission in the hands of a junior, although very capable, diplomatic officer.

13. *Britain's Insistence on Peking's Participation Endangers Japanese Peace Plans*

How much did these developments influence the British attitude toward the American peace plans for Japan? Naturally, the differences of opinion between the Anglo-American countries in their approach to the Far East and its problems were bound, in the long run, to have repercussions on the British-American dealings in connection with a peace for Japan. The British reactions to the U.S. proposals, handed by Dulles to the Far Eastern Commission countries in the fall of 1950, had already been rather noncommittal. In the beginning of January 1951 the first signs of actual differences of opinion became evident. The Commonwealth Prime Ministers, at the close of their international policy conference held in London at that time, urged a rapid conclusion of peace treaties with Japan and Germany and recommended the holding of discussions with Mao and Stalin.

This was clearly and definitely contrary to the American intentions. Washington considered this British decision a deplorable result of Russian and Chinese machinations which obviously were paying dividends. Peking had continuously stressed the absolute necessity of being consulted in any peace for Japan, threatening that Red China's exclusion would cause "a very tense situation to develop". In January 1951, mass rallies and demonstrations in China were organized against America's "provocative" actions, which were preparing Japan for "renewed aggression aimed at China under the cloak of a so-called peace treaty". The Kremlin had consistently sponsored the Red Chinese claims and had, indirectly, exerted considerable pressure in order to alienate the Western European countries from the United States, especially so far as the European policy with regard to the German and Japanese peace arrangements was concerned.

At the end of March 1951 came Britain's first official reaction to Dulles's proposals, followed in the middle of April by a completely new draft treaty — London version. The British suggestions, which were also handed to the other Far Eastern Commission countries, could be regarded as a counter proposal to the second American peace treaty draft, distributed by Mr. Dulles in March of the same year. Clearly, the British were resolved that the initiative for a Japanese peace should not reside with the United States alone. In any case they wanted to have a full and equal voice in the Japanese peace talks.

Although the British had, informally, suggested restrictions on the Japanese textile — and shipbuilding — industry, and although they had made reservations to granting Japan most favored nation rights, the British proposals, on many points, coincided with the American suggestions. The British draft was more elaborate and precise, and as such preferable to the American version. However, the British differed radically with Washington on the Chinese problem. The British Government insisted that Peking should be given an opportunity to participate in the peace-making, and London advocated that the peace treaty should contain a provision under which Formosa would be assigned to Mao's China.

These London conditions were unacceptable to Washington. The American attitude toward Red China was definitely negative. The United States had successfully sponsored the United Nations denunciation of China as an aggressor and the imposing of severe restrictions on the China trade. Notwithstanding the differences of opinion between Truman and MacArthur with regard to Formosa, an increase of aid to Chiang Kai-shek was clearly discernible. Washington adopted the position that it did not recognize Mao Tse-tung and that it entertained normal relations with Chiang Kai-shek; consequently, it could not consult Peking on the question of a peace treaty for Japan. But even an unofficial approach to Red China would have been unacceptable to the American people so long as thousands of Americans were dying at the hands of the Chinese in Korea. The American people would have resisted such a policy in case the Administration had tried to follow it. The United States was averse to any rapprochement with Communist China; on the contrary, it considered Chiang Kai-shek's Government the logical party to be consulted in connection with the Japanese peace drafting, and it accepted the division this would create between Japan and the Government in actual power on the Chinese mainland.

Not only with regard to the Chinese question, but also as far as economic restrictions were concerned the informal London suggestions were contrary to the spirit and the fundamental principles underlying Dulles's peace proposals. Dulles, however, was not inclined to give in on this question either. His firm and irrevocable opinion was that the Japanese treaty should be free of any restrictions.

Dulles refused to be disturbed by the difficulties facing his peace mission; he remained optimistic as to the chances of realizing his aims. During his stay in Tokyo in April 1951, he informed Mr. Yoshida of the British point of view, and said he hoped the differences of opinion could be ironed out.

The general trend of events indeed justified Dulles's hope. London, at the end of May 1951, showed an increasing willingness to reconcile its opinions with Washington. To expect a change in the British attitude had not been illogical. The stormy and enthusiastic reception of General MacArthur in the United States had been accompanied by widespread criticism on British policy. The British were alarmed at the extent to which the emotional wave of pro-MacArthurism in America had been directed against them. Since the start of the Korean war Britain and the United States had been drifting apart on Far Eastern policy. Now this rift seemed to become an unbridgeable gulf as passions rose in the United States. The British realized that this trend of events seriously endangered the unity of the Western world, not only in the Pacific, but also in the Atlantic area. They felt that the time had come to reconsider their attitude and to reverse their criticism on American Far Eastern policy. Britain could not risk a complete breakdown of its relations with its mighty Atlantic ally.

In order to reconcile the Americans, the British took two measures: they tightened their controls on the export of vital materials to Red China, and they changed their attitude toward Formosa. In a statement before the House of Commons on May 11, 1951, the Foreign Secretary, Mr. Herbert Morrison, declared: "It would be premature to discuss the future of Formosa, so long as operations continue in Korea". By this gesture the United Kingdom, for the time being, chose the side of the United States in neutralizing the island fortress of Chiang Kai-shek and in agreeing to some limited military aid to the Generalissimo. Morrison went on to say that Britain aimed at securing an early peace treaty with Japan, without allowing the difficult issue of Formosa to delay the negotiations.

Favored by this agreeable change in the general attitude of the British, most of the Anglo-American differences could be straightened out. The British dropped their demands for imposing restrictions on Japanese industry and they seemed willing to abandon their request for a war guilt clause.

14. *Dulles to London*

One important stumbling-block remained, however. The British insisted on consulting Communist China on the peace treaty. Recent developments in the United States, particularly the MacArthur controversy, made it still more out of the question for the State Department to consider any form of Chinese Communist participation in the peace treaty talks. In order to break this deadlock, Dulles went to London; he arrived in the British capital on June 5, 1951, determined to take what appeared to be the last hurdle on his way to the completion of his peace work.

Dulles left Washington convinced that the Chiang Kai-shek Government should be one of the original signatories of the treaty. The British Foreign Secretary, Morrison, made it clear from the commencement of his talks with the American envoy that this would be completely unacceptable to the United Kingdom. American insistence on Nationalist China's participation would mean that the United States probably would have to act alone on the Japanese pact. Dulles evolved a compromise formula. He suggested that Japan be asked to agree to conclude, within three years of the coming into force of the peace treaty, a bilateral treaty of identical or substantially equivalent terms, at the request of the government of any country which had bee nat war with Japan and had signed or adhered to the U.N. declaration of January 1, 1942. Notwithstanding the fact that this formula gave Chiang Kai-shek a better chance than Mao Tse-tung of becoming a participant in a peace arrangement with Japan, Morrison accepted the compromise. He promised to support it before the British Cabinet.

This looked like a great victory for Dulles. It had required much patience and persuasion to explain to the British Foreign Secretary the broad concepts of the treaty. Dulles pointed out that he saw the Japanese peace pact as part of a new Western strategy in Asia, aimed at the preservation of democracy for the outer rim of Asia, including India. Morrison had accepted Dulles's over-all viewpoint and consequently had agreed to cooperate with the Americans on the Chinese question.

Yet, although Dulles had convinced Morrison, the Foreign Secretary himself failed to get the agreement of the British

Cabinet. The British Government rejected the compromise formula. Again the Japanese peace talks seemed to face a breakdown. This impasse in the Japanese peace negotiations was of particular significance. It not only threatened the prospects of peace for Japan, but it endangered the basis of Anglo-American relations. It reflected not only a gap between foreign policies, but also a fundamental rift between American and British public opinion.

The British Labor Cabinet, on the one hand, under pressure from the extreme Socialist left wing in the United Kingdom, advocated a more conciliatory attitude toward Moscow and Peking than would ever be acceptable to Washington. Dulles, on the other hand, felt that he could not compromise much further on the China issue without risking the loss of the support of the Republican faction in the United States. He informed the State Department that he did not contemplate offering further concessions to the British.

His was a grave recommendation. It implied the possibility that America would have to carry on alone with the Japanese pact. Further postponement of the signing of a peace could not be risked, for it would result in powerful repercussions in Nippon. Yoshida's cabinet would probably be forced to resign. There were indications that large and influential groups of Japanese would turn to the communists to see what they had to offer. The carefully built confidence in Dulles would be completely lost. Peace had to be effected. This put Washington in a serious dilemma indeed; it could either adhere to its own course, refusing to negotiate with Peking or it could give in to British insistence on Red Chinese participation. In the former case Washington would risk a break with the British and would accept a peace with Japan without a settlement of the relations between Japan and her mighty neighbor on the Asian mainland; in the latter case, the Administration would face the most violent reaction and unsurmountable opposition in the United States; moreover, Washington did not believe in dealings with Mao Tse-tung.

15. *Moscow Tries to Exploit USA-UK Differences of Opinion*

As the controversy between the United Kingdom and the

United States continued, the Soviets stepped in to complicate matters further and to broaden the rift between the two Western Powers. In a long and bitter note the Soviet Government, on June 10, 1951, demanded that a Japanese peace conference should be convened in July or August 1951, with representatives of all nations who fought against Japan participating. There should be no separate peace for Japan according to Moscow; any peace arrangement should be based on the Cairo and Yalta agreements. Separate peace, said the Soviet Union, was nothing but a treaty with Japanese reactionaries, briefed in cooperation with American imperialists. Such a treaty would, according to the Communists, never be recognized by the peace-loving people of the world or by the people of Japan itself. Copies of the June 10 note were sent to the Far Eastern Commission countries and to the People's Republics of Mongolia, China and North Korea.

It was the third official Soviet reaction to Dulles's peace proposals. The first one had been an U.S.-U.S.S.R. exchange of notes at the end of 1950 for clarification purposes. After that the Kremlin had remained silent for a long time. It had undoubtedly followed with great interest the Commonwealth Prime Ministers' talks at London in the beginning of January 1951, where consultations with Peking and Moscow had been urged. Stalin certainly noticed the divergence of opinion between the United Kingdom and the United States of America. In the middle of March 1951, Izvestia, the official Russian newspaper, sounded a general warning that Russia had not forgotten the Japanese peace problem. The newspaper suggested that a peace treaty for Japan should be jointly shaped by the Soviet Union, China, the United Kingdom and the United States, and it said that the Russian people were greatly concerned about the plans of the West to rearm Germany and Japan.

For the rest of the anti-peace propaganda, however, the Kremlin had left it to Peking to fulminate against America's plans with Japan. The silence of the Russians in the spring of 1951 had even been the cause of concern in some circles. Questions had arisen whether Moscow, realizing that further conversations about the Japanese peace would be fruitless, had decided to revert to more forceful means and was considering

13

an all-out attack in the Far East, including an invasion of Japan.
The Kremlin was careful not to denounce these speculations;
they could be helpful in creating a useful tension in the West.
On May 7, 1951, however, the Soviet Union broke its silence.
In a note to Washington, it rejected the State Department's
invitation for unilateral peace talks with the United States. It
demanded the convocation of the Council of Foreign Ministers,
including Red China. Washington answered practically immediately. On May 19, 1951, the State Department, in a note to the
Russian Ambassador on the Far Eastern Commission, Mr.
Panyuskin, rejected the Russian proposal for a Pacific Big Four
meeting and at the same time urged the Russians to join in
completing the American-sponsored treaty.

The Russians reacted on June 11, 1951, with a proposal
for a veto-bound Four Power conference on Japan. Their
timing was perfect. Dulles's difficulties in London were at
their height. Fortunately, however, the Kremlin failed to
intimidate Washington. On July 15, 1951, the State Department
rejected the Soviet proposals definitely and firmly.

16. *Dulles's Compromise Saves Situation*

Nor was Dulles himself disturbed by the Russian proposals.
He felt, however, that something had to be done to break the
deadlock of the ticklish Chinese question. He, therefore, made
a last suggestion to the British, proposing that Japan at some
future date be allowed to decide herself with which Chinese
government she wanted to conduct relations. Dulles made it
clear once more that coming to an agreement on the Japanese —
and at the same time — the German problems was essential. He
repeated that in his opinion Germany and Japan were the two
principal goals of the Kremlin. Without these two countries,
the Soviet bloc would be hopelessly outclassed for war. In case,
however, of an Asiatic combination between Russia, China
and Japan, the Kremlin would be able to shift the balance of
world power. That, said Dulles, was the ultimate reason for
the United States to further the peace for Japan, regardless of
the attitude of others. His proposal to let Japan decide for
herself the Chinese question was a last endeavor to cooperate with Britain on the Japanese issue.

After having made his proposal Dulles left for Paris to discuss the treaty with the French authorities. The French were evidently reluctant regarding the whole question. France was busy preparing elections, and French politicians were not willing to commit themselves. The main concern of Paris was that a lenient peace for Japan could establish a precedent for German peace talks to be held later. Furthermore, the French people asked themselves if it was not better to postpone the conclusion of the Japanese peace treaty until the situation in the Far East had been clarified. The Quai d'Orsay insisted on the participation in the peace deliberations of the newly instituted kingdoms of Laos, Cambodia and Viet Nam, members of the French Union, and it made a request for reparations for Indo-China. The French objections, however, could not be viewed as insurmountable; it looked as if they could be solved in time. The position of Great Britain seemed to be the chief difficulty.

When Dulles returned to England a short time later the sky seemed cleared, however. In London the pros and cons of Dulles's last offer had been hotly debated. The British realized that they had to accept Dulles's very plausible suggestion. The American envoy had indeed gone as far as he possibly could. He certainly had displayed unswerving trust in the Japanese, viewed from the American standpoint. Would his confidence be justified? Only history will give the answer. But in those days, in the middle of June 1951, Dulles's formule was the solution. As the prolonged talks between the deputies of the Foreign Ministers of the Four Big Powers, trying to reach an agreement on an agenda for top-level East-West talks, threatened to break down after four months of fruitless conferences in Paris, and as renewed tension grew between the Soviet bloc and the Western democracies, full accord was reached between Washington and London on the Japanese treaty draft. Great Britain and the United States agreed that Japan was to make the choice between Red and Nationalist China. Dulles had gained a new and significant victory.

17. *Allison to Japan; Draft Treaty Published*

Before publishing the details of the agreement reached in

London, Dulles requested his Deputy, Mr. John Allison, to go
to Japan to sound the Japanese on the newest draft for their
peace treaty. Allison, leaving London in the middle of June,
traveled to Tokyo by way of Karachi, New Delhi and Manila.
It was the first time that a member of Dulles's mission had
visited the Indian continent. In view of the great and obvious
interest of New Delhi in the future of Japan, the question
arises whether or not Dulles himself should have consulted
Prime Minister Nehru in the course of his travels of orientation.
Such consultations, however, never took place. Personal contact
with Nehru was not established. Mr. Allison had only some
explanatory talks with officials of the Indian Ministry of
External Affairs. He got the impression that Delhi generally
agreed with Dulles's proposals, but that the Indian officials
preferred to reserve their attitude for the time being. In Manila,
Allison stressed that the U.S. position was that Japan could
not pay heavy reparations. He revealed that no plan for a
general peace conference had been made, and that the newly
composed draft would soon be submitted to all countries.

During his stay in Tokyo, Dulles's Deputy found the
Japanese authorities generally receptive toward the newest
draft; they were pleased with the results reached in London.
The compromise on Chinese participation, however, was not
appreciated by Tokyo. The Japanese contended that they would
have preferred the Allied nations to have made this difficult
and embarrassing choice, instead of leaving the problem to the
Japanese.

At the same time that Allison familiarized Tokyo with the
results of the London talks, Dulles informed the American
public of the progress made. In a nationwide broadcast the
presidential envoy explained the treaty as a non-punitive pact,
with no ban on rearmament. The treaty, said Dulles, would not
confine the Japanese, as treaty restrictions were not only useless
but defeated their own purposes. Mr. Dulles reiterated that the
contemplated peace treaty of Japan was based on justice and
loyalty; the purpose had been to establish a peace of trust and
reconciliation.

On June 26, 1951, the U.S. Secretary of State, Acheson, in a
statement before the Foreign Liaison Committee of the Senate,
stressed the military importance of the treaty by declaring that

he considered the Nippon pact essential to the security of the Pacific. He revealed that what he termed "the great crescent of Asia stretching from Japan to Afghanistan", was directly threatened by militant Chinese Communist imperialism. A peace treaty for Japan, said Acheson, with its accompanying network of bilateral security pacts, would greatly enhance the strength of the defense of the free nations.

On July 5, 1951, the draft for the peace treaty, as prepared by the United States and British Governments, was circulated among the Far Eastern Commission countries, as well as Ceylon and Indonesia, for their study and comment. The draft was based on the American proposals which had been presented in the latter half of March 1951, on the independently prepared U.K. draft circulated at about the same time, and on the comments and observations received from several governments concerned. On July 10, 1951, the new text was published in Washington. The State Department revealed that it expected the peace treaty to be signed within two months. The proposed treaty ruled out any reparations which would be beyond Japan's capacity to pay; it however required Japan to negotiate possible compensation for the Philippines and for other occupied countries by making available Japanese industrial skill and services. In its broad outline, the text followed the pattern of previous drafts. It paved the way for a separate security pact, by which the United States planned to retain troops in Japan with Japanese consent. Simultaneously, Washington revealed that the United States, Australia and New Zealand had agreed on the terms of a Pacific defense treaty, a tripartite pact, guaranteeing the security of the Australasian nations against aggression from any side. This pact could be considered as somewhat resembling a Monroe Doctrine for the Southwest Pacific.

There were some unique features in the way this set of agreements and pacts had been arranged. Diplomatic discussions had been used instead of the normal practice of calling a general conference. Secondly, the proposed peace treaty did not put Japan under any permanent restrictions or disabilities which would make her less free than any other free nation. The treaty was truly one of reconciliation. A third feature, unique in history, was the fact that no limitations were imposed upon the

rearmament of the former enemy. A new and modern approach
had been chosen in order to solve this problem; the principle of
seeking security on a collective basis had replaced the old
philosophy of punitive and vindictive action.

18. *Reactions to Draft Treaty not Favorable; Korean Peace
Proposal*

The publication of the proposed treaty was followed by an
exchange of letters between the Japanese Prime Minister and
the Supreme Commander in Japan. Mr. Yoshida took this
opportunity to convey to General Ridgway the profound sense
of gratitude of the Japanese people for the ardent endeavors of
the representatives of the United States in preparing and sponsoring a just peace for Japan.

The reactions in other countries were less enthusiastic. In
Manila, unanimous disapproval was voiced; the new draft, in
the eyes of the Philippines, did not take into consideration the
justifiable claim for $8,000,000,000 of reparations. Serious
discontent was openly demonstrated; Mr. Dulles's effigy was
burned at a public rally, and President Quirino asserted that
he would not squander the heroic heritage of the Philippines.
The Australians, mollified by the American guarantee of their
security, restricted themselves to voicing reluctant adherence.
Chiang Kai-shek's Government, however, strongly denounced
its exclusion. The United Kingdom expressed its regret that
no better solution had been reached on the China question;
it thought, however, that London and Washington had done
pretty well in leaving the decision to Japan.

The most serious opposition came from Moscow. The Soviet
Union had exhausted practically all the possibilities at its
disposal to thwart Dulles's peace work. It resorted to a last and
most unexpected measure. On June 25, 1951, Mr. Malik, the
Soviet representative in the United Nations, proposed in a
coast-to-coast radio broadcast that a conference be held to
discuss a Korean cease-fire. The basis for Malik's proposal
had been laid for a long time. As early as the beginning of May
1951 the Russian representative at Lake Success had hinted
that talks between the Soviet Union and the United States might
lead to a solution of the Korean problem. His suggestion had

been answered by a statement from the U.N. Headquarters, on
behalf of the nations fighting in Korea, that they would be
willing to end the Korean war somewhere along the 38th
parallel, if the Reds would guarantee negotiations on all
Korean problems. Apparently, the United Nations was ready
to bid for a cease-fire.

This U.N. peace move received no further response until
Malik's proposal of June 25, 1951, made shortly after the
American and British agreement on the Japanese peace proposal
had been reached. Mr. Dulles immediately suspected the
Russians of a new counter-attack on his peace work. At the
beginning of July he publicly stated that the United States
would proceed with the Japanese peace treaty, regardless of the
outcome of the Korean talks. In line with Mr. Dulles's statement, the U.S. Government, on July 15, 1951, in a note to the
Soviet Union turned down a previous Soviet proposal for a
Four Power conference on Japan, simultaneously inviting the
Soviet Union, to take part in the general treaty conference at
San Francisco. The Kremlin, however, still held some strong
cards It could make the postponement of the Japanese treaty
one of its chief political demands in the Korean peace deliberations. It might be hard for Britain or India to resist such
demands.

19. *U.S.A. and U.K. do not Waver and Issue Peace Conference
Invitations*

Notwithstanding these threats Washington, supported by
London, went ahead. It was convinced that postponement at
that time would mean the collapse of the treaty. Never again
would it be possible to induce so many nations to agree on so
much, and a postponement would almost certainly bring about
a political upheaval in Japan, with a good chance of that country
swinging toward the communist orbit. On July 20, 1951, the
United States and the United Kingdom sent invitations to 49
nations to attend a conference at San Francisco on the Japanese
peace treaty, to be held September 4–8, 1951. Attached to the
invitation was a revised draft treaty, containing 18 technical
modifications of the text published on July 10, 1951. The
invitation stated that a final draft, embodying the views of

the governments concerned, would be circulated by August 13, 1951. It was clear that only minor changes could be anticipated and it was even more clear that the Western democracies had decided to go ahead with their peace-making for Japan.

The plans were laid; the stage was set for the final act; the play was nearing its climax.

Chapter IX

THE SAN FRANCISCO CONFERENCE

The Japanese Government, pursuant to an American invitation, forms a delegation for the San Francisco Conference. The feelings of the Allied nations with regard to the invitation for San Francisco are mixed. The Soviet Union tries, unsuccessfully, to prevent the convening of the conference and creates a sphere of tension, aggravated by the reactions of Red China. The sponsoring nations, however, press forward and the conference develops into a great success for the free world.

1. *Japanese Reactions to San Francisco Invitation; the Japanese Delegation*

After many difficulties had been overcome, the work of John Foster Dulles led, as has been told, to an American-British invitation to the 49 nations which had been at war with Japan to attend a conference for the conclusion and signing of a treaty with Japan. The conference would be held at San Francisco, from September 4–8, 1951. An important milestone on the road to peace had been reached.

The defeated nation itself was also asked to participate. Referring to Yoshida's letter of July 13, 1951, in which the Prime Minister had stated that Japan was ready to take part in a peace conference, the U.S. Government, on July 20, 1951, officially invited Japan to the San Francisco Conference.

Japan accepted the invitation on July 22, 1951. Immediately thereon the Japanese Government had to decide on the Japanese representation at the peace conference. This confronted Yoshida with a real problem. First of all, the Prime Minister had not yet decided whether he himself would head the Japanese delegation or whether some other prominent public figure would be assigned that task. When, in the course of the last week of July, it became apparent that the Japanese people unanimously favored Yoshida as a representative of their country in San Francisco, the 73-year-old Premier consented, and consequently on July 27, 1951, it was announced that the

Prime Minister would go to the peace conference as the chief Japanese delegate.

But another problem of greater significance — that of the selection of the further members of the delegation — still faced Yoshida. Originally, the Prime Minister had considered the possibility of sending a small delegation on a strictly governmental basis. Although this would have been an inexpensive and easy solution, it appeared inadvisable in view of the criticism in Japan and abroad that the peace treaty was an arrangement exclusively between Yoshida and the Americans. The Japanese Government, in order to avoid this criticism, wanted the delegation at San Francisco to represent, if possible, the entire Japanese nation, unanimously sponsoring Yoshida's attitude toward the anticipated peace treaty.

This would be difficult to achieve. There were considerable differences of opinion both regarding the way the peace deliberations had been conducted by Yoshida's Government and regarding the peace provisions themselves. In particular, the U.S.-Japan security agreement was under hot debate. The prospect of an all-party delegation was not too hopeful. Nevertheless Yoshida, who could depend upon his own Liberals, instructed his counselors to contact the leaders of the other political parties and explore their willingness to participate in the San Francisco delegation.

On July 23, 1951, the Democratic Party was approached to this end. It stated that, before it could finally decide, it had to be fully and officially informed about the peace deliberations in a special Diet session. The Democratic Party said it objected to the secrecy and silence maintained by the Government on those very important questions. The Democrats' condition was hardly acceptable to the Government, which feared unneccessary complications from a public debate in the Japanese Diet on the several aspects of the peace arrangement before the treaty was signed. The problem of the participation of the Democrats developed into a ticklish and painful controversy between the two main political parties. It would have been highly regrettable if the Democratic Party had declined the invitation to go to San Francisco, particularly in view of the fact that there was even less hope that the Socialists would agree to take part. A peace treaty, signed only by Yoshida, with large groups of the political representatives of the Japanese people abstaining, would be considered of debatable value in international circles.

Yoshida, therefore, was strongly pressed to accede to the wishes of the Democrats. After some hesitation the Government expressed its willingless to comply with the Democratic Party's request for a special Diet session, on condition, however, that the Democratic Party committed itself beforehand to appoint members to the San Francisco delegation. But the latter refused to modify its position; the leaders of the party said they could not agree with the wishes of the Government. A planned personal meeting between Mr. Yoshida and the leader of the Democrates, Mr. Tomabechi, also failed to materialize.

On August 1, 1951, the Prime Minister, irritated and dissatisfied by the attitude of the opposition, unexpectedly broke off the talks with the Democratic Party. Plans for a purely governmental delegation were revived. Notwithstanding the urgent need for the Japanese delegation to be as representative as possible, it looked as if a conciliation between the parties could not be achieved. Their behavior presented a sad example of how selfish party interests can overshadow the greater welfare of the nation. The Japanese people, in general, were disappointed. They feared that Japan would be represented at San Francisco by the Liberal Government only.

As unexpectedly, however, as Yoshida had broken off his talks with the opposition, he made another move. On August 5, 1951, he paid a personal visit to Mr. Tomabechi, begging him to accept the Government's offer to hold a special Diet session. The Democratic leader could not resist this generous move. He promised that at the same time that the Government set a date for the extraordinary Diet session, he would announce his willingness to be a delegate to the San Francisco Conference. He accepted the invitation on August 16, 1951.

On July 24, 1951, the Ryokufukai Party, an independent and influential group in the Upper House, had been approached on the question of participating in the San Francisco delegation and had agreed to do so. Now only the Socialists and some small splinter parties remained opposed to nominating members.

Notwithstanding the fact that the majority of the people were in favor of the treaty, the Socialists, in view of opposition

from the left wing labor unions, did not dare to change their
attitude to the draft treaty. Nevertheless, an influential group
of right wing and centre members of the Socialist Party
were against the party decision. They formed a joint consultative organ to discuss a more practical policy of party unifi-
cation on the peace treaty issue. They realized that the Socialists
risked further loss in popularity by insisting on their so-called
three principles for peace; local elections, held earlier in 1951,
had already indicated a somewhat conservative inclination on
the part of the electorate. The right wing felt that the Socialist
peace principles were not only repudiated by the people, but
that they threatened to become a deadly boomerang which
would, in time, split the Socialist Party wide open. Certain
indications warned its leaders that dissidence of opinion was
growing within the party's ranks. One of the most significant
signs was a schism in the powerful National Railway Workers
Union, whose right wing organized a new Democratization
League, favoring the San Francisco peace talks. These developments, however, did not change the attitude of the Socialist
Party leaders. They flatly refused to join the Japanese delegation
to San Francisco.

Regardless of the dissension among the parties, there was no
doubt that the Japanese delegation would represent the
majority of the Japanese people itself, who in general were
fully cognizant of the spirit of reconciliation and trust running
through the treaty. They were willing and even eager to adhere
to the magnanimous and just peace provisions offered by
Japan's former enemies. This did not alter the fact that the
Japanese would have preferred certain aspects of the treaty to
have been different. The territorial provisions, particularly
the proposed American trusteeship for the Bonin and the
Ryukyu islands, the seizure of Japanese property abroad, the
restitution and reparation clauses — lenient as they were —
were a source of disappointment to the Japanese people.

The Yoshida Government realized that most of those
objections could not be removed for the moment. One particular issue, however — uppermost in the minds of many Japanese
— appeared to be suitable for consideration: the repatriation of
the Japanese prisoners of war still held in Soviet territory. The
insertion of a clause insisting that the remaining prisoners of

war be sent home at the earliest possible opportunity, would be gratifying to many Japanese and would, at the same time, embarrass the Russians. On July 25, 1951, the Japanese Ministry of Foreign Affairs published a White Paper, giving details on the 340,000 Japanese who had been taken prisoner by the Soviet armies overrunning the former Japanese territory in Manchukuo. According to this Japanese publication, about 230,000 Japanese had died in Soviet labor camps; it was estimated that some 78,000 persons were still being held in custody, and about 30,000 were listed as missing. In the beginning of 1951, Prime Minister Yoshida had requested the United Nations to look into this matter, and as a result of this move a commission had been set up to study the problem. The Japanese people, however, were doubtful whether anything would result from the U.N. endeavors. Some Japanese hoped that the peace conference might bring a solution.

In order to draw the attention of the world to the bitter fate of the Japanese prisoners of war — subjugated as slave laborers by their Red masters — a mass hunger strike was held in Tokyo toward the end of July 1951, urging the Government to suggest the inclusion of a repatriation provision in the peace pact. The Japanese Government officially requested the Allied nations to consider this addition to the peace treaty draft. The Japanese wishes were complied with, and the final draft for the peace pact, published on August 16, 1951, contained the provisions asked for.

2. Reactions of Free World to San Francisco Conference

What were the reactions of the other countries to the draft treaty?

So far as the *United States* was concerned, the American press and the American politicians showed a rare unanimity in welcoming the treaty draft and the plans for the San Francisco Conference. Dulles had scored a great victory from the point of view of domestic American politics.

On the international plane, Dulles's success was not unqualified. Although murmurs of approval were forthcoming from most capitals of the world, some governments voiced misapprehension or even fierce opposition.

The *British* Government was confident that it could obtain the ratification of the treaty in due course. It regretted the fact that Mao Tse-tung's China would not participate, but it acknowledged that the present solution — under which Japan herself would eventually decide the vexed Chinese question — was the best possible compromise.

Australia and *New Zealand* made the usual reservations; these were offset, however, by the prospect of the mutual assistance pact to be signed between the Australasian countries and the United States. Undoubtedly, public opinion in Australia considered the draft the most generous peace treaty ever written. The Australian Minister of External Affairs, Richard G. Casey, who visited Japan in August 1951, stated that notwithstanding the fact that his country wished to have friendly relations with Japan, it would be foolish to expect Australia completely to forget the past. Mr. Casey emphasized that the Australian people insisted on precautions against any future aggression; as such, the anticipated security pact, which according to the Foreign Secretary was not especially aimed at Japan, was greatly welcomed by Australia.

Canada was of the opinion that the treaty was reasonably satisfactory. It requested minor changes in the draft, particularly with regard to Japanese fishing rights.

On August 31, 1951, *France's* Foreign Minister, Mr. Schuman, declared that his Government had obtained satisfaction on its main proposals with regard to the peace treaty. After several consultations between Washington and London it had been decided, on August 19, 1951, that the United States would extend an invitation for San Francisco to the Associated States of Indo-China, but that the United Kingdom would abstain from joining in this move, in view of opposition from India. France consented and agreed to sign the Japanese peace treaty.

The *Latin American* countries were willing to concur with the American plans for a peace with Japan. Some, namely Peru, Chili and Mexico, requested minor readjustments in view of the fact that the provisions dealing with the liquidation of Japanese property abroad would lead to difficulties for their countries as a result of their internal legislation. Chili, moreover objected to the arrangements on Japanese fishing rights in the South Pacific and in the Antarctic.

The *Philippines* voiced serious objections to the new draft. Manila continued to press for large reparations. Availing itself of the opportunity that the reparation issue had been left open until August 13, 1951, the Philippine Government suggested that the Japanese peace treaty should recognize a definite obligation to pay reparations. Simultaneously, Manilla urged the United States that the Philippine Republic might be a party to a multilateral Pacific security pact to be concluded at the earliest possible date. It is hard to believe that Manila was actually afraid of future Japanese aggression, but the Philippine Government feared that further Red gains in Southeast Asia would outflank the Philippines and cause the United States to withdraw its protecting forces from the Philippine islands.

The *Netherlands* Government objected to the suggested waiving of reparation claims and advocated that a waiver should be restricted to official claims of the Allied Powers against the Japanese State, leaving open the possibility for individuals to file indemnity claims. Simultaneously, it advocated that not only military, but also civilian prisoners of war should be compensated for hardships suffered under the Japanese occupation. Moreover, The Hague let it be known that before formulating a definite reply to the U.S.A.-U.K. invitation, it wished to consult its Union partner, Indonesia, on the draft of the Japanese peace treaty; in connection with this it reserved its final attitude regarding to the proposed arrangement.

The *Indonesian* Government had several desiderata. It advocated that the Allied Powers should insert a clause recognizing the full sovereignty of the Japanese people over their own country and its territorial waters. Secondly, Djakarta proposed that plebiscites be held in the territories detached from Japan, in order to ascertain the wishes of the inhabitants. Thirdly, the Indonesian Government called for fair and just reparations. Furthermore, it expressed the wish that at the San Francisco Conference an opportunity be provided to discuss the final text of the treaty, and it was of the opinion that if the Chinese People's Republic and Russia should desire to participate in the peace-making, such a desire should be supported.

On August 14, 1951, the State Department answered the Indonesian Government. It accepted the suggestion regarding the insertion of a sovereignty clause. As far as reparations were concerned, it referred to its previously announced suggestion to make certain provisions under which Japan would be obliged to render assistance in the reconstruction of the devastated areas by providing technical skill and other services. The other desiderata of the Indonesian Republic, however, were politely turned down. Discussions at San Francisco, according to Washington, could not be contemplated. That would vitiate all the negotiations held before and would greatly endanger the success of the conference.

In the meantime Indonesia had consulted its neighbors on the peace treaty draft. These consultations culminated in a conference between Indonesia and Burma at Rangoon. Originally, it had been the intention to invite India and other Southeast Asian countries to attend this conference, in order to formulate a mutual Southeast Asian approach to the Japanese peace. This endeavor failed. The conference resulted in mere consultations between Djakarta and Rangoon. *Burma* appeared disinclined to attend the San Francisco Conference. It stated that any treaty which failed to provide for reparation payments would have to be rejected by the Burmese Government. It was clear that this small country, bordering on Red China, preferred not to expose itself on issues concerning the Great Powers.

Of much more significance to the sponsors of the Japanese peace treaty was the attitude of *India*, considered in many circles to be the leading country of Southeast Asia. New Delhi did not sympathize with several of the provisions of the projected draft. In a note to the sponsoring Powers on July 13, 1951, it raised four objections. It advocated that Formosa be given to China — in accordance with the Yalta Agreement — and that the Soviet claim for the Kuriles and Sakhalin be legalized. It objected to the clauses in the draft treaty which authorized the stationing of U.S. troops in Japan. Furthermore, New Delhi did not agree with a U.S. strategic trusteeship of the Ryukyu and Bonin islands and advocated that these islands be returned to Japan. In New Delhi's opinion the main objective of the Japanese settlement should be the promotion of peace in the Far East. Without specifying Communist or Nationalist China, India emphasized the desirability of leaving the way open for China and the Soviet Union to participate in the peace deliberations. New Delhi hinted that India might prefer to abstain from sending a delegation to San Francisco, as well as from signing the anticipated multilateral peace treaty, and that it might conclude a bilateral peace pact with Japan.

India's objections were of serious concern to the sponsoring parties. There was a strong feeling that New Delhi's criticisms of the draft agreement reflected the views of Asia as a whole. Hence, a situation might develop under which many of the Asian countries would hesitate to sign the treaty. There was danger that the united front achieved by Dulles would break down. The attitude of the foremost Asiatic Powers, China and India, toward the talks at San Francisco could easily lead to a last minute failure to achieve peace for Japan.

3. *Soviet and Chinese Reactions to San Francisco Plans*

Anxiety in the Western capitals about these developments was increased by the attitude of the *Soviet Union*, which skillfully exploited the situation in its usual manner. Moscow fulminated against the San Francisco plans, warning against the consequences of the "unilateral action" of Washington, and simultaneously tried to win the wavering countries over to the Soviet side by holding out an offer of general peace in the cold war.

The Korean armistice talks, initiated by Malik's suggestion at the United Nations, undoubtedly represented one of the levers by which the Soviet Union hoped to force the Japanese peace issue in a direction favorable to the Communists. The Kremlin must have realized from the beginning that whatever the outcome of the Korean talks, that outcome would always be favorable to the Communists. If the peace talks resulted in a withdrawal of foreign troops from the Korean peninsula, the fate of that country would be established, for sooner or later Korea would then fall into communist power. If the peace talks dragged on — as they actually did — those talks could be used by the Communists to bring pressure to bear on the Western countries and to blackmail them into concessions on other fronts — for instance on the Japanese peace issue. And if the

14

Korean peace talks broke down altogether, the time gained would afford the communist armies in Korea a welcome opportunity for reorganizing their forces for a renewed attack upon the U.N. forces.

During the weeks preceding the San Francisco Conference, Moscow realized, however, that the Kaesong talks did not constitute a lever powerful enough to induce the Western democracies to reconsider their plans in connection with Japan. The Kremlin then decided to open a much larger peace offensive. This new Soviet move came as unexpectedly as Malik's Korean proposals. The Soviet biweekly News, issued in English in Moscow, published an article in late July, stating: "We are firmly persuaded that there is no cogent reason why nations should not cooperate in peace and concord no matter what political structure and social systems there may be".

This was a startling news item — the more remarkable for the fact that its contents was published all over Russia. The theme of possible friendship between the U.S.S.R., America and Britain was played up in several other Soviet publications. The most striking article was by a former Soviet Ambassador to the United States, Mr. Alexander Troyanovsky, who had been recalled for his pro-Western leanings. Under the heading: "Why I believe in Soviet-American friendship", Troyanovsky emphasized the bright prospects of future Russian-American cooperation. Not only in the press, but also in many other ways, did the Russians demonstrate an apparent change in their attitude toward the West.

The next step in the peace offensive was the unmistakable endeavor of the communist delegates in Korea to come to terms with the Allies, and the simultaneous communist propaganda for a high-level conference on Far Eastern issues, to follow a possible armistice in Korea.

Even more remarkable was the publication by Pravda of an article by the British Foreign Minister, Morrison, in the beginning of August, followed by an exchange of letters between President Truman and President Shvernik of the U.S.S.R.; Shvernik proposed a Five Power pact (the United States, Britain, France, Soviet Union and Red China) for the strengthening of peace. The same proposal had been voiced at the World Peace Congress held in July 1951 at Helsinki.

The Soviet peace offensive was spectacularly staged, perfectly organized and very well timed. The Kremlin chose the right psychological moment to come forward with its general cease-fire proposal in the cold war. The Western European peoples particularly, were inclined to listen to a peace offer and to pay great attention to any suggestion likely to reduce the tension between the Communists and the Free World. They were worried by the persistence of America in seeking to conclude an agreement with Franco's Spain; they were irritated by the pressure exerted by Washington in connection with the rearmament of Europe; and they were shocked by the speed of the U.S. action regarding the Japanese peace treaty. Europe feared that those American moves might kill the last chance for an agreement between the communist world and the Western democracies. The European peoples, therefore, were greatly interested in the Kremlin's suggestions for a Big Five conference — including Red China — to be held previous to or combined with the Japanese peace talks. In their opinion, such a conference would offer a last chance to solve the differences of opinion between East and West.

Even in the United States the Soviet peace propaganda could not be ignored. Moscow's suggestions stood a good chance of affecting the Administration's program for the higher taxes and the increased controls necessary in view of the rearmament programs. In general, those Soviet moves could result in a serious retarding of the organization of the North Atlantic Treaty forces. At the same time they could lead to a postponement of the San Francisco Conference by holding out a promise of an over-all settlement of Far Eastern questions by other means.

The U.S. State Department, fortunately, stood firm. It was not even swayed by the fact that the greatly desired truce in Korea was dangled by the Kremlin before the eyes of the Western democracies as the reward for agreeing to the Soviet suggestions with regard to a peace arrangement for Japan. Washington branded the Shvernik proposals as mere propaganda and pointed out that those proposals were similar to the ones made in 1949 and 1950 by the Russian delegate to the United Nations. Those proposals had, at that time, been rejected by the General Assembly as communist propaganda.

The State Department was of the opinion that the new Russian proposals were nothing better. Consequently, the Soviet suggestion for a Five Power peace pact was turned down. Obviously it would have been plain foolishness to reopen talks with Soviet representatives at this time, when only a month earlier Soviet obstruction in Paris had caused a breakdown of the Big Four preparatory conference. Secretary Acheson declared that the United Nations had previously adopted three resolutions outlining its plans for world peace. He invited the Soviet Government to join the free nations on their road to peace through the machinery of the United Nations.

Neither the Russian Five Power pact offer nor the cease-fire suggestion for Korea had the anticipated result of delaying preparations for the San Francisco Conference. In spite of the attractiveness of the Russian proposals, the governments of the Western world stood firm. They recognized that the Kremlin, through its peace offensive, was merely promoting its policy of conquest and was trying to divide the free world and thwart the signing of the Japanese peace pact.

As the Soviet peace moves did not achieve the success hoped for by Moscow, the Soviet Union staged yet another surprise. On August 14, 1951, the Russians unexpectedly accepted the U.S. invitation to San Francisco. The Kremlin made it clear that it expected to propose at the conference an alternative text for a peace with Japan. Russia, obviously, planned to use the differences of opinion existing between the Anglo-American bloc and the Asiatic nations with regard to the Japanese peace arrangement in order to drive a wedge between the countries of the free world. With a view to paving the way for such action, the Russian newspapers viciously attacked the Western draft of the peace treaty. They warned that a conference which did not afford an opportunity for the discussion of the peace pact would be a deplorable farce. They even asserted that the mere signing of the pact, as anticipated by the United States, would constitute a significant step toward war in Asia.

Although China was not to participate in the San Francisco Conference, it is important to study the attitude of East Asia's largest country with regard to the Japanese peace issue. *Nationalist China* was greatly disappointed that it had not been

invited to San Francisco. Chiang Kai-shek, with bitter re-
proaches, reminded the world that China — which for more
than ten years had fought the Japanese aggression — was not
invited, but Russia — which had not taken an active part in
the war against Japan for even ten days — was. The Generalissimo stressed the importance of China for Japan and the role
Taipeh could play in shaping Japan's future. He emphasized
that discussions between the two countries should be opened
as soon as possible.

Red China, on the other hand, vigorously opposed the San
Francisco treaty proposals. On August 16, 1951, the Foreign
Minister of Red China, in a radio broadcast, rejected the Japanese peace draft as utterly unacceptable, making out that it
violated international agreements and threatening that its
signing would greatly enhance the likelihood of the war in the
Far East expanding. On August 17, the following day, Peking
handed a note to the representatives of Britain and other
nations concerned, rejecting the Japanese peace treaty proposals.
The Red Chinese Government stated that the American-
sponsored treaty was null and void. The Peking radio, taking
up the theme, viciously denounced the American unilateral
action for peace for Japan and sounded serious warnings
against any Japanese rearmament. Said the spokesman for Red
China: "The Chinese are determined to struggle together with
the Japanese peoples and the peoples of other nations in the
East, so that this absurd and preposterous draft peace treaty
will be consumed in the flames of wrath of the great movement
for national independence and liberation of the Asian people".
The attitude of Communist China was clear.

4. *Notwithstanding Serious Threats, United States and United
   Kingdom Proceed with San Francisco Plans*

These developments, however, did not cause any deviation
in the plans of the State Department. It did not hesitate in its
preparations for the San Francisco Conference. Secretary
Acheson, on August 2, 1951, declared that the United States
would hold the peace conference, no matter how many countries
accepted or declined the invitation.

Mr. Dulles and his staff continued working on the technical

revisions to be circulated on August 15, 1951. Trying on the one hand to satisfy those countries which had requested minor and reasonable alterations Dulles, on the other hand, did not contemplate any basic change in his peace draft. The American Government, in its consideration of the Japanese peace question, displayed firm determination and admirable courage. The decision to sign a Japanese peace treaty was a serious one indeed and could have far-reaching consequences. It could provoke an open war with Russia and Communist China. The Russian and Chinese Communists, during the weeks preceding the San Francisco Conference, openly and definitely branded the Japanese peace treaty as an imperialist plot, inviting war in Asia; they actually threatened to go to active war against Japan if the treaty were signed. It was extremely difficult for Washington to ascertain whether these statements were a bluff or whether they constituted a positive menace. The communist threat was aggravated by rumors reaching Washington of the signing in Peking of a Military Assistance Pact by Red China, Russia, North Korea, Viet Minh, Outer Mongolia and communist delegates from Japan and Burma. The pact was said to stipulate that aid would be provided for the Japanese Reds in their endeavors to "liberate Japan and to secure its admission to the world of the free and peace-loving people of communist Asia".

Moreover, following the negative attitude of the Western world, the Russian peace offensive had been stopped. The Korean armistice talks stifled, and a renewed propaganda attack on the United States was launched, highlighted by a "hate demonstration" against Western "imperialism", staged by the World Youth Congress convening in Berlin.

Those facts illustrate that the signing of the Japanese peace treaty and the security pact between America and Japan constituted a serious risk. The decision to effectuate those treaties could be taken as a pretext to start an open and all-out war.

As has been said, Washington however, did not waver and went ahead with its plans as scheduled. On August 16, 1951, the final draft of the peace pact was published. The sovereignty clause, as had been requested by Indonesia, was inserted. A new clause, prescribing that the contents of article 9 of the Potsdam Declaration should be carried out and that the Japanese military forces still held in foreign territories should be returned to their homes, had been added. A change had been made in article 14, dealing with the payment of reparations. The rewording of the reparation section made the treaty somewhat more palatable to the Philippines and Indonesia.

Mr. Dulles, during a press conference following the publication, elaborated on the final draft. He stressed the point that the 50 nations invited to San Francisco had been given to understand that the purpose of the American Government in holding the San Francisco Conference was to sign the text of the treaty as released on August 15, 1951. The San Francisco Conference, according to Dulles, was called only for the signing of the treaty and not for the discussion of it. By limiting the San Francisco meeting to this ceremony, the State Department hoped to block any attempt to obstruct the treaty-signing by what Dulles termed the "Russian wrecking crew". Dulles made it clear that if the Soviets planned to obstruct the San Francisco meeting, the United States would be prepared to deal with them.

Officially, the State Department, in a note to Moscow on August 16, 1951, rejected the Kremlin plans to present new proposals at San Francisco. The intentions of Washington were quite clear. Russia was invited to sign the treaty as it was or else abstain altogether. All the maneuvers of the Soviet Union and all the communist threats could do nothing to change this decision.

The firm attitude of the United States was backed by Britain. One might rightly ask why the British Government committed itself so irrevocably to the side of America so far as the Japanese treaty issue was concerned. The foremost reason was that Britain realized that the United States was now suddenly willing and able to speak with strength in the international arena and that it was not inclined to deviate from its course. London had already experienced this during the previous weeks, particularly in connection with Admiral Sherman's mission to Spain. Although London and Paris seriously objected to the conclusion of a military pact with the Franco Government, Washington had proceeded with its plans. Moreover, experience had taught London that Dulles seemed to be determined to go ahead with the Japanese peace pact, and that he was firmly backed by

Washington and the U.S. Congress. Apparently Britain could not change the course of events with regard to the Japanese peace, even if she had wanted to do so. London felt that it had better go ahead with the peace signing, even though it objected to some aspects of the treaty draft.

Another important factor influencing London's decision to cooperate was the fact that Britain's economic objections had been greatly modified by the successful turn of the Anglo-Japanese financial talks, which had been going on for some months. Those talks seemed to be leading to an agreement which would considerably strengthen British financial and economic position in Japan. Those circumstances made it easier to accept the returning of full sovereignty to the former enemy country.

These considerations do not imply, however, that Britain's choice was an easy one. London was as conscious as Washington of the serious risks taken by signing the San Francisco treaty. It was even harder pressed. The vigorous opposition of Red China, which, as will be recalled, had been recognized by Britain, made it particularly difficult for her to remain on the American side. Peking emphatically warned Britain of the possible consequences of her adherence to the American-sponsored Japanese peace arrangement and of her continued participation in the so-called American invasion of Korea and Formosa. With the Kaesong peace talks taking a turn for the worse, and with the hope of a Korean armistice declining, the Chinese threats were considered ominous indeed. Undoubtedly great courage was demanded from Great Britain, the United States and the rest of the free world in pressing forward with the San Francisco Conference.

5. *Difficulties and Threats Increase*

Britain's difficulties, great as they were, were still to be increased. In addition to the heavy pressure from Peking and the extra burdens resulting from the Iranian oil troubles, India, one of the foremost Commonwealth members, refused to participate in the San Francisco talks. On August 19, 1951, the State Department had sent a polite note to New Delhi refuting India's claim that the proposed peace treaty hindered the chances of a general Far Eastern settlement. Washington, in its note, reiterated the contents of the final draft of the peace treaty, published on August 16. The State Department said that it regretted having failed to find terms to comply with the Indian desiderata; Washington's note was, indeed, a refutation of nearly all of the Indian suggestions. On August 25, 1951, India answered. She informed the nations sponsoring the San Francisco Conference that India (1) would not attend the conference and (2) would not sign the treaty.

India's refusal to sign the treaty was primarily based on a general aversion to drawing the lines of the cold war in Asia too sharply. It did not want purposely to offend Peking. The Indians felt that as a result of the proposed treaty, Japan, in the eyes of Asia, would be stamped as a definite ally of America. With American bases and American troops, rearmed herself and probably treaty-bound to Chiang Kai-shek's China, Japan could easily become a permanent and definite enemy of her continental neighbor. The seeds for a long and interminable struggle would be sown and peace in Asia would become a dream more distant than even before. On the other hand, New Delhi understood the American difficulties with regard to Japan and the American wishes in connection with the peace treaty; Japan's eventual rearmament and a separate defense agreement with the United States had not been disputed in principle. Certainly, India had no desire to line up with the Soviet Union on the Japanese peace arrangements. India's decision not to attend the conference, therefore, was a question of tactics; the Indian Government, by staying away from San Francisco, hoped it could avoid being put in a position where, on certain issues, her delegates would have to take the Soviet side. It reasoned that if it were to go to the conference with the intention of not signing the treaty, it would only reinforce the Russian attempt to wreck the proceedings at San Francisco. Prime Minister Nehru clearly wanted to stand firm on his policy of neutrality between East and West.

For the Indians, who did not relish being obliged to choose between the Western world and Red Asia at the conference, staying away was indeed simplest. India's decision nevertheless aroused many controversies. Some American commentators were of the opinion that the United States should be grateful to

India for not attending the conference, after she had decided not to sign; in their opinion Stalin had more reasons to be disappointed at Nehru's decision than the West. Official Washington, however, was irritated by New Delhi's decision. The opinion of the State Department was that India, by advancing inconsistent and spurious reasons for not participating was playing into Russian hands. The Indian refusal led to an exchange of rather sharp memoranda between New Delhi and Washington. India, obviously deploring this development, tried to sound a more conciliatory note. On August 31, 1951, it sent a new memorandum to Washington, expressing the hope that the divergence over the Japanese peace treaty would not cause resentment in the two countries. The fact remained, however, that the absence of one of the most important Asiatic nations at San Francisco meant a great disappointment for the Western Powers.

Fortunately though, another of the originally dissatisfied countries, the Philippines, had changed its attitude as a result of the changes in the reparations clause. Moreover, Manila had been mollified by an American promise to conclude a mutual security pact with the Philippine Republic.

Indonesia also seemed inclined to sign the treaty. Djakarta, at least, informed Washington that it would participate in the San Francisco Conference. It preferred, however, to reserve its position on the question of the actual signing until that time.

Burma, on the contrary, persisted in her attitude. Rangoon made it known that the Burmese Government would not attend the Japanese peace conference.

The main question during the weeks immediately preceding the San Francisco Conference was, however, concerning the actual Soviet plans for the San Francisco meeting. Speculation ran high in Washington and London as to the Russian intentions; Gromyko, the main Russian delegate, had an impressive record to his name of international conferences which he had upset through delaying tactics and endless discussions. The sponsoring nations, determined to waylay any Russian attempts to postpone the signing of the treaty, had prepared a set of rules of procedure specially designed to thwart any effort to hold up the meeting. London and Washington circulated these rules previous to the actual conference and tried to induce the participating countries to sponsor the suggested procedure.

The United States and the United Kingdom had definitely set the stage for a showdown with Russia. The suggested rules aimed at limiting the debate to practically one formal statement on behalf of each country, after which the signing would take place. Getting these rules of procedure accepted at the first conference session before the actual discussions on the treaty began depended largely on the skill of the chairman and on the unity of the Western democracies. After their acceptance, San Francisco would be safeguarded against any manipulations from the Soviets or their satellites. What further steps the Kremlin might decide to take, however, remained pure speculation. This constituted the grave risk inherent in the San Francisco Conference.

The Soviet Union, in its customary manner, planned to exploit the differences of opinion dividing the free world in order to postpone a decision at San Francisco. The first step to be taken by the Russians after their arrival at New York on their way to San Francisco, was to approach the representatives of the Arab countries with a view to exploring the possibilities of alienating them from the Western Powers. Gromyko suggested to apply the Russian veto in case of any Security Council rebuke to Egypt, informing the Arabs that the Kremlin was willing to sponsor the blockade of the Suez Canal in the United Nations in exchange for an Arab refusal to sign the treaty. This attempt failed, however. The Arab countries rebutted the Soviet proposal and eventually signed the treaty. The foremost Moslem representative at San Francisco, the Pakistani Foreign Minister Zafrullah, even showed himself a staunch advocate of the principles underlying the Japanese peace treaty.

More promising for the Kremlin seemed the smoldering discontent in many Asiatic countries about the peace treaty draft. The non-participation of Red China, the fact that the San Francisco Conference did not provide an opportunity to discuss the draft treaty, and the fact that the treaty contained provisions for the stationing of American troops in Japan after the signing, were issues which had caused serious criticism in Asia. Moscow hoped to turn these circumstances to good account. Izvestia, the official Soviet newspaper, said on September 3, 1951, one day before the convening of the conference:

"It is completely obvious that the U.S. policy toward Japan, and the American-Japanese military agreement, is directed against the independence of the Asiatic people". The Red Chinese papers sounded an even stronger warning.

Simultaneously, the communist press stressed the point that a Japanese peace treaty, being dictated by the Western Powers, would be a valueless document, and as such would not be binding on the Asiatic countries.

In order to disprove the argument that the treaty was "dictated" by the United States Dulles, in a radio address for the Columbia Broadcasting system, pointed out that the extensive negotiations which preceded the San Francisco meeting should be considered as an eleven-months conference. "Communist propaganda", said Mr. Dulles, "is stigmatizing the treaty as arbitrary dictation on the part of two great Powers". Nothing — according to the architect of the peace pact — could be further from the facts. "The Allied Powers", Dulles stated, "have been conducting what in fact is an eleven-months peace conference, participated in by so many nations as to make this treaty the most broadly based peace treaty in all history". No argument was overlooked and no effort spared to strengthen the Allied front in view of the expected Soviet attempt to wreck the San Francisco proceedings.

6. *Security Pacts between U.S. and Several Pacific Countries Signed; Tension Grows*

Immediately before the convening of the San Francisco Conference several additional measures were taken further to strengthen the position of the free nations. On August 31, 1951, the United States and the Philippines initialed a mutual defense pact. This consolidation of the close ties between Manila and Washington was greatly welcomed in the Philippines. An unofficial promise on the part of the United States to use her good offices to obtain Japan's agreement for a reparation settlement with the Philippines — according to the stipulations in the peace treaty draft — further mollified the Philippines.

On September 1, 1951, the tripartite defense alliance between the United States, Australia and New Zealand was signed in

San Francisco, with the result that the ties of friendship and cooperation between the Australian and the American people were greatly fortified, and that the Australian fear of aggression was removed. The American-Australian-New Zealand tripartite pact, the Philippine-American defense alliance, the Japanese peace treaty and the security agreement between the United States and Japan formed a framework for a Pacific regional security arrangement which demonstrated the determination of the free world to oppose communism in its attempt to overrun Southeast Asia and the Pacific region.

It looked as if Dulles, through his foresight and determination, would not only succeed in creating a strong outpost for democracy in the Far East by securing Japan for the free world, but would, moreover, fit this bastion into a defensive system of military alliances covering the far-flung Pacific Ocean, even to the shores of the Asiatic mainland.

During September 2–4, 1951, the delegates arrived in San Francisco. Elaborate preparations had been made to receive them. The stage was well set.

Prior to the actual convening of the conference, the U.S. delegates took further steps to strengthen the unity of the democracies. Acheson and Dulles gave considerable time and attention to those countries which were still undecided whether to sign the treaty. Fortunately the Netherlands, Indonesia, the Arab countries and the Philippines overcame their hesitations and decided to sign.

As the free world became more united, anxiety over the communist intentions grew. Gromyko, at an official reception on September 4, 1951, successfully aroused speculations about the Soviet plans by stating that, in his opinion, the conference would take at least a month. The Japanese believed that Russia had written off Japan as lost for the Communists and that the Kremlin was concentrating on destroying any sympathy for Japan that might exist in Asiatic capitals. The Western world, however, feared that Russia harbored more treacherous plans.

There were several indications. The Russians discontinued the Kaesong talks; the Kremlin seemed to be making preparations in Iran, where the situation was rapidly deteriorating; Russian peace propaganda had been slowed down. It looked as if Russia realized that she had lost her peace offensive, and, therefore, had decided to try a more forceful way to gain her ends. Many people even believed war was imminent. There was widespread speculation whether the Soviets would turn the San Francisco Conference into a monstrous Pearl Harbor. The most fantastic stories were circulated. Some newspapers went as far as picturing Gromyko as the sinister envoy of the Kremlin, chosen to play the role of the angry and insulted representative of the Soviet Union who, protesting against the world's behavior towards Russia, might stage a walk-out from the meeting of the deliberating nations, coinciding with the arrival of Soviet bombers over American cities and the advance of Soviet armies through Western Europe. The fact that such predictions were publishable clearly illustrates the atmosphere prevailing in some circles on the eve of the San Francisco meeting.

The general tension was still further heightened by the remarks of President Truman, who on the day of the opening session, in a speech to his democratic constituents on the west coast, warned the world that unheard of new weapons might wipe out civilization in the event of a third world war.

Indeed, the impression prevailed that the Western Powers, by pursuing their anticipated course with regard to Japan, were risking the outbreak of a world-wide conflict. Yet, London and Washington were determined to go ahead. There was no road back; the die was cast; the drama would begin at the scheduled time.

7. *The Conference Convenes; Soviet Defeat on Procedural Rules*

The atmosphere was pregnant with tension, and uncertainty loomed over the War Memorial Opera House in San Francisco, when at five minutes before five o'clock on Tueasday afternoon, September 4, 1951, Dean Acheson, the U.S. Secretary of State, declared before the representatives of the 52 participating nations: The conference for conclusion and signature of the treaty of peace with Japan is convened".

After a moment of silence and prayer and after speeches of welcome by Elmer E. Robinson, Major of San Francisco and Governor Earl Warren of California, Mr. Acheson introduced the President of the United States to deliver the opening address. Offering an unmistakable challenge to Russia to prove her desire for peace by deeds and not by words, Truman said: "The United States believes the proposed treaty with Japan will show who wishes to put an end to war, and who wishes to continue it". The main theme of the President's address was a warning for Russia to keep her hands off the treaty lest she risked bringing about a new war. Truman's words indicated the underlying issue of the San Francisco Conference; it was primarily a trial of strength between the free world and the communist nations — and only secondly a peace conference.

The San Francisco Conference developed into a demonstration of the will of the peoples of the world to welcome Japan back into the family of nations. The circumstances and conditions under which this demonstration took place made it also an exhibition of the unity and strength of the free world, firmly opposed to Kremlin domination.

As has been described in Chapter VIII, the debate and the preparations for the Japanese peace pact had taken place during the preceding months, and thus at San Francisco only the official signing of the treaty was under discussion. But by that act the signatory nations openly and publicly avowed their adherence to the democratic world, for the signing of the peace treaty was, simultaneously, a confession of a political creed. This was the reason for Russia's opposition, Burma's aloofness and India's neutrality; and this was the reason that Indonesia's attitude, the Philippines' decision and the Arab world's participation were of such great significance. The sponsoring nations had carefully prepared the procedure for the San Francisco Conference; they aimed at making the ceremony of signing the treaty a demonstration of the unity of the free world, highlighted by a crushing defeat of the Soviets and their sinister aims. The course of the conference was to show how successful Dulles and his assistants had been in setting the stage for the peace signing.

On September 5, 1951, the first and probably most important session of the conference was held. It was then that the U.S.-U.K. draft for the rules of procedure was submitted to the conference. The outcome of the debate on those rules would be decisive for the future of the conference, and thus for the future of Japan — and to a large extent, even for the future of the world. The Soviet representative could be expected to concentrate all his efforts on thwarting the British-American procedural plans and on preventing the passing of the proposed stringent conference rules, which would practically deny the Communists any chance of obstructing the conference.

After the rules of procedure had been submitted to the conference at the beginning of the morning session on September 6, the debate was opened. Mr. Gromyko almost immediately took the floor. But his reaction was quite different from what had been expected. Instead of limiting himself to the point under discussion — the rules of procedure — he exhausted all his arguments against the American treaty draft itself in an hour-long, vicious attack on the Western intentions with regard to Japan. Instead of submitting his proposal for the admission of Red China at the proper moment, he raised it at the beginning of the meeting — at a time when that issue was not under discussion. Concluding his harangue, he submitted and explained the Soviet proposals for a peace with Japan, requesting their immediate discussion and consideration. The question under debate — the acceptance of the American-British proposed procedural rules — however, was barely touched on by the Russian delegate. Eight times that morning Mr. Gromyko took the floor, but as the debate progressed, he found himself outmaneuvered by Acheson, the U.S. Secretary of State, who had been elected president of the conference. Acheson skillfully handled the discussions according to a time schedule.

In fact, the rules of procedure were adopted by conference vote even before Gromyko and his henchmen — the Polish and Czechoslovakian representatives — realized what a decisive defeat they had suffered. Had Gromyko been outwitted and outmaneuvered? Had he made a wrong estimate of the situation? Or had the Russians decided, prior to the debate, that their case was lost, and that it was not worthwhile to fight for a change in the proposed procedural rules — or for that matter, in the treaty draft in general?

The Russians had considerable opportunity to obstruct the conference. There was a possibility of driving a wedge between the East and the West. The people of Asia were afraid of renewed Japanese aggression; they were doubtful about

American intentions, and they were sensitive to the threat of a war between America and the Soviet Union; their attitude of reserve toward the San Francisco proceedings was demonstrated by the absence of China, Burma, and India and by the criticism of Indonesia and the Philippines; it was emphasized by the fact that China had not even been invited and by the vigorous attacks of Peking on the treaty draft. Furthermore, the Western nations themselves were not so firmly united on the treaty draft as their San Francisco attitude indicated. On the contrary, many differences of opinion remained unsolved.

The Russians, undoubtedly, were cognizant of these facts. Yet, Gromyko failed to obstruct — seriously and efficiently — the acceptance of the decisive conference rules. He neglected the chances to do so. He even blundered. He made his main speech at the moment he should have suggested an amendment to the rules of procedure, and he submitted his amendments to the treaty draft at the time that this item was not under discussion, and could, according to the approved rules, be omitted from consideration.

The Russian attitude was entirely incomprehensible. On the one hand, it was hardly conceivable that the Russians would acquiesce in plain defeat. On the other hand, it was not very probable that they had come to San Francisco only to give their views on the Japanese treaty. Their tremendous propaganda campaign prior to the conference, their elaborately staged peace offensive, their hidden threats — all had indicated their intention to put up a stiff fight. Their preparations for a month-long stay in San Francisco — where they had rented a luxurious mansion — gave the impression that they intended to do their utmost to prolong the discussions and take a prominent part in them.

It was, therefore, difficult to imagine that they would not exploit all possibilities to obstruct the conference — that they would accept an open dafeat which would result in a serious loss of face in Asia. However, that was actually what happened.

The conference, during its morning session, adopted — without a change — the rules of procedure as drafted by the United States and the United Kingdom. Those rules severely limited the debate and barred the revision of adopted measures.

15

Thus they stifled any communist effort to wreck the treaty-signing.

Notwithstanding this Western victory, however, a general feeling of uneasiness and perplexity prevailed in view of the relative ease with which the skillful Russian delegate had been beaten. The question arose whether probably the Russians did not care what rules were adopted and what procedure was set for the conference. The free world wondered if the Soviets actually planned to stage a dramatic exit at the next session. They feared that this would be followed by a spectacular declaration of war, a war "forced upon" the Kremlin by so-called aggression from the side of the free world, which the Russians would pretend they could answer only by force.

8. *Conference Ends in Victory for Free World*

Yet nothing like that happened in the Wednesday afternoon session of September 5. Mr. Dulles explained the contents of the treaty. He did not hesitate to heckle the Russians and to stress his conviction that the treaty would be welcomed by all the sincere nations of the world.

The Thursday session also proceeded according to schedule. Gradually the tension lessened; one could even discern a feeling of anticlimax. The speeches by the delegates of the participating countries proved that Dulles, in stating that peace for Japan was generally favored by the free democracies, had been correct. The only dissenting voice during that day was that of the Czechoslovakian delegate. The boring and repetitious propaganda statements of the satellite representative were in sharp contrast to the inspiring and courageous address by another speaker of the day, Mr. Jayewardene, the Ceylonese delegate, who stressed the fact that the treaty assured the people of Japan those fundamental freedoms which the people of the Soviet Union would dearly love to possess and enjoy, but which, unfortunately, were denied to them.

The Friday, September 7, session also went off as planned. Mr. Gromyko vainly attempted to put a last spoke in the wheel. He asked the conference how it intended to deal with the amendments submitted by him during the morning session of September 5. Acheson then again ruled Gromyko out of order. He said that no amendments had been tabled by the Russian representative at the proper time. Firmly adhering to the adopted rules of procedure, the Secretary of State side-tracked the Russian objections and closed the debate. He then announced the last speaker of the day, Prime Minister Yoshida of Japan.

Without omitting to mention some of the remaining deside-rata of his people, Yoshida stressed the general feeling of gratitude and happiness which prevailed in Japan at so mag-nanimous and reconciliatory a treaty of peace offered his country by the victorious nations.

The Prime Minister stated that the treaty commanded the overwhelming support of the people of Japan. Yoshida empha-sized that the Japan of 1951 was quite different from the one of 1945.

Said the Prime Minister: "It is with feelings of sorrow that we recall the part played in that catastrophic human experience — World War II — by the old Japan. I speak of the old Japan, because out of the ashes of the old Japan there has arisen a new Japan. Purged of all untoward ambition and of all desire for the path of military conquest, my people burn now with a passion-ate desire to live at peace with their neighbors in the Far East and with the entire world".

A new nation, a reborn Japan, stood ready to enter the family of nations as a respectful and promising new member, dedicated to peace, democracy and freedom. Prime Minister Yoshida's words drew a warm applause from the combined delegations; only the communists remained silent.

On Saturday, September 8, 1951, at 10.15 a.m., the formal signing of the treaty pact took place. Gromyko, who had told the press that the Soviet Union had dissociated itself from the conference, was absent; so were the delegates of Poland and Czechoslovakia. The other 49 nations signed the pact. Mr. Yoshida was the last to affix his signature — in Japanese charac-ters — to the document which ended the state of war between his country and the nations of the free world.

Significantly, the conference which confirmed the admission and entrance of Japan into the family of free nations constituted the worst diplomatic defeat suffered by communism in the postwar era. The former aggressor — Nippon — crushed, defeated and humbled after five years of bloody war, had eventually restored itself, had gained a place among the democracies of the free world, and was welcomed by them as an equal. One of the war-time Allies, however — Russia — had chosen the path of aggression and imperialist policy and for that reason she was excluded from joining the family of free nations. A serious warning not to pursue this path was given to the Soviet Union during the San Francisco Conference. This conference, by accepting Japan as a member of the free world community was clear evidence of the growing unity amongst the democratic nations and of their determination to frustrate any further communist attempt to conquer Asia.

Yet those nations themselves had still to confirm the decision taken by their Governments; the peoples of the free world, through their parliaments, had still to adhere to the policy laid down at San Francisco.

The following chapter will reveal what were their reactions. At the same time the description of the developments in the first months after the signing of the peace treaty will indicate some of the problems soon to face Japan.

Chapter X

JAPAN AWAITS PEACE

Japan, followed by six of her former enemies, ratifies the peace treaty. The treaty comes into force on April 28, 1952, upon the depositing of the instruments of ratification with the State Department in Washington. In the meantime, Japan concludes an administrative agreement with the United States on her security arrangements. She faces the problems of her rearmament, her relations with China and the USSR, and the regaining of her economic independence. These matters foreshadow the difficulties awaiting Japan as a sovereign nation.

1. *Japan Ratifies the San Francisco Treaties*

The signing of the peace treaty, although marking the beginning of a new era for Japan, did not mean an immediate return to full sovereignty. The treaty had still to be ratified by Japan herself and by at least six of the eleven signatory nations that had actually been at war with her.

Moreover, during the period between San Francisco and the coming into force of the treaty, the Japanese Government was faced with many pressing problems, which foreshadowed the difficulties awaiting Japan in the post-occupation years. Japan's economic situation and her relations towards her neighbors in Asia were the most important ones.

One aspect of the former of these two main problems was the question of how to compensate Japan for her lost trade with China. Others were the reparations issue, the clearance of Japan's foreign debts and her rearmament.

This latter problem was closely linked with the question of Japan's security. As has been described before, Japan had arranged with the U.S. Government for the continued stationing of American armed forces in Japan in order to guarantee her security until such time as she herself would be in a position to assume the responsibility for her own defense. In order to formalize this matter a security pact between the United States of America and Japan had been signed on the same day as the peace treaty. This pact prescribed that an administrative

agreement be concluded between the two Governments to
determine the conditions which would govern the disposition
of the U.S. forces in and about Japan. The Japanese Government had the task of negotiating this agreement.

Besides, several other agreements with third countries had
to be entered into concerning reparations, fishery and commerce.

Last but not least, post-treaty Japan faced the problem of
regulating her political status with China (Peking or Taipeh),
India and Burma.

The Japanese people realized that San Francisco was only a
first, although a very important step on the road to peace, and
that many difficulties still lay ahead. In spite of the very generous
spirit of the peace treaty, there was some strong criticism of it
in Japan, and a feeling of nervousness and disappointment that
no solution was presented for Japan's relations with her most
powerful Asiatic neighbors. Japanese reaction to the signing of
the treaty was in accordance with these feelings; no exuberant
joy was demonstrated in Tokyo on the occasion of the San
Francisco ceremony. Moreover, no spectacular events occurred
to mark the signing of the treaty. Some days after, on September 16, 1951, the Supreme Commander and his Diplomatic
Adviser, accompanied by Mrs. Ridgway and Mrs. Sebald,
lunched with the Emperor and the Empress, this being the
first time Their Majesties had received the occupation chief
officially and socially at the Imperial Palace.

On September 8, 1951, the day of the signing of the peace
treaty, the occupation authorities changed the signs on occupation buildings to read: "only authorized persons permitted
to enter", instead of: "Japanese nationals prohibited from
entering", and they discontinued special train coaches and
waiting rooms for allied personnel. But for the rest no obvious
changes took place, although the program of a gradual
restoration of sovereign rights to Japan would be speeded up in
the months to come.

Yet the Japanese people generally appreciated the difficult
task, accomplished by their venerable Prime Minister on his
peace signing mission. Yoshida's dignified and friendly
attitude at San Francisco had greatly enhanced his popularity
and strengthened his position. The Japanese extended a warm

welcome to him and his party upon their return from the Golden
Gate city on September 14, 1951. A member of the Imperial
Household was present at the Tokyo airfield to represent the
Emperor; Prime Minister Yoshida received a box of imperial
cigars and an invitation for an official lunch at the Palace.
These signs of royal appreciation expressed the public feeling
towards their 74 year old leader.

Yoshida's most important statement upon returning to his
country was his emphasis on the need for Japan to realize and
to assume her greater responsibilities towards other nations,
whose confidence she had to regain. He revealed his intention
to convene as soon as possible an extraordinary Diet session
for the ratification of the treaties, and he denied any plans for
Japan's rearmament in the near future. The Minister of Finance,
Ikeda, and Mr. Ichimada, the Governor of the Bank of Japan,
referred to Japan's manifold economic problems connected
with the approach of her independence. The words of the
returning statesmen indicated the great task waiting Japan in
the coming months.

The first and most important step to be taken by Japan was
the ratification of the San Francisco pacts. Delay in Tokyo
could easily lead to postponement elsewhere.

The Japanese Government launched a large program of
lectures and meeting in order to familiarize the people with
the peace treaty and the security pact and to prepare the country
for the Diet discussion. Although the majority of the Japanese
nation supported the treaty and also the pact, several questions
remained unanswered. Many Japanese were not satisfied with
the San Francisco arrangement. The security pact in particular
seemed to meet with feelings of doubt and disapproval.

In Socialist circles, opinion was divided as to whether the
party should or should not support the ratification of the
peace treaty. The security pact, involving Japan in the military
consequences of America's foreign policy in the Far East, met
with practically unanimous Socialist disapproval; they feared
the consequences of the clear-cut choice between the free
world and the communist camp, made by Japan at the San
Francisco meeting. They doubted the wisdom of drawing the
dividing line of the cold war in Asia as sharply as implicated
by the San Francisco agreement. Their leftist wing was very

outspoken in its opposition. Susuki, one of the more extreme leaders of the party, favored the Indian socialist aims of establishing a third force in Asia, striving at the elimination of all Western influence. He warned against the danger of a definite break between Japan and her Asiatic neighbors, stressing the impossibility of an economically independent Japan unless she retained the closest ties with China, India, Burma and Indonesia. A visit of prominent Indian socialists to Japan, during the month of September, 1951, strengthened the position of Suzuki and his followers.

Several of the more moderate Socialists, however, were inclined to accept the peace treaty, although rejecting the security pact. Discord in the Socialist ranks, long dormant, flared up; an attempt by the Policy Council of the Party, on September 19, 1951, to attain a compromise between the right and left wing, failed to produce definite results. As a consequence of this lack of unity in the Socialist Party and of the uncompromising and doctrinaire attitude of many of its leaders, the Socialists gradually lost much of the confidence they had won from the people soon after the war.

The ever widening gulf between the left and right wing socialists and their loss of influence marked a deplorable development in the parliamentary history of Japan after San Francisco.

Moreover, the problem of Japan's relationship with her Asiatic neighbors formed one of the main issues in post-treaty Japanese foreign policy.

The Democrats were generally in favor of the peace treaty. As far as the security pact was concerned they were of the opinion that, although the pact was indispensable to cope with the power vacuum in Japan after the end of the Allied occupation, it should not last long, and should not compromise her independence. They advocated Japan's speedy rearmament, followed by withdrawal of the security forces and a return to complete sovereignty in matters of defense and military policy. The Democrats further urged the early conclusion of a collective security system in the Pacific, to include Japan.

The Liberals and the Ryokufukai Party sponsored both pacts.

On October 10, 1951, the 12th Extraordinary Session of the National Diet, called mainly for the purpose of seeking Diet approval of the San Francisco treaties, was opened. The discussions took a fortnight and all prominent issues were seriously contested. Japan's sovereignty, the problem of her security, her rearmament, the military agreement with the United States, her future diplomatic relations — in particular with her Asiatic neighbors — her reparations duties and her economic prospects were all hotly debated. In addition, the question of Japan's "frozen rights" on the Ryukyu- and Bonin-Islands, — temporarily under American trusteeship — and the position of Sachalin, the Kuriles and the Habomai Islands — still in Russian hands, although not recognized as Russian by the signatories at San Francisco — were earnestly considered.

Sponsored by the Liberals, the Ryokufukai, most Democrats and some Socialists, however, the peace treaty was accepted by an overwhelming majority.

The security pact gained less support. The fear that it might irritate Moscow and Peking, and involve Japan in a war, the uncertainty about the implications of the pact, combined with the fact that many people considered its consequences might prove contrary to the new Japanese Constitution, resulted in considerably more opposition than in the case of the treaty.

On October 26, 1951, the House of Representatives approved the peace treaty by 307 votes in favor and only 47 votes against; the security pact was adopted by 284 votes to 71.

The Upper House passed the peace treaty on November 18, 1951, by 174 votes in favor and 45 votes against, and the security pact by 147 votes to 76.

The two pacts, after having been accepted by the Japanese Parliament, were duly ratified by the Government and submitted to the Emperor. On November 19, 1951, Hirohito affixed his signature to the instruments of ratification. A special envoy of the Japanese Government was rushed off to the United States with the ratification document, which was deposited in the State Department on November 25, 1951.

Japan was the first country to ratify the San Francisco peace treaty; six more nations had to follow before it could come into force; as far as the security pact was concerned only the United States' ratification was still required.

2. Japan-United States Administrative Agreement and Japan's Rearmament

The next step to round off the San Francisco pacts was the conclusion of an administrative agreement between the United States and Japan, provided for in the security pact. The pact was rather vague and it was therefore necessary to elaborate the conditions governing the disposition of United States forces in and around Japan.

The vagueness of the security pact was one of the reasons for criticism by several Japanese politicians, who accused the Government of secret dealings with Washington on such a vital question as the stationing of foreign troops in the country. The issue was complicated by the fact that the controversial problem of Japan's rearmament was closely connected with this matter. The pact, stressing the provisional character of the arrangements chosen for Japan's defense after the coming into force of the peace treaty, said that it expected "that Japan will itself increasingly assume responsibility for its own defense", thus clearly indicating its eventual rearmament.

Public opinion was further disturbed by rumors of differences of opinion in Washington. It was suspected that the State Department and the Department of Defense were somewhat divided on the contents of the administrative agreement. The State Departement favored giving Japan the widest possible independence; it realized how sensitive the Japanese people were with regard to anything which would look like a continuation of the Occupation in a disguised form. It wanted to avoid a situation from which the communist press could derive useful propaganda material by painting Japan as a country dominated by western imperialists, and a mere tool of America.

In the view of the Defense Department, Japan was primarily a vital base for the United Nations campaign in Korea. The military considered it necessary to retain as many privileges as possible in order to guarantee their troop-facilities in Japan. The abandonment of these privileges was felt to be detrimental to the efficient execution of the operations.

The Japanese, however, were becoming increasingly irritated by the favored position of the occupation personnel. The

Dai Ichi building, SCAP's Headquarters, and the Imperial, the most prominent Tokyo hotel, occupied by high-ranking allied officials, became symbols of the wish of the military to keep their power. The Japanese were most anxious for these properties to be handed back to them. Consequently, the question of which of the buildings now being occupied by the Americans should be returned, became one of the main issues between the two countries. Another important problem was whether the American officers and men should come under Japanese jurisdiction. The American military authorities objected to such an arrangement and wanted their personnel to be tried by their own courts. It could not be avoided that these demands were interpreted as a wish for extra-territorial rights, an issue which for generations has been one of the most thorny affairs in the Far East.

A third prominent question was what would be the respective shares to be borne by the United States and Japan in the expenses necessary for the maintenance of the forces and buildings and the upkeep of bases and other facilities in Japan.

In order to get firsthand information on these problems, Dean Rusk, Assistant Secretary of State for Far Eastern Affairs, came to Japan, arriving on November 23, 1951. He reached preliminary agreement on a date for holding an official conference for the conclusion of the administrative agreement, and on January 28, 1952, the talks started. Rusk, nominated Special Ambassador, and Earl Johnson, the Assistant Secretary for the Army, represented the American Government, the Japanese delegation being headed by State Minister Okazaki.

Although public opinion in Japan was greatly interested in the outcome of the discussions, nothing was revealed until February 28, 1952, when the negotiations were succesfully ended and the United States-Japanese Administrative Agreement was signed in Tokyo; on the same day its text was announced. It conformed in general to similar agreements concluded with sovereign countries throughout the world where United States forces are maintained.

The share of Japan in the expenses for her security arrangment would, to begin with, be 17% of her total budget for the next fiscal year. The judicial rights over their personnel, granted to the United States military authorities, were extensive indeed; it could not be denied that such personnel, although

they were obliged to respect the Japanese laws, enjoyed extra-
territorial rights, being subject only to their own jurisdiction.
A comparison with NATO practices and a promise to revise
this judicial arrangement at such time as agreements regarding
the status of NATO troops in foreign countries were concluded,
did not soften this fact. Altogether, however, nothing in the
agreement was definitely detrimental or unfair to Japan. For
practical purposes, the arrangement was the most workable
solution to be found.

Criticism, however, was strong; it centered round the secrecy
with which the Government had handled the deliberations and
had agreed to the judicial provisions. Even the United States
delegation was surprised at the strong anti-American feeling
revealed in the Diet and the press. A more open attitude of the
Japanese Government could probably have prevented many
of these deplorable developments, as most Japanese recognized
the necessity of keeping American forces in Japan and regulating their position.

As could be expected, the reactions of the Japanese population were exploited by the Communists, and the issues
raised by the conclusion of the agreement provided welcome
propaganda material for the Soviets. A rather unfortunate
coincidence was the fact that at the same time a serious crisis
in the British-Egyptian relations over the defense of the
Suez Canal and the stationing of British troops in Egypt had
arisen, providing a ready comparison for unfriendly critics.

In addition to criticism on its handling of the agreement
negotiations, the Government was attacked on its attitude
towards the rearmament question. Most Japanese understood
that, eventually, their country had to rearm in a world where
irresponsible militarism was still rampant. They had accepted
MacArthur's 1951 New Year's statement that "the law of
self-preservation" permitted the Japanese people "to mount
force to repel force", despite the provisions of their new Constitution. They had also accepted the clauses of the peace treaty,
recognizing Japan's right as a sovereign nation to self-defense.
Dulles's warning that Japan must not expect "a free ride" as
far as her security provisions were concerned, was generally
seen to be logical, although not accepted with enthusiasm.

When, however, Prime Minister Yoshida, on January 31,

1952, revealed that the Government was considering plans to establish a Defense Corps, which would take the place of the National Police Organization, loud criticism was voiced. Practically every Japanese knew that this police force, constituted by Government decree of August 9, 1950, had always been an army in disguise. Most Japanese, however, had conveniently avoided facing this fact and had hidden behind their Prime Minister's repeated statements "that Japan could not afford and was not considering rearmament". Now they were rudely awakened and had to face the unpleasant fact of openly accepting the return of an army and a military administration, the latter euphemistically being called a "Security Ministry". In addition, they had to countenance a considerable increase in security expenditure; the budget covering the expenses of the planned security forces and the expenses resulting from the administrative agreement would take nearly 25% of the national budget.

The opposition parties, the Democrats and the Socialists, fiercely attacked the Government on its plans. They objected to the way the plan was presented, and they accused Yoshida of acting under pressure from the Americans, which to a certain extent, was true. Several critics remarked that rearmament was contrary to the Japanese Constitution, although competent lawyers denied this. One of the main issues, however, was the fact that it would have considerable repercussions on the economic situation of Japan.

Moscow quickly recognized the possibilities of arousing Japanese feelings of aversion towards rearmament. Combined with her attacks on the presence of American troops in Japan, the Soviets continued to stress the "desperate plight of the Japanese, pressed by Wallstreet bankers to rearm for use as cannon-fodder in their imperialistic wars".

The question of Japanese rearmament and of the presence of American security forces in Japan, would remain two outstanding problems to be solved in the years after the peace treaty had come into force.

3. *Japan Looks South for her Economic Future*

Another very important problem facing Japan during the post-

San Francisco days was the re-establishment of a healthy and independent economy.

Although after the policy change of 1949, the Occupation had strongly supported the rehabilitation of Japan's industries and the revival of her overseas trade, Japan's economic structure was markedly behind, compared with European standards — to say nothing of those of America. The out-of-date workshop practices and technical knowledge had been somewhat improved, but as far as marketing procedure, organization and management of industry and trade were concerned, Japan still lagged far behind.

Despite these handicaps, upon the ratification of the peace treaty, when Occupation responsibility for sustaining her would come to an end, Japan would still have to find a way of solving her own economic problems. In pre-war days these had been huge and complicated tasks; for the future they were to prove even more difficult.

Before the war Japan had at her disposal the iron-ore, coal and soya-beans of Man Chu-kwo and Korea; she had access to the huge Chinese mainland as an export area; her Empire extended from the South-China Sea and the South Pacific to the Sea of Othotsk and the Bering Sea, and she held sovereignty over rich Formosa, several other Pacific island groups, Sachalin and the Kurilles.

The peace treaty limited Japan to her four main islands; and the political situation in the Far East closed the Asiatic mainland to her trade. In addition, the San Francisco pact presupposed that Japan assumed a share in the expenses for her security arrangements. It imposed reparations on her and prescribed repayment of her foreign debts. The above circumstances, combined with the country's lack of reserve funds, caused the loss of a great deal of economic freedom for Japan and greatly enhanced her problem of regaining economic independence.

The solution of this problem was complicated by the fact that during the year 1951 Japan enjoyed a large but artificial war boom in business. The Korean conflict brought Japan an unexpected windfall in the way of procurement orders for the United Nations forces.

The result was a favorable budget, due entirely, however, to unstable war circumstances. During the first nine months of the Korean war, direct procurement by the United Nations Command made up for more than one-third of Japan's total export; procurement orders were valued at $250,000,000, of which roughly one-third were in services, and two-thirds in goods, mainly metal and metal products, machinery and textiles. During the next year this amount was greatly increased. In 1951 Japan received roughly $950,000,000 from procurement orders for the Korean war and for the maintenance costs of Allied troops in Japan.

Two consequences of this development are worth mentioning.

In the first place the war boom obscured the fact that Japan's normal trade pattern with the dollar area showed a constant dollar shortage. Under the influence of the American financing of Japan's import of raw materials and foodstuffs, Japan's import trade during the Occupation had become focused on the dollar area. In 1951, 56% of her total imports came from hard-currency sources. For that same year, however, only 22% of her total exports went to dollar countries, thus causing a dollar shortage.

As for the sterling area, this pattern was reversed. 43% of Japan's total exports went to sterling countries, whereas imports from sterling sources accounted for only 24% of her total imports, resulting in an accumulation of sterling in Japan. By no means, however, was the dollar shortage counterbalanced by the value of the sterling surplus.

This unfavorable situation was made worse by the non-convertibility of the pound sterling. Although the Japanese-British Payments Agreement of September 1951 made it possible for Japan to trade in sterling with the so-called transferable area — an area comprising many more countries than those belonging to the sterling bloc — the high rate of exchange of the pound, enforced for countries with transferable currencies in their trade with Japan, neutralized many of the potential advantages of the Payments Agreement.

Up to the end of 1950, Japan's deficit in dollars had been offset by American aid provided by the Occupation. Her recurring sterling accumulations over and above the permitted swing had, from time to time, also been cleared with United States help.

This dangerously unbalanced state of affairs was gradually

reversed by the ever-increasing procurement orders from the
United Nations forces in Korea. American aid through grants
and loans was replaced by United Nations war orders paid in
dollars, the scope of these orders becoming so large that for
the first half of 1952 Japan's budget even showed a surplus in
dollars.

A second consequence of the war boom was inflation. The
healthy tendency towards deflation, resulting from the stern
measures advocated by the Financial Adviser of SCAP,
Joseph M. Dodge, during his stay in Japan in 1949, assumed an
inflationary character shortly after the outbreak of the Korean
conflict.

The wave of prosperity in Japan clearly could only be
temporary.

A stern warning was given by Dodge, who paid a fourth visit
to Japan from October 28 to November 29, 1951. He seriously
warned the country that unless it tightened its belt and cleaned
up its economy, it faced economic collapse. He stressed the
artificial character of the Korean boom; he warned that in case
of a Korean peace, the rehabilitation of that unhappy country
could never balance the amount received from procurement
orders; he urged the Japanese to cut imports on non-essential
items and to lower production costs — Japanese heavy industry
products being relatively highly priced compared with world
market prices —; he advocated measures to attract foreign
capital investment, he criticized the planned reduction of
taxes, and he seriously warned the Japanese to curb the inflation
which was threatening their country.

Dodge did not mince his words in revealing a rather unpleasant truth. Obviously, his remarks met with criticism,
although well-informed Japanese were conscious of the fact
that his warnings were worth the most serious consideration.
Said Prime Minister Yoshida, on the occasion of the Detroit
banker's departure: "Mr. Dodge, the Japanese people will
be thankful for what you did 50 years from now; we, the
Government, already realize the great work done by you for
our country".

During the latter half of 1951, the war boom slowed down;
the economic situation was aggravated by the general depression
in world markets and by shortages of electric power and coal

resulting from excessive drought, which crippled Japan's hydro-electric power stations, and from strikes in her coal mines, combined with transport difficulties.

This reversal of the economic situation awoke the Japanese to the fact that they would have to concentrate on finding a sounder and broader basis for their economy. They would have to look for cheaper raw material markets, not situated in the dollar area; they would have to modernize their economic structure and their workshop equipment, for which purpose capital investment — foreign and national — would be necessary; and they would have to increase the volume of Japan's overseas trade and commerce.

It was obvious that many Japanese were inclined to look towards the Asian mainland for a solution of their economic problems. We have already seen in a previous chapter that, as a result of her close pre-war ties with Man Chu-kwo and China, Japan considered Asia as her historical and foremost hinterland. This, however, was a somewhat exaggerated picture. Although Japanese imports and exports to China in 1938 accounted for nearly 50% of her total trade, in the 1920's and mid 1930's this trade covered only 13% of her imports and roughly 22% of her exports.

At the end of the war the China trade came to a complete standstill.

As from May, 1949, this trade had been revived by foreign commercial houses, Japan importing iron-ore, coal, soya-beans and salt in exchange for steel products and some textiles. The average annual volume reached $60,000,000 in 1950. But following the outbreak of the Korean conflict, export restriction on strategical goods to Communist China were enforced followed, in January 1951, by an increase in the list of export items required to be officially authorized. This resulted in the trade virtually being crippled.

Chinese Red propaganda did not fail to make the most of this fact, stressing how America's imperialist policy in the Far East — the Japanese peace treaty and American intervention in Korea — obstructed the smooth economic growth of Japan and imposed undue restrictions on her trade with neighboring countries. The occupation authorities, recognizing Japan's particular position with regard to China, lifted several of these

16

restrictions in September 1951, some days after the signing of the San Francisco treaty.

As prices differed from 16 to 17 dollars per ton cif for Chinese coal against 30 to 35 dollars per ton cif for American coal, and also Chinese iron-ore was highly competitive in price, great hopes were entertained in Japanese circles for an increase in the China trade. These hopes, however, were obviously exaggerated. What could be expected from China, closely linked with Soviet Russia, and with a communist regime in power, consciously linking China's economic interests with those of the Soviet bloc? Even if the Japanese had been given absolute freedom to trade with Communist China, no spectacular results could have been expected. Trade with any member of the free world was, in communist eyes, to be used only as a weapon in the over-all world struggle, and the conditions imposed by the Communists would prevent normal development.

At the same time, the Russians tried to rouse Japan's interest in possible trade with the Soviets. In the autumn of 1951, the Commercial Attaché of the Soviet Mission in Tokyo visited the National Diet for the purpose of discussing the possibility of trade between the two countries. This move was clearly a part of the general peace offensive, launched by Moscow in the midsummer of 1951, and intensified after the failure of Soviet policy at San Francisco. Practical results from these Russian trade offers could, therefore, hardly be expected.

In view of the fact that the prospects of trade with the Asiatic mainland were like a dream, ending only in disillusionment, the Japanese people had to seek a solution in a different direction. Their most obvious choice was South and Southeast Asia.

As early as April, 1951, the Americans had advocated Japanese trade expansion in this direction. General Marquet, the capable and hardworking Chief of SCAP's Economic Staff Section, in a report stressing the need for Japan to formulate her long-term economic policy, stated: "The United States believes that Japan's industrial potential may be utilised advantageously to a maximum extent in order to increase raw material production and industrialization in Southeast Asia. An attractive opportunity exists for Japan to supply

Southeast Asia and other areas with capital and consumer goods not now available from normal sources in countries engaged in war production. To these ends, efforts should be exerted to enlist the support of the various United States economic aid and technical missions in Southeast Asia to develop programs linked to over-all U.S.-Japan economic cooperation plans.

This program was followed when the plans for Japan's economic revival were being drafted. Japan was seen as the workshop of Asia, importing raw materials from under-developed areas and producing consumer goods and capital equipment fit for the low-prized South and Southeast Asia markets. With United States participation in the rehabilitation of Japan's industry, as well as by using Point Four and similar programs — with the aim of sponsoring her trade development — Japan could become as important an ally in the economic sense as in the political and strategic sense.

The program, however, was beset with many difficulties. Japan was likely to meet with resistance on the part of the South and Southeast Asian countries, which feared a resurgence of Japanese imperialism, and she could anticipate opposition from the vested foreign interests in these areas.

Notwithstanding these difficulties the Japanese undertook the carrying out of their plans with great energy.

As a first step, they opened negotiations with the Indonesian and Philippine Governments on the implementation of their reparation obligations as laid down in the San Francisco peace treaty. Japan hoped, moreover, that she could further her economic relations with the receiving countries through the execution of these reparations.

Although the negotiations turned out to be extremely difficult and no definite agreements had been reached by the time of the coming into force of the peace treaty, the Japanese Government persevered. An ambitious plan was drafted to assure Japan's raw material supply from Southeast Asian sources. It aimed at a $50,000,000 investment in the Philippines, Malaya, India, Pakistan, Indo-China, Borneo and Indonesia, in order to develop new sources of iron-ore, non-ferrous metals and coking-coal. In India, Japanese technicians were granted permission to survey iron-ore deposits in the Orisa Bihar region; Japan hoped eventually to export from this source to the extent of a million tons or more a year. Negotiations were opened with the Philippines to invest $1,000,000 in iron mines. Preliminary studies had convinced the Japanese that Southeast Asia, with sufficient foreign aid, could produce all the iron-ore and a considerable part of the coking-coal Japan would need.

This reorientation of Japan's economy, away from China and towards South and Southeast Asia, became one of the most important problems to be solved by independent Japan.

4. *Japan's Relations with Soviet Russia and China*

Unfortunately, Japan's preparations for her return to inde-pendence were not undisturbed. Moscow did not fail to realize that many opportunities existed in Japan which could further Soviet aims in the Far East, aims, which were dia-metrically opposed to the lines along which Japan's future development had been drafted.

After her defeat at San Francisco, Russia had to decide upon the new tactics she would employ to gain her ends; her choice lay between the use of greater force or the granting of apparent concessions. The first course meant running the risk of a world war. The second offered a chance of dividing the free world and of slowing down the growth of its ever-increasing strength. Moscow chose the latter. In the period after the San Francisco meeting it became more and more evident that the Soviets were on the "peace path", trying to lull the free world into imagining that the danger was diminishing and that there was less need to close its ranks.

As far as Japan was concerned, the Soviet Union decided to drive a wedge between the Japanese people and their Govern-ment. At the end of 1951 the Soviet press published the new program of action, adopted by the Japanese Communist Party in August of that year. From a rather moderate policy under the occupation regime, Japan's communists had changed to a frankly militant attitude in order to effect the setting up of a "national-liberation democratic government" and the with-drawal of all American forces from Japan. The program stated that there was no peaceful way of "liberation" and that it was necessary to organize "a serious revolutionary struggle of the people against reactionary forces in Japan".

Although Russia's expectations of her appeal to the Japanese masses were high, the response was negligible. Moscow's declaration of war on the eve of Japan's collapse was still generally resented; her huge reparation claims not forgotten; her attacks on the Emperor, her failure to return or account for roughly 300,000 Japanese war prisoners and her occupation of Sachalin, the Kurilles, and in particular the Habomai Islands, had deeply offended the Japanese. Last but not least, the communist attack on South Korea, clearly a communist threat towards Japan, had aroused anti-Russian feelings. Moreover, it was a wellknown fact that the Soviet Union was assembling strong forces in Manchuria, in the north on Sachalin and Kamchatcha, in the south around Vladivostok and Khabarovsk. Those forces, estimated at 40 divisions at least — of which many were airborne — and a large bomber fleet, looked like a huge nutcracker, waiting to crush Japan.

The Soviets did everything to counteract these unfavorable impressions, and to lure the Japanse away from their American friends. By his 1952 New Year message to the people of Japan Stalin himself speeded up the cold war in the Far East, and thus revealed the primary importance attached by the Soviets to the disruption of relations between Japan and the free world. Said Stalin: "The people of the Soviet Union have themselves in the past experienced the horrors of foreign occupation, in which the Japanese imperialists took part. They, therefore, fully appreciate the suffering of the Japanese people, deeply sympathize with them and believe that they will achieve the regeneration and independence of their country, just as the people of the Soviet Union did".

A clearer indication of the communist course of action was hardly possible.

The implementation of the Soviet policy took two forms: the first being a friendly approach to the Japanese people. It stressed the economic plight of Japan, caused by her "obligatory" rearmament and the denial of her freedom to trade with the Asiatic mainland, in particular China; it deplored the fate of the Japanese, "suffering under a continued American occupation and their own capitalist rulers"; it expressed pity for them, cut off from their Asiatic neighbors, and it urged the Japanese to throw off the heavy yoke and take their destiny in their own hands. In this "friendly" category lay the Soviet offer of autumn 1951 for the extension of trade between Japan and Manchuria; the "peace prize" offered to a leading Japanese leftist; the Soviet invitation to attend the International Economic Conference to be held in Moscow and the sudden press campaign in Russian newspapers, describing the miseries of the Japanese people. All were part of a planned propaganda program.

The second way Moscow chose to implement her policy was to instigate mass violence in Japan. The Communists embarked on a program of sponsoring strikes and creating disturbances; they provoked clashes between the police and the occupation forces on the one hand and the Japanese people on the other. Numerous instances of violence against the police occurred all over Japan. Residences of prominent Japanese, known for their support of Japanese rearmament, were attacked. On February 21, 1952, organized mass demonstrations were held in Tokyo and twenty-five other large cities, during which many people were injured.

Foreseeing such events, the Japanese Government had drafted an Anti-Subversive Activities Law, combined with a Suppression of Violence Bill. In addition it considered a revision of the labor laws which would restrict the rights of the Japanese workers to strike as a method of collective bargaining. The Governments plans met with fierce opposition from labor circles; several unions called for nationwide strikes. The first of these strikes took place on April 1, 1952, involving a quarter of a million workers. The second round, on April 18, 1952, was on a much larger scale; roughly three million workers went on strike.

Communist propaganda skillfully used this labor unrest to further its aims. It looked as if the Communists were purposely inviting stricter enforcement of law and order, thereby hoping to start a process by which the Government and the police would be forced into taking increasingly stringent measures, and thus involuntarily find themselves adopting pre-war totalitarian methods. The Communists could confidently expect the Japanese people to resent this development and consequently become more responsive to Moscow's "liberation" propaganda.

One of the most violent outbreaks of these communist-inspired actions occurred during the May Day demonstrations of 1952, three days after the coming into force of the peace pact. The actions of the Japanese Reds in turning these peaceful demonstrations to their own account led to disturbances and bloodshed. American property was damaged and several Japanese killed.

Although the Russian tactics failed to have the expected results and the Japanese people as a whole resented their actions, particularly after this last outbreak of communist rioting, Russia's activities in Japan remained one of the determining factors in Japan's political development after the restoration of her sovereignty.

5. *Japan's Formal Relations with the Communist Powers*

As the date of the coming into force of the peace treaty approached rapidly, so the problem of regulating the formal relations between Japan and the Soviet Union arose.

A large Russian mission had established itself in Tokyo under the guise of members of the staff of the Soviet Representative on the Allied Council. When, upon the coming into force of the treaty, this Council would cease to exist, the members of the mission would automatically lose their right to stay in Japan. On April 23, 1952, the Allied Council held its last session; the Soviet Delegate, General Kislenko, vigorously protested against its closure; but he was overruled by the Chairman, the American Representative, Niles Bond. The Council was dissolved.

There were only two ways left to the Russians, either to negotiate a peace arrangement or to quit the country. Moscow could conclude a separate peace with Japan which, according to article 26 of the San Francisco treaty, had to be "on the same or substantially the same terms as are provided for in the present treaty". This procedure had been followed by India, which signed a bilateral treaty with Japan on June 9, 1952. Obviously, Russia was not inclined to take such a step. Consequently, the Soviets were, theoretically, obliged to leave Japan, and the world wondered if Tokyo would force them to go. The solution of this ticklish problem was left to independent Japan.

Another problem was Japan's relationship with China — either Peking or Taipeh. The provisions of articles 21 and 26 of the treaty indirectly left the choice to Japan.

As long as the United States did not recognize Peking, and as long as the Korean war went on, it was obvious that the prospect of Japan recognizing Red China would seriously endanger the ratification of the Japanese peace treaty by the United States Senate. This fact was stressed by Senator Sparkman during his visit to Japan in December, 1951. Said the Senator: "Any agreement between Tokyo and Peking would seriously endanger the Senate's ratification of the San Francisco pacts."

Mr. Dulles, in Japan at the end of 1951, discussed with Prime Minister Yoshida Japanese-Chinese relations and their possible repercussions in the United States. In order to put America at ease and to preclude the possibility of a rejection of the San Francisco treaties by the United States Senate on this ground, Yoshida, on December 24, 1951, addressed a letter to Dulles, stating that Japan was ready to negotiate and conclude peace with the Nationalist Government and that Japan would not make peace with the communist regime.

Yoshida's letter was seriously criticized, both in Japan and in Britain, when it was published on January 16, 1952. The Japanese Prime Minister, however, withstood the storm. Openly declaring that: "Japan could not associate with communist countries, which in collusion with the Japanese Communist Party, disturbed Japan's domestic peace, order and stability", he started deliberations with Formosa. One of the main issues discussed during these talks, which started in Taipeh in mid-February 1952, was the question of Nationalist China's sovereignty over China's mainland. In the pact between the countries, signed on April 28, 1952, it was stipulated that the treaty "shall, in respect of the Republic of China, be applicable to all the territories which are now, or which may be hereafter, under the control of its Government". This was as far as the cautious Yoshida was willing to go.

6. *Peace at Last*

In the meantime, extensive preparations were made by the Occupation authorities for the return of full sovereignty to Japan.

After San Francisco, SCAP greatly speeded up his program of abolishing occupation restrictions. On September 13, 1951, the Supreme Commander authorized the Japanese Government to negotiate directly with the 23 foreign diplomatic missions represented in Tokyo; on September 28, restrictions heretofore imposed on the Japanese Government Overseas Agencies, were rescinded; and on December 27, 1951, General Ridgway, in his "goodwill memo", stressed the need for American forces personnel to realize their gradually changing status in Japan and to act accordingly. On January 24, 1952, SCAP began to release "procurement demand property", until then requisitioned for occupation use, and on April 7, 1952, the famous Imperial Hotel, occupied for more than six years by Occupation V.I.P.'s, was returned to the Japanese, and preparations were made to quit the huge Dai-Ichi building, the Supreme Commander's Headquarters since 1945. It is to the credit of General Ridgway that, with tact and energy, he effected a gradual change in the status of American troops in Japan from that of occupation forces to invited security troops.

Japan's return to full sovereignty was also prepared in the international field. Her first step towards return to the international community had been as far back as July, 1948, when she was re-admitted to the International Postal Convention; in October, 1949, followed her re-entrance in the International Telecommunications Convention; on May 16, 1951, she was granted membership in the World Health Organization. Of particular economic importance to Japan was her admittance to the International Wheat Council on June 14, 1951; on June 16, 1951, she became a member of the International Material Conference and on June 21, 1951, her admittance as a member of UNESCO was made possible. Japan's re-entrance into world affairs, even before the peace pact had been signed, was in itself a rare phenomenon in international relations.

One of the most interesting features of this process of a gradual return to independence was the granting to Japan of "ad hoc sovereignty" on the occasion of the International

Fisheries Conference between Japan, the United States and Canada, held in Tokyo from November 5 to December 14, 1951.

The changed attitude of the Americans towards their former enemy was highlighted by the visit of former Admiral Nomura, Japan's special "peace Ambassador" to Washington at the time of Pearl Harbor, to the U.S. battleship "Wisconsin", on March 12, 1952, on the occasion of Vice Admiral Robert P. Briscoe's taking over command of the U.S. Seventh Fleet. The warm welcome extended Nomura, still on the purge list, was particularly significant in view of his role as sponsor of Japan's rearmament; he aimed at an army of 250,000 men, an airforce of 1800 planes and a navy of over 350,000 tons, including four small-size flattops. Times had certainly changed; United States authorities were openly favoring a return of Japanese strength.

As the year 1951 came to its end Britain, as the first of her former enemies, took the lead in ratifying the peace treaty with Japan. In the middle of November, 1951, discussions on the San Francisco treaty were opened in the House of Commons. Opposition was raised on behalf of the British export trade, in particular the pottery and Lancashire textile interests, both of owners and workers. They feared Japan's future competition and tried to insert new restrictions in the peace arrangements. This endeavor, however, failed. After some debate the Bill approving the treaty was passed by the House. On December 4, 1951, the House of Lords followed suit and the way was then open for formal ratification by the Crown, effected soon after.

New Zealand quickly followed. On December 5, 1951, the Lower House of the New Zealand Parliament passed the treaty pact, although it took until April 18, 1952, before the New Zealand instrument of ratification was deposited with the State Department in Washington. The Australian ratification document arrived at the same time, subsequent to acceptance of the San Francisco treaty by the Australian Parliament in March 1952.

In the United States, extensive preparations were made for the ratification debate, scheduled to begin in January, 1952, immediately after the coming into session of Congress.

Vice-President Barkley, and Senators Sparkman and Smith, visited Japan in December, 1951, for firsthand information on the attitude of the Japanese people regarding the peace treaty and the security pact. Mr. Dulles also went to Japan in order to familiarize himself with the latest developments and with Japan's attitude towards China, the administrative agreement and several other problems connected with her return to full sovereignty.

On January 22, 1952, the Secretary of State, Dean Acheson, presented four treaties to the Senate Foreign Relations Committee, for the advice and consent of the United States Senate: the Treaty of Peace with Japan, the Mutual Defense Treaty with the Philippines, the Security Treaty with Australia and New Zealand, and the Security Treaty with Japan. On March 14, 1952, deliberations in the Senate commenced. Senator Tom Conally, opening the debate, hailed the San Francisco arrangements as "setting Japan free so that her people could join with the United States in the all-important task of building the collective strength of the free world". This remained the main theme of the discussions, which ended on March 20, 1952, when the peace treaty was ratified by an overwhelming majority of 60 votes to 10. The Senate also ratified the security pact by 58 votes to 9.

Ceylon was the fifth country; it ratified the treaty at the end of March, 1952.

One more country had still to ratify before the peace treaty could come into force. At the beginning of April, 1952, Pakistan became the sixth nation, apart from Japan herself, to ratify the San Francisco treaty, France and Canada following shortly afterwards.

On April 28, 1952, the seven necessary ratifications had been deposited in Washington and peace and full sovereignty were now officially returned to Japan, ten years, four months and twenty days after the Pearl Harbor attack had plunged the Far East into one of the severest wars of modern history.

What will the future bring? Will the lesson be understood and the opportunity grasped? Will Japan show herself a dependable and trustworthy ally and will she go forward as a peaceful, democratic nation and a respected member of the free world? Or will all the misery and the bloodshed of World War II have been in vain, and will all the energy, good will and faith, displayed during the occupation, fail to bear fruit? The next chapter will deal with these questions.

CHAPTER XI

WHERE WILL JAPAN GO?

The aim of the Occupation and the hopes of the signatories of the San Francisco treaty were for a democratically inclined Japan, willing to cooperate with the free world. Has this been accomplished and will it last? Only the future will provide an answer to this question. A rough estimate of the results of the Occupation indicates that there is good hope for further development of democratic tendencies in Japan and for continued adherence of this country to the family of free nations. On the other hand, the evaluation will show the existence of many dangers, present and latent, threatening such a development. It will, moreover, reveal the fact that if Japan and the free world are earnestly determined to seek genuine cooperation, the future holds a significant promise for a prosperous Japan, a respected and prominent member of the free world. This fact constitutes a challenge to the Japanese people and the people of the free world alike.

1. *San Francisco; an Expression of Hope*

In order to understand the attitude of the world towards Japan, attention has to be given, once more, to the San Francisco conference of September 1951. This conference constitutes a milestone in world history. Japan was welcomed back into the family of nations and her welcome was sanctioned on April 28, 1952, when peace was formally restored to Japan. The reception given to the former enemy country was, on the whole, a hearty one. This in itself was remarkable in view of the fact that the bloody and fanatical war against the Japanese had ended only six years before.

It will be remembered that among the many sympathetic and encouraging words spoken by the representatives of the nations present at San Francisco, some dissonance was heard.

The communist bloc had opposed the envisaged treaty. It had pretended to favor a peace for Japan and a return of this nation to full sovereignty and freedom — but on entirely different terms from those of the other 49 nations. The sincerity of its peace plans had been questionable.

Britain had voiced fear of future Japanese competition in the economic field. The Philippines, Australia and New Zealand had recalled Japan's aggression and had reiterated their firm determination to check any renewal of Japanese ambitions in a southward direction. Several countries had stressed the moral duty of Japan to repay some of the unmeasurable damage caused by the Japanese warriors in Southeast Asia.

Notwithstanding these apprehensions with regard to the future and these reminders of the past, the general feeling had been that the time had come to withdraw the Occupation and to readmit Japan into the community of free and sovereign States. This feeling had been concreted by the signing of the San Francisco treaty and its ratification by the majority of the countries involved.

It would be unrealistic to pretend that self-interest did not play an important role in this matter. International developments since the end of World War II have created a situation whereby two opposing camps, the communistic and the democratic, dominate the world scene and face each other in an embittered struggle, just short of an all-out war with arms. In the battle for power between these two groups, the former enemy countries, Germany and Japan, will play an important role. Their position may well be the decisive factor in this struggle. The free world hopes that Japan will be on its side and that it can rely on the Japanese nation as a firm ally and a strong bulwark against the communist threat in East Asia. The democratic nations, therefore, in determining their attitude toward Japan, have showed willingness and readiness to forgive Japan her actions during World War II. By extending a welcome to Japan as an equal member in the society of free democracies they hope to assure her voluntary adherence to their aims.

2. *Future Uncertain; Depends on Permanence of Occupation Reforms*

At the time of the signing of the peace treaty and its coming into force, Japan's future adherence to the free world community could only be a hope. The way Japan will go is shrouded in the mist of the future and depends on the circumstances. The answer to the big question: "Will Japan fulfill the hopes and expectations of the free world?" will only be determined in the years to come. On the other hand, by ratifying the peace treaty and the security pact, the Japanese people have definitely and openly chosen the free world. Japan today is not only formally committed to the family of democratic nations but actually and voluntarily belongs to it. In the words of her Prime Minister: "We are definitely and irrevocably on the side of the free world. If that does not suit the other side, we cannot help it".

It is a different question whether the Japanese people — in the long run — will favor continued adherence to the free world, and if so, whether their leaders will comply with the wishes of the people.

Predictions on these matters would at this point be vain reflections and as such of no real value. On the other hand, the answers to these questions will greatly influence the future of Japan as well as the future of the other nations of the world. It might, therefore, be useful and even important to recapitulate some indications of Japan's future development and to make an estimate of occupation results. A consideration of certain trends of thought, and an evaluation of past events might point to the road Japan will choose in the years to come.

In the following pages an endeavor is made to analyze some of these points and to assess the positive achievements of the Occupation. In so doing some subjects, covered in the preceding pages, will have to be reviewed; some questions, only superficially treated or even omitted previously, will have to be studied more extensively. Where in the foregoing pages the international aspect of the Occupation has been given most attention, in this last chapter its influence on the Japanese nation itself will be dealt with more thoroughly. Thus it will be endeavored to give a verdict on the ultimate success of the Occupation.

Some persons are convinced that the Occupation has been a great success. Others are doubtful about the endurance of the occupation reforms. Still others criticize the Occupation altogether.

The last verdict originates — in most cases — from a misunderstanding of the aims of the Occupation. It is frequently presumed that the Occupation had the task simply "to democratize Japan". This is a wrong point of view. The Potsdam Declaration of July 26, 1945 — the official document of general principles upon which the occupation policies were based — only stipulates on this subject that:

"The Japanese Government shall remove all obstacles to the revival and strengthening of democratic tendencies among the Japanese people. Freedom of speech, of religion, and of thought as well as respect for the fundamental human rights shall be established".

It further states that there had to be established in Japan "in accordance with the freely expressed will of the Japanese people, a peacefully inclined and responsible government". The Potsdam Declaration, therefore, does not speak of "the democratization of Japan"; it only suggests that the development of democratic tendencies be encouraged.

This careful wording reflects an understanding of the fact that such a centuries-old culture as that of the Japanese cannot be completely overhauled and reconverted in a few years, especially under the circumstances of an occupation.

History shows, on the other hand, that it is possible to change a society by external influences. In fact, this process can be observed constantly. A specific change, at a specific time, however, can only be effected if such a change is in conformity with the over-all pattern of development of the particular society.

If the Allied nations — following their victory over Japan — aimed at introducing their own philosophy, their own social ideas and their own system of government in Japan, they could only hope to be successful if they found a way to graft their reforms upon existing tendencies in the Japanese nation and to influence and foster such tendencies with care and insight.

The post-surrender directive, issued to the Supreme Commander as a general outline for his occupation policy, was based on these considerations. The directive said that the Occupation was to "*encourage* the democratization of Japan". The ultimate objective of the policy was stated as "to bring about the eventual establishment of a peaceful and responsible government which will respect the rights of other states and will support the objectives of the United Nations". But so far as "instituting a democracy" was concerned, the policy directive only "desired that this — the new government — should conform as closely as may be to principles of democratic self-government. It is however not the responsibility of the Allied Powers", continued the directive, "to impose upon

Japan any form of government not supported by the freely
expressed will of the people".

Summarizing, one can say that the post-surrender policy
directive expressed the hope that a liberal government could
be instituted in Japan, and the directive stated that such a
measure should be "encouraged". The original drafters of the
post-surrender policy — wise and experienced former Ambassador Joseph Grew and his advisers — were competent and
able men who understood that a procedure whereby a democratic doctrine was forced upon the Japanese could never bear
fruit. Democracy is a political philosophy, a conception of
life which cannot be superimposed on a nation. Democracy has
to be understood by the people; it has to be accepted by the
people; it has to grow and develop and become an inherent
part of a nation before that nation can be so called.

Not only must such a process therefore be in accordance
with tendencies already existing in a nation, but such a process
requires considerable time — especially in Asia, where the
beginnings from which a democratic society may grow have
still to be created. Furthermore, it requires a favorable atmosphere; it asks for conditions which stimulate the wishes and the
opinions and activities out of which the inclination toward
democracy naturally grows. An occupation, in general, does not
create the atmosphere required for a process so subtle as the
inception or evolution of democracy. The drafters of the
post-surrender policy directive realized this. They, therefore,
explicitly prescribed that the Occupation should try to create
a sphere favorable to the introduction of democracy in Japan
and that it should endeavor to be instrumental to such a
development.

In fact, the Occupation was charged only with the duty of
introducing to Japan a new way of life — a new social, political
and economic pattern of society.

In this light, the Occupation has most certainly accomplished
its task and in so doing has been a success.

Some persons, in judging the Occupation, have been misled
by the public addresses of the Supreme Commander. His
statements have frequently given the impression that MacArthur
claimed to have effected the democratization of Japan. The
Supreme Commander probably meant that he had completed

Fuji-san, Japan's Sacred Mountain

His Majesty the Emperor of Japan

his part of the task in Japan. In his flow of oratory, and with a definite and clearly realized purpose, MacArthur frequently pictured the aim of the Occupation as much more ambitious and elevated than the post-surrender directive implied. He saw his duty as a crusade against the totalitarian, aggressive and reactionary forces which had misled the Japanese nation. His was a mission to reshape Japan into a free and respected democracy and into a dependable ally of the free world. Moreover, in order to inspire his staff and the Japanese people and to win the world for his lofty aims, MacArthur had to maintain a high ideal for his undertaking. MacArthur's statements may have been somewhat high-sounding, his style somewhat rhetorical and spectacular, but as such his words were particularly suited to the Japanese mind. The Supreme Commander urged the Japanese to overcome the spiritual and moral disillusionment resulting from their defeat in war. He wanted to rouse their spirits. He set the Japanese nation a high goal. He created for the Japanese a new ideal and a new mission. "As Japan goes so will go Asia", said MacArthur in one of his public addresses. This stirred the deepest feelings of the Japanese people. Theirs could be a new and great responsibility — one of spiritual leadership in the Far East. By thus encouraging the Japanese people to choose a government which closely conformed to democratic principles, MacArthur greatly contributed to the success of his difficult mission.

A careful study of SCAP's public statements, however, reveals that MacArthur clearly realized that his work in democratizing Japan was limited to the erection of the framework, to the introduction of democratic ideas and concepts and to guidance in creating a new government and a new political, social and economic structure for Japan. MacArthur repeatedly stressed the fact that the Japanese people themselves had to continue, deepen, enlarge and accomplish the work begun by the Occupation. General MacArthur showed the Japanese a new road, but he knew that the Japanese themselves had to elect to set foot upon this road.

3. Occupation Introduces Democracy

With these considerations in mind one certainly can say that the Occupation has done a significant, benevolent and successful work. It, indeed, introduced democracy to Japan. With remarkable energy and skill, SCAP formulated many reforms covering practically all fields of public life. With insight and determination and with much tact and restraint the Occupation introduced these reforms to the Japanese people and, during the years of development, carefully guided and supervised them. One has to follow the history of several of these reforms in order to appreciate the painstaking labor involved in their drafting, the enormous work connected with their introduction, the understanding and determination required to familiarize the Japanese with them, and again the labor involved in re-modeling and "Japanizing" them after they had been tried out. Lastly, great restraint had to be insisted upon in letting the Japanese "play" with them, criticize them — even sabotage these reforms, until they had become a real part of the daily life of the Japanese people.

4. Six Significant Reforms

Six of the occupational reforms stand out as being of particular significance to the future of Japan:

(a) The political reform
(b) Freeing of the press
(c) Educational reform
(d) Woman suffrage
(e) Organization of labor unions
(f) Land reform

The political reform, described in Chapter III, has given Japan a Constitution and an administrative framework which provides her with a legal base for a democratic government, comparing favorably with that of any democratic nation of the free world. The post-war elections — combined with changes enforced in the administrative branch — have brought into power a democratically inclined Government which has functioned for several years as satisfactorily as is possible under occupation circumstances.

One can say that in post-treaty Japan the machinery for a democratic Government exists and has been tried out long

enough to be judged. Its reception has been favorable, although
this does not mean that an actual democracy has been established,
but only that the possibility thereto has been opened. The
Japanese people must grasp the opportunity offered them.

It is not correct to say that the Japanese have had the same
opportunity before and failed to grasp it. It is true that in the
early thirties steps were taken to set up a liberal and representative government in Japan, and it is also true that nationalistic and aggressive forces succeeded in checking these
advances and in imposing their own totalitarian system on the
nation. But the Meiji Constitution, then the basis of the
Japanese Government, contained so many inconsistencies
and fundamental defects, and opened so many possibilities for
a group of reactionaries to promote their policies that a comparison with the situation today is hardly possible. Moreover,
the present Constitution provides the necessary safeguards to
ensure the perpetuation of the new liberties: it will be far more
difficult from now on to override its provisions and to revert to
a totalitarian system of government.

While a comparison with the fate of liberalism in the years
before World War II is pointless, yet the fact that the liberal
trend in politics is not new in Japan is of great importance for
the future development of democracy in this country. The
circumstance that many of the concepts underlying the "new
Japan" existed before, though they were not put into effect,
makes their realization much more probable now.

In this connection it is important to bear in mind that in the
years preceding the Manchurian Incident in 1931, many
Japanese intellectuals were definitely progressive, even leftist
inclined. There was great interest in the teachings of Marx
and in the socialist systems as practiced in Europe. In particular
the students followed with enthusiasm the developments of
socialist politics in other countries. Many of those who at that
time were students or young officials today hold executive
positions in private business or in the Government. Moreover,
the number of people who never approved of the ultra-nationalist
and imperialist tendencies of the militarists — but were forced
to follow the general trend of affairs — was relatively great.
These people are now ardent supporters of the new democratic
system.

In view of these considerations it is possible to speak of a revival of liberal tendencies in Japan. Thus the endeavor to
create a democracy obviously has a much more solid foundation
than would be the case if the liberal outlook was entirely new
and unknown to Japan.

The existence of these facts constitutes the historic base for a
liberal government and the legal base for a representative
democracy — it does not imply, however, that the democratic
form of government in Japan is guaranteed to remain in existence. In order to provide a solid foundation for a free and
representative government, the Japanese people first have to
recognize the value of such a government; secondly, they have to
maintain a healthy party system for voicing their opinions and
enforcing their will; thirdly, they must be willing and resolved
to fight for their liberties.

An investigation into the actual or possible existence of these
conditions can best begin with a review of the present position
of the political parties of Japan.

5. *Political Parties of Present-Day Japan*

As mentioned before, the major political parties were forced to
dissolve during the years immediately preceding World War
II. In the beginning of the war the great majority of the so-
called representatives of the Japanese people were forced to
form a single, government-controlled party. During this period
the political life of Japan was strangled. With the restoration of
political liberty, instituted by the Occupation in 1945, the
leaders of the Japanese people formed new parties, based on
the old political groupings of the early thirties.

Today there are in Japan four main political parties: the
Liberal Party, headed by premier Yoshida, the Progressive
Party under the leadership of Shigemitsu, the Social Democratic
Party with Tetsu Katayama as its most important member,
and the Japanese Communist Party.

The *Liberal Party*, which has held the reins of government
since October 1948, is based on the former Seiyukai, a political
group which represented the interests of the landlords and the
aristocracy, and which was sponsored by the powerful commercial house of Mitsui. The party is conservative and forms

a rallying point for the majority of the — traditionally conservative — Japanese people. Even though several former ultra-nationalists have undoubtedly found a place in the Liberal Party, it would be wrong to suspect the Liberals of ultra-nationalist or imperialist tendencies. The Liberal Party is a moderate nationalist and conservative group, opposed to the practices of the extreme right. In general, it is important to realize that although many old leaders are again available for office and several of them would prefer a return to pre-war policies — or are just plainly opposed to any innovation introduced by the Occupation — the direct and immediate political influence of the extreme right is negligible; the possibilities for its revival are definitely limited.

The *Progressive Party* was formed on February 8, 1952, as a merger of the Democratic party of Tomabechi and the Farmers' Cooperatives; the Democratic Party, whose former members exercise the greatest influence amongst the progressives, was more or less the continuance of the pre-war conservative opposition, the Minseito, which represented the commercial and trade circles and the interests of the great cities.

The Progressive Party, after a difficult start, gained rapidly in influence, in particular after the nomination of Shigemitsu, former Minister of Foreign Affairs in Japan's surrender-cabinet, as its president. The Progressives form a second large group of conservatives in Japan. They are anti-communist; although they differ with the socialists on most issues, they sponsor the so-called "wellfare community". As far as rearmament is concerned they go further than the Liberals; they advocate a speedy rearmament of Japan in order that their country regain its "real independence". In general they favor a nationalist policy. Where Yoshida stresses the importance of Japan's ties with the Western world, Shigemitsu sponsors relations between Japan and her Asiatic brothers, with which she has the closest racial ties. Both parties, however, have a great deal in common. It would be wrong to consider the Progressive Party as "progressive" in the Western political sense of the word. It cannot even be seen as a "middle of the road block". That it will play an important part in shaping Japan's political future is obvious in view of its large and important membership and the prominence of its leaders.

The *Social Democratic Party* of Japan was established by the well-known Christian Socialist Katayama, immediately after the surrender in September 1945. It formed a rallying point for many Japanese people who favored a progressive policy, giving substance to their hopes for a socialist Japan. As such it held great promise.

The Socialists, however, were faced with great difficulties in the following years. One of the first setbacks the Party suffered was the failure of its leader, Katayama, to hold the Government after a difficult premiership during 1947 and 1948. Another blow resulted from the developments in connection with the peace treaty. The Social Democratic Party, which adhered to its so-called three principles of peace, laid itself open to severe criticism by its right-wing members, who accused it of an unrealistic approach to the peace problem. Its left-wing members, on the other hand, were of the opinion that the Socialists should take an even firmer stand against the peace treaty provisions. The leaders of the party failed to find a formula to cope with the communist tendencies of many of its members, who exercised their influence through powerful communist-inclined labor unions.

These difficulties led to a schism in the Social Democratic Party and to a considerable loss of power and influence.

This is an unfortunate development; the Socialist Party could have formed a useful opposition, and would be ideally suited to counterbalance tendencies both toward the extreme right and the ultra left. On the one hand, it could restrain conservative inclinations, on the other hand, it could offer a political home to the millions of Japanese industrial workers and low-paid white-collar workers whose present-day political outlook is rather distorted. A healthy Socialist Party would be the solution for many people whose lack of political stability now forms a dangerous avenue of approach for communist infiltration.

It would, therefore, be of real importance for the political future of Japan if the unity and the standing of this party were restored.

This would, moreover, enhance the possibility of a close contact between the Japanese socialist leaders and their political counterparts in other countries. The international organization of the socialist parties of the world and the international socialist congresses offer ample opportunity for mutual enlightenment. These contacts would have a stimulating and at the same time restraining influence on Japanese politics. They would provide Japan with a political window to the outside world and they would give the outside world ready access to the politics of Japan and their developments. The restraining influence of such contacts would be of great importance in assuring a political balance in Japan.

The *Japanese Communist Party*, dating from July 1922, but suppressed in the mid twenties, was reinstituted in October 1945 by its former leaders, who were released from prison as a result of the occupation directives.

The Communists staged a spectacular comeback. Radiant with the glamour of martyrdom, the communists leaders attracted many followers. They increased their parliamentary strength from 5 seats in the first postwar elections to 35 seats in the general election of June 1949. Correspondingly, communist influence in Japan's newly organized labor unions grew rapidly.

When, however, towards the end of 1948 and the beginning of 1949 the general change in occupation policy toward Japan was effected, the Japanese Government, in concurrence with the Occupation, took large-scale measures to curb communist activities. Communists and leading leftwingers in the powerful Government Railway Workers Union and in the National Communications Workers Union were discharged. Furthermore, the Government dissolved the League of Korean Residents, a communist stronghold in Japan.

The most serious setback the Communists received was in the spring of 1950 when Moscow instructed the Party to resort to the use of force and violence in staging demonstration and organizing strikes. By their actions the Communists antagonized the Japanese people and lost much sympathy. This was demonstrated in the election returns. From 35 seats in the Lower House during 1949–50, the Communists in November 1950 fell back to 23 seats.

On the instigation of SCAP, the Japanese Government in mid-1950 expelled the leaders of the Communist Party from public office; at the same time the most important party publication, the Akahata, was suspended.

Although the Communist Party has not been outlawed in Japan, its official position has become insignificant. There is only a very small number of Communists in the Diet, and union leaders who are official members of the Japan Communist Party are far in the minority in the labor movement. Most industries and government agencies have cleared their payrolls of membership card holders and refuse to employ them.

Communist tactics in the days of the coming into force of the San Francisco treaty have been described before. Neither Stalin's peace songs, however, nor the violent reactions of the Communists towards the peace and security treaties, frequently underlined by unruly demonstrations, disturbances and bloodshed, had the sympathy of the Japanese people.

The communist danger in Japan, however, must not be underestimated. Indirectly and subversively, the Communists exercise considerable influence. It is difficult to assess their power. Some people see the communist organization as an iceberg, with a small visible top but an enormous hidden substance. This seems to be less true than the fact that the small but strongly organized and well-disciplined Communist Party exercizes an unproportionally powerful, though indirect, influence through its shrewd handling of leftist tendencies in the Socialist Party, the labor unions, and leftist-inclined intellectuals, schoolteachers and students. A large group of Red-inclined Koreans in Japan adds to the number of potential Communists. Moreover, the Communists scare weak officials and wavering individuals into assuming a lenient and sometimes even a cooperative attitude toward their activities. There have been, for instance, rumors that some parts of the Japanese police force were not reliable and would, in an emergency, be unwilling to check really serious communist disturbances for fear of reprisals.

The real and great danger threatening Japan through communism results, however, from other circumstances, which will be mentioned later. Just as, for the time being, the forces of the extreme right are successfully neutralized, so also are the forces from the extreme left. Yet their potential power is still great; future developments could give these forces unexpected stimulus, through which they could become an acute and actual danger.

In order to complete the picture of the political parties in post-treaty Japan it is should be mentioned that in the Upper House, 59 seats of the 250 are held by the *Ryokufukai*, which is less a political party than a group of old peerage members of the Japanese House of Lords. These gentlemen have been chosen to the present Upper House as a result of their personal influence and standing. In view of modern circumstances they formed a party organization. Their attitude is conservative, but definitely not extreme. They exercise a moderate and dignifying influence on the Upper House. A few other parties form small minorities with little influence.

6. *Some Remarks on Functioning of Party System*

As a next step to the understanding of Japan's political life, it might be useful to study the present day political system and the manner in which it functions.

In the autumn months of 1945, immediately after the armistice, the political trend in Japan was definitely toward the left. The Communists, who claimed that they alone had opposed the totalitarian imperialist group of the war years, received an enthusiastic welcome as they emerged from prison and exile. Left-wing literature enjoyed great popularity because many Japanese, in their bewilderment during the early days after the war, sought a solution to their problems in communist materialism, which had been totally suppressed during the war years. The communist's success, however, was shortlived. The course of action adopted by the Japanese Communist Party greatly disillusioned and alienated the Japanese people. Its unmistakable subordination to Moscow and the lack of sympathy which it received from the Occupation destroyed their myth. In the first postwar general elections of April 1946, the Communists won only 3.8 percent of the vote.

Socialism, on the other hand, won the day. The socialist program and its standing in the Allied world formed a great attraction for many Japanese, especially for the white-collar workers, the government employees and the city population. The Socialists won 17.5 percent of the vote in the April 1946 elections and 25.8 percent in the April 1947 elections. The 1947 success secured them 143 seats in the House of Representatives. The Socialist Party had become the strongest party in the Diet, and its leader, Katayama, became Premier. The circumstances, however, did not favor the Katayama Government for, as has been described in Chapter V, serious economic difficulties rocked Japan in 1947–48. The Socialists were not able to realize their election program, and they were blamed for the troubles besetting their country. They rapidly lost their popularity, and in February 1948 Katayama was forced to resign. After an unsuccessful endeavor by Ashida, the head of the Democratic Party, to lead a coalition Cabinet, Yoshida and the conservative Liberals returned to power in October of that same year.

The middle-of-the-road parties declined in influence. A trend to the extreme right and ultra left developed in the domestic politics of Japan.

In the third postwar national election of January 1949, the Liberals won an outright majority of the total of 466 seats in the Lower House. The Communists tripled their strength and conquered 35 seats.

In the following years the Communists were not able to retain their influence. The Liberals, on the other hand, representing the most conservative party in Japan, firmly re-established their position in Japanese politics. As has been described before, their policy might give the impression that they favor a return to pre-war circumstances.

This, however, is not true. Though the Liberal Party leaders are definitely conservative, the political and economic philosophy underlying their policies is based mainly on the liberalism of the 1920's and 1930's, which advocated parliamentary and civil government and a peaceful constructive foreign policy.

Summarizing, one can say that the postwar electrorate of Japan has shown itself predominantly conservative and will most probably remain so in the near future.

In the meantime one has to realize that the political party system of Japan is not yet mature. Many of the old defects still survive. Program and ideals are frequently secondary to personal matters. The political ruffians of the old days have again come to the foreground. At the same time, several of the actual leaders prefer to remain behind the curtains. Inside the party machinery, personal friendships, the feudal ties of family clan and the feudalistic relationship between the protecting master and the protected retainer are frequently more important than party interests. Large-scale corruption in political and government circles has undermined the confidence of the public. A feeling of responsibility toward their constituents is sometimes completely lacking in the chosen representatives. The Diet itself has been the stage of some undignified scenes and disgraceful occurrences.

Moreover, a return of pre-war leaders, who are gradually being depurged, might strengthen the as yet dormant influence of the still existing militaristic and imperialistic elements. Although their voices are silenced for the time being, they might gradually and inconspicuously reassert themselves by penetrating into the conservative parties or even by aligning with leftist forces. The last development is not inconceivable, especially in view of the anti-capitalist prejudices in Japanese army circles before the war, and in view of the international prospects through cooperation with the Soviet Union. The success and the actual danger of such developments, however, are largely dependent on external circumstances which are not present today.

It is quite understandable that the political life of Japan, freed overnight from its shackles and resurrected under circumstances as abnormal as those of postwar days, has had difficulty in keeping its balance. Obviously, the development of sound political leadership in Japan will take time, as the majority of the older leaders were trained in a police state, and the younger men are without experience.

There is, however, no reason for despair. Rather, the general trend of political life in contemporary Japan is hopeful. There are improvements in the working of the Diet as well as in the functioning of the party system. The developments of representative government are encouraging.

Consequently, it is justifiable to conclude that Japan, in addition to the requisite legal basis and governmental machinery, also has a party system which may well become the smoothly working institution necessary in a free and democratic country.

7. *Japanese Appreciate Political Freedom, but Economic Crisis Might Kill Interest*

The next question is whether the Japanese people are convinced of the values of a free and representative government, and whether they are willing and resolved to fight for their political liberties.

The general impression is that a large percentage of the population are conscious of their newly gained political freedom and their political rights, and that they cherish them and are resolved to deepen the meaning and to expand the scope of these rights, and furthermore to better the political system of new Japan. They would undoubtedly resent any encroachment upon their newly acquired democratic liberties.

The Japanese people have exercized their democratic rights with great vigilance. The percentage of votes cast in the postwar elections has been surprisingly high. At the first postwar general elections for the Lower House, in April 1946, 72.08 percent actually polled their votes; in April 1947, the percentage was 67.95 and in January 1949, it was 74.04. For the Upper House elections the numbers have been approximately the same.

This does not mean, however, that as many Japanese really understand the fundamental responsibilities of adult franchise, or that they take a real interest in national political affairs. Many questions of vital importance to Japan as a nation fall outside the comprehension of the majority of the population. A public opinion poll in the mid 1950's disclosed that as much as 30 percent of the population — a percentage which consisted mainly of women in the farming and fishing villages — lacked any interest in or understanding of even such a vital question as the signing of the peace treaty. An intensive educational program in the political field will therefore be necessary in order to deepen and broaden the interest of the Japanese people in their national and international problems. Many of the Japanese party bosses, unfortunately, purposely retard this educational process. They prefer an uninformed group of voters, easily handled and uncritical of the actions of their representatives in the Diet. Yet the increase in the percentage of voters points to a growing interest in national affairs, and this is further stimulated by a far-reaching, free and constructive press and radio service. Furthermore, the educational programs for the Japanese youth contribute to the development of the future electorate.

On the local level, the interest of the Japanese people in politics and public life is, and has always been, much greater than on the national plan. The percentage of voters in prefectural and local elections increased from approximately 70 percent in 1947 to more than 90 percent in 1951. Even in pre-war days the local government in Japan was more representative than the national government. The decentralization measures of the postwar days, instigated by the Occupation, have greatly enhanced the power and significance of local government. Consequently, democracy has taken root more deeply on the local level than on the national level.

Moreover, locally the Japanese have been less disappointed in their expectations from the blessings of the new, democratic government. Nationally the corruption, the old party defects and the irresponsibilities of some of the representatives have reappeared more frequently and have caused more disillusion than locally. In general, more sincerity and more understanding have been displayed in prefectural and local councils than in the Diet. These local institutions can form a fertile training ground for responsible and wise leadership.

The lack of understanding of the complex problems of the nation, the disappointment in the results of the new democracy and the danger of the revival of the old guard, emphasized by the return of several depurgees, undoubtedly constitute a danger to the healthy development of political life in Japan.

The most serious danger, however, lies in an economic crisis, or even a decline of the present economic situation. Such a development would hamper the growth of democracy and might even shatter its existence. When the struggle for daily bread becomes very severe, when only a meager living can be eked out through hard and constant toil, people lose their interest in broad political questions. The development and the survival of democracy presupposes a reasonable standard of living and a certain degree of security. When life becomes intolerable, when the battle for existence becomes hard and difficult and when great numbers of the population live on the verge of misery and poverty, a nation loses its feeling for political proportions and values. Its interest in democracy declines. That is the time when the demagogues and the dictators get their chance. Then the slogans of the extreme right or the ultra left find a willing ear. Then the people grasp at the words of irresponsible politicans as a last straw and follow any creed which promises improvement in their bleak circumstances. Under those conditions modern totalitarianism — communism or fascism — takes root and thrives.

Hence, the most significant danger threatening the success of the political reforms in Japan lies in the economic instability of the country. If a healthy economy is retained, however, the future holds a promise of a moderate, responsible and representative government in Nippon.

8. *Second Reform: Freedom of the Press.*

One of the most important prerequisites for the maintenance of a healthy political system is a free press, and in general the freedom of the people to express their opinions, to discuss and to criticize political developments and to receive and exchange factual and unbiased information. The new Constitution of Japan guarantees these freedoms.

As has been mentioned in Chapter III, a satisfactory system of enlightening the public with regard to general affairs and world news has been erected in Japan. Obviously, during the occupation years an indirect censorship had to be maintained. Outright criticism of the Occupation by the Japanese press could not be tolerated; this would have been contrary to the very nature of such an operation. Yet, notwithstanding the limitations set by MacArthur's directive for a press code, issued September 19, 1945, considerable progress was made toward a responsible, free and objective press. The publishers and editors in Japan have given vigorous and constructive assistance to the development of a representative Government, and there is a firm determination on the part of the most of them to continue on this road.

The Japanese have a natural curiosity about the happenings in the world. The large Japanese newspapers are read throughout the country, although not always understood; even in the small villages their subscriptions amount to one copy for every three to four households. News by radio fills the gaps.

In addition to Japanese news agencies and publishing companies, foreign magazines have opened offices in Japan or have entered into special contracts with Japanese editors. Moreover, all the more important international news agencies are represented in Japan. The way their news items are published and the treatment they receive will be indicative of the way Japan is going.

Although the outlook for the continuance and growth of a free, responsible and liberal press is hopeful, this constitutes a danger in itself. Some circles — particularly the Communists — are inclined to misuse this freedom. They produce so-called free, but actually highly controlled publications which give distorted news, false teachings and misleading interpretations of events. They preach dangerous political doctrines and poison the minds of the people. Some publications with communist leanings have already been suspended. The government might feel the necessity of curbing all their activities. This urge to prevent the publication of dangerous matter might lead to the institution of censorship. The fear of communist propaganda might even be misused by certain groups in order to advocate and sponsor such a censorship. Once instituted, it would be very difficult to restrict its activities and to exercise the necessary restraint in its execution. After the first steps on the road of controlling the press have been taken, the next ones are not so difficult to take, and petty officialdom and reactionary influences in the government may resort to an easy way of checking healthy and constructive criticism.

From the above it seems that the press and public information services of present-day Japan are undoubtedly on the road to becoming a constructive and indispensable part of the new Japanese nation. The greatest danger threatening this development is an overestimation of the communist danger, followed by the gradual stiffening of a reaction to the misuse of the press freedoms by communist elements.

9. Third: Educational Reform

The future of a free and democratic society and of a democratic government depends largely upon the education of the youth of the country.

Among the determining factors which led Japan astray in the pre-war days were the defects in Japanese education. These defects were to be found mainly in its spiritual foundation and only to a certain extent in the system itself.

The system itself — from a technical point of view — was not entirely unsatisfactory. It had much in common with old-fashioned disciplinary European systems. There was compulsory education for the first six years of schooling, and there was ample opportunity for continued and higher education, although the entrance examinations for higher educational facilities were exceptionally difficult. There were no rules which excluded any Japanese for reasons of social standing from the highest educational institutions. On the contrary, the government sponsored promising young candidates by financing and facilitating their studies. The so-called "dead alleys" in the educational system were more the result of its serious competitive character than a consequence of class distinction. The system was defective only in the way that it facilitated and helped the central government in controlling the education of Japanese youth.

Ideologically, however, Japanese education was unsatisfactory from a democratic point of view. It was based upon the "Imperial Rescript on Education", issued by Emperor Meiji. In itself this rescript contained many sound principles for the moral behavior of Japanese youth. The rescript, however, defined the aim of the Japanese educational system as training the Japanese people to protect and further the Japanese nation and the Imperial line, "unbroken for ages eternal". Instead of striving after the personal perfection of the individual and the pursuit of universal truth, education was intended to prepare the youth of Japan for the service of the State. Education formed an important part of the totalitarian system of pre-war Japan. The leaders of the Japanese nation did not seek the happiness and prosperity of the individual; on the contrary, they aimed at the aggrandizement of the nation through the strengthening of its economy and national defense, without any consideration for the people as individual beings. The Japanese people were trained and educated to fit into the State machine; truth, morals and culture were harnessed to serve the greater glory of Nippon.

The basic philosophy underlying this concept of nationhood was a vague, mystical doctrine preaching a mighty and powerful

Japan inhabited by a master race, which was charged with a sacred mission to save the world — and which, under the leadership of its all-powerful Emperor, had the divine duty and exclusive right to enforce a world hegemony.

This doctrine greatly influenced the Japanese educational system — in particular the teachers of the primary schools. In fact, it influenced the life and actions of the masses of the Japanese people. A simplified version of this doctrine was presented in the so-called "Kokutai no Hongi", a pocket book of "the basic principles for the Japanese nation", written for the general public. Although this document was hastily and even carelessly composed and did not meet the approval of the higher intellectual circles of Japan, the militarists managed to have 2,000,000 copies of the "Kokutai no Hongi" printed and distributed by 1940. The most important parts of this document were inserted into a textbook for the Japanese youth, who had to memorize the contents verbally.

The powerful position of the Japanese Ministry of Education which financed the majority of the educational facilities of Japan and controlled the educational system, the teachers' training, examinations, the admittance to higher educational institutions, the textbooks and even the curriculum of all State schools, greatly facilitated the indoctrination of the youth of Japan with government prescribed ideas and morals.

A noteworthy exception to the complete subordination of education to the aims of the government was demonstrated by the courage — and even the partial success — with which several private universities and some state universities fought for their freedom. This fact indicates that in the higher educational and intellectual circles of pre-war Japan several groups remained opposed to the spiritual captivity which the totalitarian and militaristic leaders sought to enforce upon the nation. This constituted a hopeful basis for the liberalization of education undertaken in postwar days.

In general, however, the strongly centralized, totalitarian regime of pre-war Japan crushed any deviation from its rules and prescriptions; the majority of the teachers, successfully regimented to militaristic training and strict obedience, blindly followed the imperialistic teachings.

Indeed, through the educational system the totalitarian

18

leaders of Japan exercised a powerful and decisive influence upon the Japanese nation.

The measures taken by the Occupation to change the education of the youth of Japan, as mentioned in Chapter III, can be divided into two groups: (1) The measures taken to change the system in such a way that it would be less fitted for the misuse of education for totalitarian purposes and better suited for a democratically inclined education; (2) the reform of the spiritual basis of education.

So far as the *changes in the organization* are concerned, in cooperation with the Japanese Government the educational ladder was reorganized, and the so-called 6–3–3 system was introduced — based on the American pattern. Under this system every boy and girl spends six years in grammar school and three years in a junior high school. By law, these nine years of schooling are compulsory and free. After that, three years of senior high school and later college or graduate professional schooling may follow; for higher education a relatively great number of universities — for both sexes — are available.

Simultaneously, the curriculum and the methods of teaching were changed. The courses in "ethics", an indoctrination in the "Spirit of Greater Nippon", were abolished. The old ways of memorizing innumerable facts under pressure of the rod were replaced by a more liberal and flexible system, aiming at the encouragement of initiative and an individualistic approach to a problem. Co-education was instituted throughout the country. In addition, steps were taken to abolish the predominant position of the Ministry of Education. School boards of democratically elected private critizens are now charged with making the decisions previously vested in the Ministry. Since 1949, textbooks have been privately written and published. The Japanese schools can make a free choice of books instead of having to accept the ones imposed by the Education Ministry. The teachers make out their own curriculum, and the inspection, administration and financing of the schools are now the task of the prefectural government or the municipal councils.

The Educational Reform Council, an all-Japanese organization of prominent educational leaders under the chairmanship of Professor Nambara, has done outstanding work in advising on the nature and implementation of the educational reforms and has supervised — and in many instances directed — their execution. In short, the educational reform in postwar Japan has certainly contributed to the democratization of the country and to the improvement of education.

The new system of education has been put into operation — step by step — over the past several years. It is generally acknowledged to be sounder than expected, although in the rural areas it might be less advantageous than in the cities. The financial consequences, however, are heavy and might lead to a revision of the nine years of compulsory education.

There is even more chance that some other aspects of the educational reform will be changed. To begin with, the present school board system is not popular. The school boards lack the necessary prestige to attract the right people; they have no budgetary power, which limits their activities to the advisory field. The rate of voting-abstention for the boards has been rather high. An improvement in their status in the near future is doubtful, because the influence of the Ministry of Education has not been completely eliminated. The Japanese people, accustomed to the fact that some government agency should handle such affairs as the education of the youth of Japan, might easily yield to pressure from Tokyo for the re-establishment of the power of the central government in educational matters. This is even probable because of the financial plight of the local administrations, now responsible for the financing of education. The requirements for the nine years compulsory education in terms of school buildings and teachers, the issuance of revised textbooks, matching the changed curricula, and the necessary overhaul of the educational facilities after the years of negligence during the war, constitutes a huge financial problem. Although the Japanese people are generally willing to make sacrifices for their children, it might be impossible for the prefectural governments to carry the financial burden of the new system. This, inevitably, would necessitate large central government subsidies, which in turn would strengthen the position of the Education Ministry.

Certain aspects of the educational reform may, therefore, be changed. Yet this in itself is no reason for undue concern, so long as such changes do not imply a definite return to the rigid pre-war education of Japanese youth.

So far as the *ideological side* of education is concerned, — where the actual causes for the grave defects of the pre-war system lay — the question is of much greater importance. The educational reform of the post-war days eradicated the totalitarian aspect of pre-war education. Education is no longer a strictly controlled and regimented institution, aiming at the training of willing subjects working in the interest of the nation, and at indoctrinating the individual as an obedient citizen of greater Nippon.

In order to be of real and permanent value, however, the reform should have introduced a new spiritual basis upon which modern education in Japan can rest. Whether education can perfect personal qualities, whether it can successfully preach universal moral standards and an understanding of the rights and the responsibilities of the individual depends on the spiritual platform upon which it is founded. In introducing such a platform the Occupation has been less successful.

The general upheaval following the defeat in war and the introduction of an avalanche of new ideas and new principles of life resulted in spiritual confusion for many people. Old patterns of thought and of moral discipline were relaxed or completely abandoned. A new conception of life, however, did not easily take shape. This has been particularly true in the lower intellectual circles to which the majority of the teaching class belongs. The teachers, faced with the difficult problem of providing a new doctrinal basis for their educational work, superseding the old familiar doctrine, were completely at a loss. The new democracy introduced by the Occupation did not offer an easily comprehensible set of rules ready for use in pocket book form. Its basic concepts were scarcely understood by the average Japanese. The result was the appearance of a widespread spiritual vacuum.

This vacuum has been shrewdly exploited by communism. The communist doctrine offers an easy — and after the years of regimentation — even somewhat familiar hold, whereas other ideologies are too difficult, vague, or unfamiliar to be understood. This unfortunate development is demonstrated by the fact that the teachers unions of the first postwar years definitely leaned toward the left. Although during 1951 most official members of the Communist Party were expelled from the unions, the fact remains that communist doctrines have unmistakably infected the educational circles of Japan.

The remedying of this tendency, emanating from the spiritual confusion prevalent in post-surrender Japan, and the establishment of a sound moral and spiritual base for Japanese education — and in general for the Japanese nation — are difficult problems facing the development of a democratically inclined Japan.

If time and circumstances are favorable, there are reasons to hope that the newly introduced ideas can be successfully blended with the deep-rooted, morally lofty ideologies descending from old, historical Japan, which have been transmitted through the generations to our age. The qualities demonstrated in the pre-war days by some of the educators of Japan — particularly in private schools and universities — constitute one of those reasons. While then there have been notable reforms in education, there is at present a lack of fundamental ideology, which — as will be explained later — presents an obstacle to the full development of democracy in Japan.

10. Fourth: Woman Suffrage

The great strides taken by the women of Japan in establishing their newly acquired equality with men and their newly gained political rights have already been described in Chapter III. Such changes had become more or less inevitable, as a result of the difference in circumstances brought about by industrialization and by the employment of women in factories.

In a social sense, however, this equality has not yet been completely accepted. In many instances the man is still the undisputed head of the family; the father is still the master of his children. Though a gradual change is discernible, full equality of men and women in the Western sense is still a thing of the future. Socially, the position of women — especially in rural areas — has not changed much. Politically, however, their equality has been established by law and it is hardly conceivable that in the future the political equality of the Japanese women will be abolished.

This does not imply, however, that their freedom cannot be

encroached upon in other ways. Today the women of Japan form a promising force for the development of a true democracy. The movement to promote the emancipation of women and the women's organizations have greatly contributed to the creation of a moderate and representative government. The women constitute an important group which, basically, is strongly opposed to imperialistic and aggressive tendencies. Their organizations, however, are still young. The number of well-trained, experienced women leaders is small. The standard of political and social education of the women of Japan is low, and its furtherance is a gigantic task, hardly begun as yet. If increased economic difficulties should arise, if the question how to obtain their daily bread should prevail over the other interests of the Japanese women, they could easily be misled by false promises and deceitful slogans of demagogic leaders. Communism, promising an easy way out of their difficulties by picturing a poor man's paradise, would undoubtedly prey on the women's organizations of Japan. And their political equality and the existence of their organizations would constitute an even more menacing danger than ever had been possible in the days of their social suppression.

In this connection the importance of contact between the Japanese woman's movement and similar organizations in other countries cannot be stressed enough. Free and frequent interchange of views and data on the status of women and their role on the political and social plane will have a stimulating and, at the same time, a moderating influence on the development of a healthy woman's movement in Nippon. As the position of women in the United States is exceptionally far advanced, contact with corresponding European organizations, where more similar problems will be met, might be particularly beneficial. These contacts might constitute one of the important safeguards for the furtherance of a free and democratic way of life in Japan. The sponsoring of such contacts is a challenging task facing the woman leaders of Japan and of the free world alike.

11. *Fifth: Organization of Labor*

The instantaneous and astonishing response of the workers or

Japan to the policy of the Occupation, which encouraged the organization of labor and collective bargaining with employers, has already been described in Chapter III. While it is outside the scope of this book to make a more comprehensive study of the labor movement in Japan and of the manifold laws and provisions which today safeguard the rights and well-being of the Japanese worker, a few remarks are still required to indicate the importance of the labor movement for the future of Nippon.

Theoretically, the labor standards of Japan compare favorably with any labor legislation in a modern democracy. In particular the institution of the labor relations board system — which requires a board in each prefecture and one on the national level, each consisting of members equally representing the employers, labor and the general public — forms an outstanding feature of the postwar labor movement in Japan. These boards are charged with the protection of labor; their strong position and extensive legal rights make them one of the important bastions of democracy in Japan.

In practice, some of the unions have shown admirable progress in the five years since their establishment. The Japan Teachers Union — with more than 500,000 members — and the powerful Union of Railway Workers are outstanding examples. Generally however, labor is somewhat less advanced than in the West. The old paternalistic tendencies and practices are still very strong. The Japanese worker subconsciously feels more attached to his master than to his union — the latter often being too impersonal a relationship and too vague to his taste; too insecure and unreliable, in his opinion. Moreover, the execution of large construction-projects has facilitated the survival of the old labor-boss system, an institution not compatible with modern labor standards. In the many small-scale industries of Japan — such as the textile, paper and toy fabrication, performed as home industries — there is hardly place for a labor union. Moreover, the weak financial position and the lack of trained leaders in many unions have not favored their sound development.

Yet, the labor movement had become an important factor in post-treaty Japan. Its development forms an indispensable prerequisite for the furtherance of a free and representative system in Japan's economic and political life. This development

however, is still in its initial stages. Its way will be fraught
with many difficulties. Obviously, the labor movement is
progressive and even leftist-inclined; this is inherent in its
character and might constitute a healthy and balancing factor
in the interplay of social forces in the country. At the same
time this tendency contains a dangerous possibility of communist domination of the movement. Only a harmoniously
developed, mature labor movement understands that communism is fatal to its ultimate aims.

The communist influence in Japan's labor unions, which
reached its peak in the middle of 1948, gradually declined
since the beginning of 1949. From that time the disaffection of
the Japanese unions for communist-dominated organizations,
for instance the National Liaison Council of Trade Unions,
representing the W.F.T.U. in Japan, became discernible. This
disaffection increased in intensity in the middle of 1949, due
to a series of communist excesses; and it received great impetus
from the clear display of communist intentions in the aggression
against South Korea. When the National Liaison Council was
dissolved in August 1950, by order of the Attorney General,
communism lost its grip on the labor movement in Japan.

So far as present-day Japan is concerned, the communist
influence in the labor unions seems to be under control, and
the acute danger of subordination of the Japanese labor
movement to the Communists seems remote. In this connection
the General Council of Trade Unions of Japan, drawing its
inspiration from the organization of the International Confeder-
ation of Free Trade Unions in London, plays an important
role as a center for non-communist Japanese unions. It includes
the major national industrial unions and numbers far over
3,000,000 members.

Yet the Communists still form a dangerous minority in the
labor movement, deriving particular strength from their rigid
organization and discipline and their unity of purpose; they
remain a latent force, continuing to propagandize and to
maneuver in order to regain control of the labor movement.

So long as circumstances provide the Japanese population
with reasonable prosperity and secure their contentment and
the existence of a state of law and order, the labor movement

of Japan has a good chance of developing into a healthy and beneficial institution for the country, protecting the workers and exercizing a moderating influence on labor and management alike.

The great danger threatening labor in Japan lies in the economic structure of the country. Japan's labor force is practically the only source of natural wealth the nation possesses. Through the employment of her labor, Japan has to gain the foreign exchange needed to import necessary additional foodstuffs. Japan, indeed, depends on her workshops — and by that fact on her workers. As has been said before, if the workmen are expensive — as a result of social legislation and a high standard of living — the workshop might become too expensive and the profit insufficient to cover the needs of the country.

Even at the present moment the demands and the wishes of labor in Japan are frequently in direct contrast to the requirements of a balanced budget, more so than in many other countries. Therefore, the position of labor in Japan is somewhat unstable. If the economic situation deteriorates, management will try to reduce the costs of production by lowering the costs of labor. If labor protests, as it can normally be expected to do, and if it resorts to its most powerful weapon in collective bargaining, the strike, management might appeal directly to the Government over the heads of the labor relations boards, on the pretext that such strikes endanger the national economy. The Government, frightened by the prospect of a further loss of badly needed foreign income, might easily choose the side of management and take measures to force labor back into the workshops. This, inevitably, would incite the workmen to acts of violence and the Communists would be blamed for stirring up trouble — as they would undoubtedly do. And for the sake of law and order and for the national welfare, severe restrictions would be imposed on the freedom and the rights of labor. By that, the road leading back to pre-war circumstances of exploited labor would been opened again, and the new conception of life in Japan would receive one of its most serious setbacks. In short, economic distress — combined with an exaggerated fear of communism — forms the most serious danger to the present-day promising labor movement of Japan.

An important factor in fostering a healthy labor movement

is the maintenance of close and extensive contacts with the several labor unions in other democratic countries as well as with the international labor movement of the free world. Such contacts can have a stimulating and at the same time a restraining influence on the Japanese labor movement, and might be instrumental in preventing its deterioration or its encumbrance by reactionary forces.

12. *Sixth: Land Reform*

As Japanese aggression, culminating in World War II, indirectly found a basis in the discontent of the rural population, and as the poverty and backwardness of the Japanese tenant farmer constituted one of the main factors upon which Japan's totalitarian system was based, the elevation and liberation of the peasant population of Japan has been a further highly important factor in sponsoring the establishment of a healthy, stable and progressive Japanese society.

The Occupation, through its land reform, has succesfully accomplished the task of liberating the Japanese tenant farmer and of raising him from the status of an exploited agricultural laborer to that of a free and independent member of Japanese society. The way in which this has been done forms one of the best examples of the method used by the occupation authorities to introduce reforms in Japan. As has been mentioned in Chapter III, the reform was based on SCAP's directive of December 9, 1945, ordering the Japanese Government to institute a program of transferring land ownership from landlords to tenants and protecting the new owners from reversion to tenancy. The organization of the nearly 11,000 local committees comprising more than 400,000 Japanese required to execute this reform, was a challenge in itself. Convincing these many thousands of cooperators of the usefulness and practicability of the land reform required the utmost patience and a thorough understanding of the Japanese mentality. Once initiated, the work had to be followed up, checked, and rechecked. The many committees had to be encouraged, assisted in solving their problems and sometimes restrained. Law enforcement problems were multitudinous and difficult; the landlords put up a stiff resistance to the reform; the tenants were timid and slow to understand the method of execution. As the program progressed, many inadequacies became evident; these had to be corrected. Local conditions had to be taken into consideration; personal feelings and subtle relationships had to be respected. Sometimes it was very trying to let the Japanese muddle along, but this was essential to the success of the reform. Measures had to be taken to guarantee its endurance; financial safeguards had to be established, cooperatives had to be erected and the farmers had to be taught to manage their own affairs. The central government had to be induced to draft the laws necessary to establish and guarantee the new situation, and the Diet had to be prepared for the passing of the Land Reform Bill.

From the foregoing the enormous scope of the work should be clear. The new situation has taken deep root in the Japanese nation, and the majority of the farmers are proudly conscious of their new position as small but independent landowners. A visit to rural villages reveals the fact that the farmers of Japan generally realize the significance of land reform and associated affairs, that they believe in its value and that they are resolved to maintain it. The reform, moreover, has created a large class of small landowners, tilling their own soil. As such it has opened the possibility of erecting a strong bulwark against the inroads of communism in rural Japan.

The problems of the Japanese farmers, however, have not yet been solved. The rural population of Japan is still increasing; the size of the farm holdings is still excessively small; the work required is still unbelievably hard, and the profits made are scarcely sufficient to sustain the large peasant families and, at the same time, to pay the relatively high taxes. The farmer is still dependent on the rice broker and the supplier of fertilizers, notwithstanding the activities of the farmers' cooperatives in these fields. During difficult years the farmer will inevitably be faced with the problem of either borrowing money in order to secure a bare existence for his family, or selling his land. Although the newly instituted cooperatives and agricultural associations can give him some financial help, the temptation might be great to mortgage his land to a rich rice broker or a more successful neighbor, or to sell it outright to get the badly needed cash.

The fluctuating market situation and the relatively high taxation of land have already forced many farmers to sell some of their recently acquired plots. It is a well-known fact that most farmers deeply resent taking this step. Some have even reverted to the old practice of selling their daughters, as preferable to selling their rice fields. This fact illustrates the seriousness of the problem.

The leaders of Japan, who by tradition are inclined to consider the peasant population as that part of the nation which can easily and profitably be squeezed in order to sustain the country, might not be too willing to protect the farmers or to erect strong safeguards protecting their rights. The farmers do not form a special political group or party; their main vote is cast on the basis of personal preference and is mostly conservative. The only exclusive peasant party, the Romo To, is very small and does not exert any real power. Consequently, there is no political influence of any significance which automatically defends the farmers and their interests. The attitude of the parties toward the farmer problem is decided chiefly by political opportunism.

The present regulations of the Japanese law prescribe a further division upon his death of the already tiny plots of land belonging to one farmer, between his children or heirs. This is a definite disadvantage of the new system. Another danger, already mentioned, is the temptation for the farmer to sell his land in order to get ready money. A prohibition law on the alienation of land, as issued in the former Netherlands East Indies in the early twenties, would be of great help to guarantee the results of the land reform. Some changes in the Land Ownership Law would, under certain circumstances, be desirable.

A definite reversal of the situation toward large-scale land ownership, however, would constitute a grave danger for the future of democracy in Japan. Such a deplorable development would be greatly stimulated by economic difficulties in the country. Its consequences would be very serious. A large increase of communist membership in the rural areas could be expected, for the farmer, greatly disappointed by such a turn of events, would be apt to try his luck elsewhere. And he is less docile and more alert to political possibilities than before the war. In executing the land reform program he has learned to take part in the management of his affairs, and he has tasted political power and what it implies. Losing his responsible position as a small landowner, he might easily embrace a political creed which promises him a return of privileges, regardless of how false the creed itself might be. Deception, discontent and distress might throw the traditionally conservative farmer of Japan into the arms of communism or bring him back into the hands of ultra-nationalistic totalitarian leaders.

13. *Additional Occupation Benefits*

The Occupation has not only introduced the "democratic way of life" to the Japanese by initiating important reforms, by introducing a wealth of modern technology and by making the Japanese familiar with the progress of modern business, agriculture, medical science and social and educational systems, but also by setting a living example of democracy. MacArthur once said: "It — the defeat in war — left a complete vacuum, morally, mentally and physically. And into this vacuum flowed the democratic way of life. The American combat soldier came with his fine sense of self-respect, self-confidence and self-control. They — the Japanese — saw and felt his spiritual quality — a spiritual quality which truly reflected the highest training of the American home".

Although the General's words sound somewhat rhetorical, the essence of his remarks is true. The American occupation forces have indeed introduced to the Japanese people the "American — democratic — way of life". They have done this mostly indirectly, by acting just as they are and by behaving just as they do at home. Many Japanese expected a severe and even a cruel occupation — and feared an enemy that would plunder the country and feast on the vanquished. Instead, the Americans behaved on the whole decently and correctly. They not only imported most of their needed supplies and nearly all of their own food — forbidding the use of the much needed Japanese food to their troops — but they even imported large quantities of foodstuffs for the Japanese population and later extended billions of dollars of outright aid to the Japanese nation for reconstruction and rehabilitation purposes. By 1951, approximately $2,000,000,000 had already been spent for this purpose.

As individuals, the "occupationaires" were unexpectedly kind and helpful to the Japanese. Not only were children spoiled, poor people helped, old women treated with esteem — but when calamities of flood, earthquake, or typhoon struck the country, the Occupation extended a helping hand. Later, after MacArthur had lifted the fraternization ban in September 1949, the assistance and charity administered by the Americans became even more extensive. Orphanages were adopted by military clubs, Christmas gifts were sent to schools for poor children, and Boy Scout troops were organized. The lifting of the ban only legalized a long existing situation. Everywhere the "hidden friendships" between the Japanese and the Americans sprang into the open — especially between the American soldier and his little, dark-eyed girl friend, who from now on ostensibly took him by the hand and guided him through Japan —learning a lot and teaching a lot. The frequently difficult consequences of these relationships are outside the scope of this study.

Not only in the great cities did the Japanese learn to know the Americans; the dispersion of the occupation forces and of the military government teams throughout the country presented a broad field of contact. Moreover, the endless stream of advisers, technicians and inspectors in the medical, agricultural, educational, and industrial fields, and those occupationaires engaged in land reform, fishery, forestry, mining, labor organization, public health, civil information and education and other activities have exerted great influence upon the Japanese way of life and have brought to the most remote corners of Japan some tenet of the work of the Occupation. And nearly always those officials brought advice and assistance, demonstrated their great interest in the country, showed their love for the people and manifested their own decency of attitude and purpose.

After the arrival in Japan of the families of the many officers, civilian employees and non-commissioned officers of the occupation forces — the "dependents" — in the middle of 1946, the influence of the Occupation upon the Japanese became even stronger, as in the thousands of American households throughout the country one of the best sides of America, its home life, was demonstrated.

Obviously, there have been exceptions. Some people have misused their powers, others have enriched themselves, or have shown the reverse side of a free society. Many Japanese had cause to wonder, looking at the luxurious life, the parties, the amount of liquor and the free manners displayed in some occupation circles. These bad examples have been followed by some Japanese, especially the youth. The American movies have unfortunately stimulated a deterioration in morals. But it is wrong to overestimate the influence of these facts; they are in the minority and are outshone by the advantages. The Americans in Japan have demonstrated the great blessings inherent in a free and democratic society which respects and sponsors the freedom and dignity of the individual.

One of the most spectacular demonstrations of unselfish interest and assistance is probably the work of the Public Health and Welfare Section, previously mentioned. Immediately after the war an epidemic of typhus struck Japan; aid was rushed from the States and 8,890,000 Japanese were vaccinated, a truly unprecedented number. The typhus mortality rate was reduced from 41.5 per 100,000 persons in 1946 to only 0.6 per 100,000 in 1948. The vaccination program for smallpox was even more astounding; after the appearance of 17,800 cases in 1946, the entire population of 80,000,000 was vaccinated. In 1948 only 29 cases of smallpox were reported in Japan. Other medical activities of the Occupation include the reduction of dysentery by 87 percent, of typhus by 86 percent and of diptheria by 85 percent. This unparalleled activity in preventive medical care has impressed the Japanese deeply and convinced them of the rightness of the ideology introduced to them.

The spirit of democracy has been demonstrated also in the Natural Resources Section, which has done work of a similarly distinctive and important character through its programs sponsoring the preservation and cultivation of the natural resources of Japan — in agriculture, fishing, forestry and mining. The civil Information and Education Section, the Labor Division of the Economic and Scientific Section, several other agencies of SCAP, the many temporary missions in the financial, technological, industrial and other fields — each has contributed to the great work of construction in Japan.

The influence of "things American" was further enlarged by

the long lists of Japanese who were invited to the United States to see and study for themselves how democracy works. Teachers and students, correspondents and publishers, engineers and executives, bankers and industrialists, private business men and government officials, Diet members and mayors of small towns, sportsmen and artists, men and women — all went to the States and came back with new impressions, knowledge, understanding, hopes and—undoubtedly—also disappointment.

Several other countries followed the American example; France and England in particular have extended many invitations to Japanese for study and orientation in their countries.

Indeed, two cultures — the Eastern and the Western — have touched each other on many planes; two ways of life have been mingled in many respects. The influence of the American way of life on Japan must not be overestimated, but underestimation would also be a mistake. As a whole it has been constructive, wholesome and favorable and has facilitated the introduction of a new way of life to Japan.

Lastly, it must not be forgotten that the Occupation has brought to Japan a very valuable gift — especially important to a defeated and disorganized nation — law and order. The years immediately following the surrender could have been a period of serious disturbances, political upheavals, murder, chaos and social turmoil. MacArthur, however, imposed upon the Japanese nation a wise and restraining order, based upon a liberal law and backed by the presence of the occupation forces. This circumstance, which has enabled Japan to get on her feet again, has to be considered one of the great benefits of the Occupation of Japan.

14. *Japanese Welcome New Way of Life*

The Japanese people in general realize and acknowledge the blessings of the Occupation, although some may grumble. Prime Minister Yoshida, in an article "Japan and the Crisis in Asia", published in Foreign Affairs of January 1951, has expressed these thoughts by saying: "The munificence of the American Government and people has conferred untold benefits upon Japan. We are deeply grateful to the Allied authorities for guiding and assisting us in the difficult task of national reconstruction. The presence of the Allied forces has been the prime factor for ensuring the country's tranquillity and internal security". The above is the opinion of most Japanese people. This attitude toward the work accomplished during the post-war years in close cooperation between the Occupation and the Japanese people favors the endurance of the new way of life and of the reforms, introduced during the occupation years.

The interest of the Japanese people toward these reforms cannot be explained as an artificial attitude assumed by them in order to make the best of the occupation years, but with the underlying determination to throw all the changes overboard at the end of the Occupation. This presumption is definitely belied by the facts. A large-scale hypocrisy has not been enacted in Japan, although small groups of Japanese die-hards might have wished it that way.

The Japanese attitude has undoubtedly been influenced and facilitated by the Japanese character and by the fact that the Japanese mind has always been malleable and easily swayed. The Japanese adore new fashions, and democracy, to a certain extent, was a new fashion. The ease and sometimes astonishing rapidity with which the Japanese familiarized themselves with many of the new reforms, can certainly be ascribed to the aptitude of the Japanese people for assimilation and to their gift for copying new and foreign methods. But deeper and more durable feelings underlie the interest taken by them in the reforms sponsored by the Occupation.

The basic reason for the enthusiasm displayed by the Japanese in accepting the reforms is the fact that the Japanese — following the surrender — had a profound and sincere desire to reconstruct a better country. The Japanese were anxious to build a new and different Japan after the grim and dark war years had passed and utter defeat had left their country prostrate. The nightmare of the last war was felt much more intensely and deeply than is sometimes realized abroad. The gray and trying days of preparation for Japan's expansion into Asia and the Pacific were followed by the black years of continuous defeat and of gradual retreat from positions conquered in the first onslaught of Japanese aggression. A rapidly increasing shortage of the most essential goods and materials and an everlasting menace by fleets of bombing planes, devouring the woodbuilt Japanese cities in a holocaust of flames, destruction and death, have burned deep scars into the souls of the Japanese. By the end of the war Japan was utterly defeated — physically, economically and morally. If their leaders had called on the Japanese to stage a last suicidal fight against the invader, the Japanese would have obeyed. This does not mean, however, that when the war ended the Japanese were not greatly relieved that the nightmare was over. Their attitude was that the future could hardly be worse than what had happened in the past.

The Japanese, nearly seven years after their defeat, have not forgotten these facts. They feel that they were deceived and misled by their militaristic leaders. They do not want these leaders back nor their totalitarian methods. The Japanese are aware of the advantages of the newly established free society and of their present existence. Yet the Japanese people will need time to familiarize themselves with the consequences of the new way of life and to assimilate the reforms instituted in Japan. These reforms need time and a favorable sphere to mature.

15. *Maturing of Democratic Concept Necessary*

Fortunately the reforms and the ideas underlying them were not entirely new to Japan. The seeds for a more liberal government and a freer society were already present sometime before, as previously pointed out.

The small shoots, however, nurtured in the first years after the war have to be sheltered and cared for so that they can grow and become stronger, and take root in the Japanese nationhood. In this regard it has been fortunate that the Occupation was not withdrawn after a relatively short period of time. As a rule, a long Occupation should be avoided, especially if its aim is to bring the occupied country back into the family of nations and to re-establish promising and useful relations with the former enemy, instead of plundering and pilfering the country; a long drawn-out occupation is apt to result in serious antagonism and irritation, even though the possibilities for mutual understanding are present.

MacArthur was always conscious of this fact. Repeatedly he advocated a speedy withdrawal of the Occupation and a restoration of Japan's independence. The previous chapters

have shown that international circumstances prevented this for
many years. On several occasions MacArthur, who noticed the
growing confidence and rapprochement of the Japanese people
toward the United States, warned against the danger of
annoyance which would result from a continuous presence of
American forces and American administration in Japan.

He realized that after the Occupation had lasted for a few
years the Japanese should be permitted to run their government
on their own initiative and responsibility. He warned that a
protracted Occupation, no matter how efficient, wise and
benevolent, tends to destroy the people's self-respect and their
spirit of self-reliance and creates resentment and irritation.
MacArthur emphasized that with such results the Occupation
would militate against the growth of true democracy in the
country. When in 1948 a peace treaty was not forthcoming and
could not be expected for a long time, MacArthur had looked
for other ways to minimize these dangers. He found a solution
in the piecemeal peace policy.

Through this policy the execution of government and other
business became largely the responsibility of the Japanese,
who made their own decisions, managed their own affairs and
became more and more independent.

The process of the piecemeal peace granting, already
described in detail, has been instrumental in avoiding some of
the drawbacks of a long occupation and in smoothing the
process of Japan's return to independence. Through the
piecemeal peace policy the cold, outside air of "independence"
was gradually admitted into the "glass house" in which the
small plants of the Occupation were nursed. Before those
plants were transplanted into the cold ground, and before they
had to stand on their own, they had already been acclimatized.
Therefore, even though a long military occupation is generally
prejudicial to the fostering of initiative and enterprise and to
the sense of responsibility of a people, and even though it is apt
to curb the spirit of self-reliance and independence, the
continued presence of the American forces and of the American
administration in Japan has had its good sides, along with its
less favorable consequences. It has ensured the reforms a much
needed time to grow and to mature, and it has offered the
Japanese people ample opportunities to familiarize themselves

with the new conception of life. In general, the bad and the good sides of the prolonged Occupation are equal — thanks to the wise manner in which it was carried out and the restraint and understanding of the Japanese.

The same balance exists with regard to the change in occupation policy as effected in 1948. It has been described before that the necessity of speedy economic reconstruction in Japan resulted in a change of several of the originally instituted reforms, especially in the economic and labor spheres. The decentralization of big industries and the granting of many rights and privileges to the working classes had to be somewhat restricted. It is important, however, to realize that this in itself would have been inevitable under any circumstances. The economic and social structure of Japan necessitates a rather centralized system of enterprise in industry and commerce. We have seen that the scarcity of natural resources and the dependence on export trade as an earner of foreign exchange for the purchase of badly needed foodstuffs force Japan into the position of a workshop, with labor as practically the only asset. Raw materials have to be purchased abroad, have to be brought to Japan for processing and then sold again abroad. The smooth and profitable execution of this process implies the existence of centralized concerns for the organization and the handling of this trade. The language difficulty, the scarcity of money and the lack of knowledge of foreign countries are circumstances which add to the inevitability of this system. The fact that in Japan only a very small percentage of the population has enough training and has mastered enough knowledge and experience to cope successfully with the problem of international trade and commerce, big industry, shipping and finance, is another factor necessitating the centralized structure of Japan's commercial and industrial enterprises.

Hence, the change in policy from intense deconcentration, as initiated in the first years of the Occupation, toward a more moderate situation was to be expected in any case. The same applies to the restriction of some of the rights and privileges of the laboring class. Normally, this would have taken place after the Occupation had left, as a "reaction" to occupation measures branded as less fitted for Japanese circumstances. Now the Occupation itself, in cooperation with the Japanese Government and the Japanese people, effected these changes and "japanized" many of the originally somewhat too far-reaching reforms in industry and commerce. Now these changes took place gradually, without any disturbances or without being a spectacular reversion to the old ways. This in itself might outweigh the disadvantages which undoubtedly occurred as a result of the stiffening and gradually more conservative attitude of the Occupation.

16. *Democratic Progress Threatened by Dangers*

As has been described above, the record of the postwar years reveals the great possibilities for the development of a democratically inclined Japan, willing to cooperate with the free world. It also reveals that, in general, the Japanese people appreciate their new way of life and are willing and resolved to keep it.

At the same time the review of this period shows that several dangers threaten this development — dangers which might create circumstances thwarting the good intentions of the Japanese people and even killing their will to fight for their new liberties.

Some of these dangers are not yet present. Yet they may appear if circumstances, unfavorable to the furtherance of democracy in Japan, develop. The gravest of these dangers is an economic crisis which would arise if Japan were denied the necessary economic freedom for the rehabilitation of her overseas trade; another is that of a rigid state control, which might result from an overestimation of the communist menace.

Apart from these potential threats to the progress of democracy the most important dangers actually existing at the present time might be said to be: the ideological confusion, the return of the old guard and the activities of the Communists.

Some persons consider also the post-treaty tendency to change the reforms instituted during the Occupation as an actual danger to the further development of democracy. Undoubtedly the tendency contains a danger, but not so great or significant as is frequently asserted. The reforms may be "japanized", shaken up and changed in details. They will most certainly be exposed to more serious criticism than during the occupation years.

The Japanese people, after more than six years of Occupation, need a period to "blow off steam" in order to assure themselves that they are free and independent again. Consequently, their utterances and actions during the time immediatly following the coming into force of the peace treaty should not be taken too seriously or as indicative of their permanent attitude; furthermore, a "japanization" of the postwar reforms might even be helpful in assuring their endurance. Only where the reaction of the Japanese people would imply a return to pre-war totalitarian practices, or where modifications in the reforms would mean a change in basic principles would real danger exist. This, however, is not likely if the other dangers, mentioned above, fail to materialize.

The greatest danger of the several threats to democracy is, however, that they might stimulate each other — that one favors the development of the others. The overestimation of the communist menace, for instance, could lead to stringent political measures; such measures might be considered by foreign nations as an indication of reactionary trends; these nations might become suspicious of Japan's intentions and therefore less willing to cooperate with Japan; this, in turn, would thwart the rehabilitation of Japan's overseas trade and such a development could result in an economic crisis, which again could open the gate to communism. While, therefore, studying these various dangers separately is somewhat difficult because of their interactions, the importance of each singly still requires that some of them be considered separately.

In the following pages the danger of a possible economic crisis, of overestimating the communist menace, of the spiritual confusion, and finally the danger that arising difficulties are exploited either by the extreme right or the extreme left, will be reviewed.

17. *Danger of a Possible Economic Crisis*

It has already been pointed out a number of times that one of the most serious dangers to the future of the new Japan would be the occurrence of an economic crisis or even a sudden aggravation of post-treaty economic difficulties. Such a crisis is possible. The normal trade balance of Japan falls far below the level required for even the immediate needs of the country. Japan has to feed more than 80,000,000 persons, who increase at the rate of 1,500,000 a year. Japan's domestic food supply provides for only 80–82 percent of her population. The remainder of the food has to be imported and purchased by foreign exchange. Obviously, Japan needs trade in order to subsist.

This situation has existed in Japan for the last decades. In pre-war days, however, Japan's problem was different. Japan — while locally poor in natural resources — had access to large overseas supplies of raw materials, some of which came from her colonies and some from areas under her direct influence. Moreover, in addition to the financial gains from her export trade, Japan had a source of foreign income through the services she rendered, especially her shipping, and through her foreign investments.

Post-treaty Japan possesses no overseas territories; she has a small merchant navy and no financial investments in foreign countries. Her only source of foreign income is her export trade, which has to provide the money for about 19 percent of her needed foodstuffs, to buy the raw materials for her industries, to repay her debts and to pay the numerous overhead costs which are necessary to sustain her governmental agencies and her trade organizations abroad. The temporary windfall of the Korean war does not alter this fact.

Moreover, Japan has to modernize her technology and re-construct her deteriorated industrial apparatus. This involves a large capital investment which Japan lacks. She needs to attract foreign investors.

The natural wealth of Japan is limited. It consists mainly of her trained manpower and her hydro-electric resources. The latter must be more fully developed to meet Japan's require-ments; this again means a considerable outlay of capital invest-ment.

Consequently, Japan's economic situation is very tenuous and precarious. But it is not hopeless. Japan has still the potential power of functioning as the "the workshop of Asia", and thereby earning the foreign exchange she needs. Notwith-standing the heavy destruction wrought in Japan during the war, and notwithstanding the relatively small amount of overhauling and replacing of worn-out or outdated tools of production in the last 10 years, her industrial apparatus is still far superior to anything elsewhere in Asia. Her labor is unsurpassed in number, in standard of training and experience, and in aptitude for industrial employment. Japan's trading and manufacturing organizations suffered during the war and have been seriously threatened by the deconcentration measures after the war, but much of their potential has been left intact and is available. Japan's experience in foreign trade is many years behind that of most Western countries, but her business leaders are ready, eager and capable of catching up when given sufficient opportunity.

Japan, however, needs opportunities to trade, sources of raw materials and buyers for her finished products. As mentioned previously, before the war Japan's trade rested on three bastions, the America's, China and the Sterling Area. Today, trade with China is reduced to a minimum — far less than the pre-war volume — and under the present political circumstances no large increase can be expected, even if such an increase were sought. Japan has to find a compensation for all or part of her pre-war trade with the Asiatic mainland, China, Manchuria, Siberia and Korea, which amounted to about 25 percent of her export trade and 15 percent of her import.

As has been described in detail in Chapter X, Japan looks for a compensation for this loss of trade to Southeast Asia, South America and Africa. As a matter of fact, trade with Southeast Asia was characteristic of Japan's economy up to 1930. This trade lost its significance when Japan turned to Manchuria as her major source of raw materials after she had brought this area under her control.

However, Japan will first have to overcome opposition to her expansion of trade in these directions. She will have to overcome the distrust and reluctance of the peoples of these areas, who — particularly in Southeast Asia — are still very mindful of the experiences of World War II, who remember Japan's plans for the creation of a "Greater East Asia Co-Prosperity Sphere" and who suspect Japan of being ready to start all over again, although for the present only financially and economically. These people are inclined to close their frontiers to the Japanese and to resist close economic relationships with Japan. Their fear of the consequences of close economic ties with Japan may well be greater than their appreciation of the advantages of such a development.

In addition, these areas are traditional spheres of economic and financial influence of Western democracies. Southeast Asia belongs for the most part to the Sterling Area, with additional Netherlands and French interests; South America forms an important field of economic expansion for the United States; and Africa is claimed by Europe, especially by Britain, as a sphere of economic development. Japan, by entering those fields, will assuredly meet with competition and resentment from vested interests.

If the reluctance and opposition of the autochthonous populations and counteractions on the part of third interests become too strong, if Japan is not granted a fair and reasonable chance of restoring her international trade and of finding compensation for the loss resulting from the inevitable restrictions on her economic relations with the mainland of Asia, then the economic problem for Japan becomes practically insoluble. Continuous American help to bridge the gap between necessary imports and total exports cannot be expected, nor is it advisable. Japan rightly desires to regain her economic independence, even though she will gladly accept American help so long as the present situation exists.

An economic strangulation of Japan, followed by an economic crisis, would create dangerous tensions in the country. It would threaten and strangle the development of a healthy political life; it would endanger the promising evolution of the position of women; it would result in a lowering of the standard of living and of the social security for the workers and lead to severe restrictions on their rights and freedoms. These developments would breed opposition, disturbances, disappointments and instability and would create an ideal climate for communist activities. Moreover, economic difficulties would bring poverty and misery to the farmers and would drive this large section of the Japanese population into the arms of communist or ultra-nationalistic leaders.

In short, an economic crisis, or even a serious deterioration of economic conditions would destroy the reforms of the post-war years, would kill the young but promising sprouts of democracy, would tear down the framework of a free and responsible society and would deliver the individual into the hands of totalitarian leaders — be it left or right — who would bring the Japanese nation back to the dangerous and deplorable status of a police state consisting of a regimented, impoverished and sullen population ready to be used in any imperialistic endeavor.

18. *The Danger of Overestimating the Communist Menace.*

The second serious threat to Japan's future is the possibility of overestimating the communist menace. Also this might result in grave dangers for the future development of democracy in Japan. The turn of world events has created the fateful circumstance of one totalitarian State having been defeated, and another, more powerful and threatening, having arisen. In order to cope with the Communists, the democratic governments of the world are forced to take restrictive and prohibitive measures, which in themselves are opposed to the spirit of democracy. Protecting the country against the inroads of communism and preventing open violence and disturbance are obviously necessary. Consequently, some freedoms have to be curbed; some restrictions have to be imposed and the police organization has to be reinforced and given greater power than normally would be necessary.

In Japan this constitutes a particular danger. Japanese authorities are naturally inclined to an exaggeration of bureaucracy and to overorganization. This in itself leads to unnecessary interference in the rights and freedom of the normal citizen. The careful and tactful handling of extra powers is definitely not one of the assets of Japan's petty officialdom. One of the most striking examples is the Japanese policeman. A London bobby, through his restraint and self-assurance, will have a soothing effect on an excited public, but the quarrelsome and aggressive Japanese policeman, with his underlying lack of self-confidence, will irritate the public and encourage it to show its feelings. From fear that he might not be able to handle the situation — and hence lose face — the Japanese police officer will revert to unnecessarily severe measures. He will request an overwhelming force to execute his duties. A minor incident might easily become a serious issue.

This state of mind is not only significant of the Japanese police; it prevails in the minds and character of many lower officials in Japan. Their lack of self-confidence, initiative and the power of decision results in a querulous and difficult bureacracy which is apt to resort to stringent measures and totalitarian procedures.

These factors, the communist threat and the inclination of the officials to exaggerate eventual counter-measures, can easily be exploited by sinister forces of the extreme right or ultra left. By stimulating these developments, such forces could again reduce Japan to a totalitarian police state — the ultimate aim of both groups.

Everywhere in the free world, the problem of dealing with the internal threats of communism constitutes a possible danger and threatens to turn a country into a regimented society. In Japan in particular, where the character of the people lends itself to such a development and where the forces to exploit and misuse these circumstances are potentially large, this danger against the spirit of democracy is unusually great.

19. *The Danger of Spiritual Confusion*

Hand in hand with the danger of a possible economic crisis and an over-estimation of the communist menace, the spiritual confusion in post-treaty Japan has constituted one of the greatest impediments to the development of a healthy democracy in that country.

In the years preceding the war, the Japanese people, by and large, found satisfaction for their spiritual needs in surging nationalism and in reverence for their Emperor. Shintoism had been chosen as the official doctrine to guide the spiritual life of the Japanese. In this organized cult, preaching the rise to glory of the nation, and Emperor-worship, the ethical principles forming the basis of the "national teachings" of the Japanese nation were codified. By virtue of its origin it even provided some religious background for Japanese nationalism. Where Shintoism lacked deeper religious concepts, it was supplemented by Buddhism or Confucianism, teachings which were tolerated so long as they did not interfere with the aims of the Government to institute a nationalistic and totalitarian society. In

general, the Japanese people are not religious in the Western
sense of the word; for instance, the lack of a clearly defined and
understandable dogma as the religious basis of their conception
of life does not constitute a problem for them.

We have seen that a thorough indoctrination of the people
and a deliberate regimentation of the Japanese youth, through
strictly controlled education, assured the successful imposition
of this ultra-nationalistic doctrine upon the minds of the Japanese. Furthermore, the totalitarian leaders had a relatively easy
task in regimenting a nation which, during its long history, has
been characterized by its vertical social structure, the submission of the individual to the community and the unquestion-
ed authority of the superior over his subordinate. The
amenable character of the Japanese people, who are normally
docile and willing to follow instructions and orders, was easily
perverted and exploited by their leaders.

Those who doubted the values and the future of the imperialistic, ultra-nationalistic ways formed only a small minority,
and — except for a very few — lacked real influence, power and
the courage of their convictions. In any case, they were easily
suppressed by the forces of the totalitarian regime; they
fell victim to the thought-police, to the "neighborhood-organi-
zations" and to other totalitarian institutions which sharply
curtailed the liberty and freedom of the individual.

The crushing defeat at the end of the war violently shook
the vestiges of this imposed ideological system. The tradition,
and particularly the faith, beliefs and concepts on which it
rested — the whole fabric of Japanese ultra-nationalism and the
"Spirit of Greater Japan" — seemed to come crashing down
and disintegrate completely. As the war leaders were exposed,
as the true story of Japan's defeat was revealed, as the institution
of power and authority were torn down, as fear and suffering
were removed and the constant and burdensome pressure
exerted by the police and by the military authorities was
abolished and freedom restored, the Japanese realized that
they had been misled and deceived. They were stunned and
utterly confused by this unexpected turn of events. Their
imposed traditional conception of life, with its many forms and
sacred rules and regulations, was ruthlessly exposed — its
barrenness forcefully demonstrated at the crucial moment. The

poignant misery and poverty of the masses of the Japanese people — particularly the urban population — prevented them from realizing that the strong and healthy moral core deep within the soul of the Japanese nation would in due time enable them to return to a normal life and to restore their country. An intellectual confusion, therefore, had embroiled them in the autumn days of 1945. This, combined with the dreary spiritual vacuum overshadowing the majority of the Japanese in the days following their defeat, constituted a serious danger to the future of Japan and was certainly detrimental to the furthering of the over-all aims of the Occupation.

The latter, recognizing the danger of this situation, endeavored to find a new ideology to fill the vacuum. It tried to introduce democracy as a basic concept of life; the inalienable rights of all men to life, liberty and the pursuit of happiness were the ideals which had to replace the former Japanese moral and ideological code.

From the very first the Japanese were eager to learn about this new, strange and apparently powerful ideology called democracy, which had inspired the Allies in their fight against the Axis forces and which had formed the basis — yes, the secret — of the Allied victory over their powerful enemies.

The Japanese, however, failed to grasp the underlying philosophy of the democratic way of life. This surely is understandable. How could a nation by nature so obedient, submissive and easily led, understand — overnight — an ideology based on recognition of the individual? How could the Japanese people comprehend the teachings of freedom and dignity of the individual, when they had been brought up in the rigid spirit and strict ethical teachings of the "moral code of greater Japan", whose vague, unrealistic but absorbing doctrine stressed the subordination of the individual to the Empire and its greater glory? How could the Japanese follow the creed of pursuit of personal happiness when their education had been centered on an indoctrination aimed at passionate worship of, and unquestionable service to the Emperor and the nation, and which at the same time had neglected the interests, the dignity and the freedom of the individual?

The Americans, furthermore, took their ideology as something so natural and simple that they failed to explain their

doctrines and to elaborate on the principles of democracy. In
their endeavors to clarify its underlying philosophy and to
teach its basic principles, the majority of the reformers lacked
the necessary intellectual background to undertake such a
monumental task and frequently resorted to the preaching of
an oversimplified and somewhat sterilized notion of their
conception of democracy. But in general, the Americans
considered the question so self-evident that they thought the
Japanese people would immediately recognize the values and
blessings of the new way of life.

This, however, did not happen.

In the days following the war, democracy remained a vague,
strange and incomprehensible ideology. And notwithstanding
the fact that since then many reforms have been accepted and
adopted readily by the Japanese and are now generally appreciated by the common people, notwithstanding the fact that the
feeling of freedom and liberty, the absence of fear and terrorism
and of interference in one's individual life are circumstances
which are cherished by practically every Japanese, and even
though the Japanese people generally approve and rightly
evaluate the benefits of the new way of life — most Japanese
still lack a clear comprehension of the true nature of Western
democracy, still fail to realize its rights and privileges, duties
and restrictions and its underlying philosophy.

And this is likely to remain so in the future, as far as the
comprehension and adaptation of democracy in a purely
Western sense of the word are concerned. There are several
reasons to support this opinion.

In the first place, democracy in the West is based upon, and
is permeated with Christian culture and philosophy. Although
Christianity, as a religion, has lost much of its former dominating position in the West, as a philosophy it is still the most
important influence in shaping the Western concept of life.
Christianity in Japan, however, is a negligible force; its
teachings have never reached the masses and have never greatly
influenced the nation. Christianity, as a basis for the development of a purely Western pattern of democracy in Japan, is,
therefore, not present.

Another important aspect of Western democracy — especially in the American version — is a strong tendency toward

individualism combined with a feeling of duty toward the community. Basically, the Western democrat is an individualist. The ideal of freedom of the individual is the result of a long and eventful historical growth. So far as America is concerned, the search for freedom was the basic reason for the emigrants to find a new world, and — later — to fight for their independence. Freedom of the individual is one of the foremost principles of the American way of life. Notwithstanding this strong emphasis on individuality, in the West there is, as has been said, a strong sense of duty to produce and to cooperate with and for the community. This attitude forms a very important tenet of Western life. The Westerner has an urge — a feeling of necessity — to act, create and improve; in fact, typical examples of primary American virtues are individual initiative, individual responsibility, duty to the community and honest citizenship.

As has been described before, the Japanese, for ages past, have been indoctrinated with a concept of life under which the individual was completely subordinated to the community. The Japanese society was the prototype of a vertically organized society, as opposed to the horizontal structure of modern, Western democracy. In Japan, the father was the undisputed head of the household; the household was part of the clan, headed by one of its older male members; and the clan belonged to the nation, reigned over by the Emperor, whose absolute power was the key to the entire ideological and moral system upon which the "national" teachings of the Japanese nation were based.

This concept of nationhood was codified in the Imperial Rescript, promulgated in 1890. Although originally drafted as a description of the broad principles of educational policy, it was in fact a document setting forth basic ethical directives which would henceforth govern the thoughts and the actions of the whole nation. Its beginning reads as follows:

> "Our Imperial Ancestors have founded Our Empire on a basis broad and everlasting and have deeply and firmly implanted virtue. Our subjects ever united in loyalty and filial piety have from generation to generation illustrated the beauty thereof. This is the glory of the fundamental character of Our Empire and herein also lies the source

of Our Education. Ye, Our Subjects, be filial to your parents . . . . . ."

The Rescript stresses the complete submission of the individual to the community. It lays down the doctrines of ancestor-worship, of filial piety, of duty to the nation and loyalty to superiors. These teachings could never have exerted the great influence they did, had they not been founded upon deep-rooted ideologies which had governed the Japanese nation from time immemorial.

At a later date these teachings were made more stringent, were systematized and exploited to serve the imperialistic aims of the totalitarian leaders. Although the doctrine created opposition and indifferentism in some circles, its influence on the Japanese people has been so predominant that the creation and development of individualistic tendencies in Japan present a most difficult problem.

The Japanese people have always displayed a strong feeling for social duty, and they certainly are not lacking in energy and diligence; in that respect at least they resemble the Westerners. They are a very industrious people and they have even demonstrated an amazing power of initiative, combined with great imagination and organizational talent. The masses are capable of working hard and relatively efficiently; they have an instinctive sense of order, loyalty and obligation toward their masters. Owing to their lack of a strongly developed feeling of individualism, however, these outstanding and highly valuable qualities make them an easy prey for a few determined and domineering leaders, who could exploit these assets either for the better or for the worse. In themselves, these qualities are not conducive to turning the Japanese into democratic citizens. Only in combination with a restrained and responsible individualism can the feeling of duty and the industrious and conscientious character of the Japanese people form an asset for the development of democratic tendencies in their country.

The Japanese society, based upon and developed in accordance with these principles of life and characteristics of the Japanese people, is obviously not fitted to embrace Western democracy. On the contrary, its structure is so far removed

from that of the modern Westen democracies that it is doubtful
whether a purely Western conception of democracy will ever
evolve in Japan, and even more, whether the vast and complicated machinery of Western democracy in all its political,
social and economic aspects could ever be developed.

The questions arises, however, as to how far this situation
is to be regretted — or even whether the institution of a
purely Western democracy would ever be very desirable in
Japan. There may be a much better and more promising
solution. In fact, such a solution has been attempted by the
basic directives issued to MacArthur as Supreme Commander.
As has been described before, the basic post-surrender policy
did not aim at the simple democratization of Japan. It aimed at
the development of democratic tendencies and at the establishment of a peacefully inclined and responsible government.
The nations at San Francisco did not express the wish that
the Japanese nation should become an exact copy of a Western
democracy; they only voiced the hope that Japan would
become a respectable and trustworthy member of the free
world.

The hopes for such a development are most promising:
The Japanese leaders themselves realize that the rehabilitation
and the further development of Japan in a modern world
require a greater personal freedom and responsibility of the
people; a satisfactory machinery for a representative government in Japan has been created; many reforms have been
instituted which in themselves augur well for a democratically
inclined society; the Japanese people — in general — have
become accustomed to and have learned to appreciate the new
way of life. But more important still — history reveals that the
spiritual life of the Japanese nation, in the old days, was
characterized by a high level of moral virtues. It was based on
the three aforesaid teachings of Shintoism, Buddhism and
Confucianism, which — before their philosophy had been
distorted and their ethics misinterpreted — provided a perfect
background for a morally high-founded and balanced society.
This was the spirit and the moral tone which attracted Francis
Xavier, the great missionary of the 16th century, and this was
one of the reasons why Christianity in those days found so many
ardent disciples in Japan. This spirit guided such famous

20

spiritual leaders of the 19th century as Fukuzawa Yukichi; it formed the moral base for such great and enlightened statesmen as Prince Saionji; and more recently it was one of the underlying reasons why the Japanese people generally responded so eagerly to MacArthur's appeal.

These qualities have had few opportunities to develop since the gigantic Tokugawa attempt to secularize Japanese life; they have had even less chance to assert themselves since the Meiji Restoration harnessed the individual — spiritually and physically — to the service of the State. But still, this deep undercurrent of the Japanese nation has — in many instances — survived the vicissitudes of Japanese history. Subconsciously, these concepts are still alive in the hearts and minds of many Japanese. This has been the basic reason why the Japanese nation has rehabilitated and restored itself so remarkably well and quickly after the war. Without this moral foundation the work of MacArthur would have been doomed to failure. Indeed, immediately after the surrender the Japanese people had lost practically all their self-confidence. Even the wise words of their Emperor, spoken on August 15, 1945 — a fortnight before the arrival of the occupation troops — proclaiming that he expected that in post-war "Japan tradition would be transmitted from the son to the grandson, with a solid faith in the indestructable character of the Land of the Gods" failed to lift the morale and spirit of the nation. Later, however, it became evident that these words had not been spoken in vain. Slowly, the Japanese regained some of their confidence and responded to their Emperor's appeal — and with the progress of the years Japan has gradually restored herself, and the people of Japan have rediscovered some of their old virtues.

Consequently, if time permits and if circumstances are favorable, the newly introduced concept of democracy may be successfully blended with the philosophy of the old Japan and be shaped into a doctrine which will form the basis for a Japanese interpretation of democracy.

At the time of the coming into force of the peace treaty, however, this process was still in its initial stages and the underlying ideology an as yet unstable foundation.

20. *Extreme Right and Ultra Left Ready to Exploit Difficulties*

The time and circumstances needed to foster and develop such a spiritual concept will, however, not be available if the threat of communism stifles the atmosphere or if economic chaos strangles the freedom and welfare of the population. As has been outlined before, these two factors, an overestimation of the communist menace and an economic crisis, can easily suffocate the young shoots of democracy. The situation resulting from such developments is particularly favorable for the expansion of the forces of the extreme right or of the ultra left. Moreover the destructive work of these forces would be greatly facilitated by the existing ideological confusion in many circles in Japan. If this unfortunate contingency should materialize, then Japan would rapidly revert to a centralized police state and fall prey to communism or to some other totalitarian system geared for aggressive and expansionist aims.

The *extreme right* has a definite chance of success under present-day conditions. There is no shadow of a doubt that some of the ultra-nationalistic leaders are still amongst those in power in Japan, ready and willing to have another try — hopeful that this time they will succeed. Their ranks will probably be reinforced by some of the purgees who are returning to public life in great numbers. The purgees constituted the majority of the trained brains of the country. As such they represent a latent force of considerable proportions. Furthermore, one can expect that many of them are opposed to the Occupation and what it has done. Upon the instigation of the Occupation the purgees were deprived for several years of practically all means of existence; their fate was a very hard and difficult one. It is understandable that they are not inclined to look kindly on the Occupation or the new Japan. Their obvious choice would be the reactionary camp. Several of them, however, were merely faithful public servants who served the nation in the way their superiors desired. They cannot be considered as hard-boiled, ultra-nationalistic imperialists. Moreover, many of the purgees are too clever and realistic not to understand that times have changed and that the new Japan asks for a completely new approach to the problems of nationhood. Quite a number of the depurged Japanese may be resolved to cooperate, sincerely, in rebuilding a new Japan; many will have learned a lesson and will choose the new way. Some, however, will strengthen the ranks of the ultra-nationalists, where bitterness or misunderstanding of the changes wrought in Japan will lead them to carry on in their former manner.

The great chance for the extreme right to gain supremacy in Japan lies in the fact that its leaders — temporarily hiding their true intentions — can so easily and so inconspicuously penetrate and partake in a democratically inclined government by pretending to favor active cooperation with the free world in its struggle against communism. Emphasizing the economic difficulties and the communist danger, they can easily propagate the necessity of a stiffening of controls. They can instigate a process of action and counter-action under which severe police measures and government regulations would seem logical for the sake of the internal security and the economic survival of the country. Through such a process the safeguards of democracy would be eliminated one after another; the opposition would be crushed step by step. The extreme rightists would gradually and without spectacular changes increase their power and, under cover of their so-called cooperative attitude with the free world, could regain their predominant position and reinstitute a society and a nation which would emerge as dangerously and as aggressively as ever before.

The *extreme left* constitutes another danger. Just now it would appear that the chances for the leftists are smaller than those of the rightists. Japan is officially committed to the free world, where leftist tendencies are looked upon with more suspicion than a conservative rightist inclination. The leftists do not progress very far by trying to penetrate a democratically inclined government under cover of cooperation. As soon as they start to emphasize their tendencies, they will be unmasked — in contrast to the rightists, who can continue their preparative work to a relatively far-advanced stage through a process of cooperation and gradual changes. The growth of rightist influence can be easily hidden and safely covered, but the extreme left must soon expose itself.

Moreover, the official Japanese political organization for the sponsoring of ultra left policies, the Communist Party, is practically outlawed. Its actions are looked upon with much suspicion, and its leaders are fugitives. Furthermore, the Communists, even if they were in a position to pretend to temporary cooperation with a more moderate government, could never do so without — in due time — insisting on severing Japanese ties with the free world, suggesting a complete reversal of Japan's present-day foreign policy, and advocating the disposal of the Emperor, one of the most effective obstacles to the realization of communist plans in Japan.

Consequently, the rise of communism in Japan cannot be covered and would be immediately noticed. Only the groundwork for a leftist movement can be prepared in secrecy.

Notwithstanding these disadvantages, the prospects for the extreme left in present-day Japan are comparatively favorable. Communism can voice a magnetic, emotional and demagogical appeal to the masses. It can stir the nationalist feelings of the people. It can openly attack the presence of foreign troops on the sacred soil of Japan. It can stubbornly emphasize the so-called foreign domination of Nippon by "capitalist" America. And it can, on the other hand, picture the prospect of a mighty, nationalist, modern and leftist Japan playing her role in Asia — side by side with the Soviet Union and the People's Republic of China — a combination forming an irresistible bloc against the imperialistic West. Stalin himself has boasted, "With Japan, we are invincible".

Furthermore, communism can promise the Japanese masses a short cut toward improving their standard of living and their economic status through the advantages of its economic system. It can add to its propaganda appeal the attractive prospect of Japan cooperating with the Sino-Soviet bloc, with at the same time a free hand in Southeast Asia. Moreover, the leftists can incite the Japanese people against any restrictions on their rights and privileges. It can promise the workers greater rights and better privileges after they — the working class — have gained power.

These things the leftists can do openly, instantaneously, without need for restraint. They do not share any responsibility in the government. They do not have to reckon with the complication of having temporarily to veil their real aims. But, most important of all, the leftists have the help of a foreign Power — the Kremlin — which is anxious for Japanese com-

munism to succeed and which continuously calls upon the
Japanese people to break "the chains of their enslavement by
the West" and to join the "free, peaceful, and democratic
people's republics".

These appeals will become more powerful as the position
of Moscow and Peking solidifies. The Japanese have a tendency
to follow the strongest Power and to favor the winner. If
the determination of the Western world to assert itself in the
Far East should decline — as in the days of Secretary
Royall — the Japanese could easily swing toward more promising
Powers.

In this connection it is important to realize that the Japanese
people earnestly follow the course of events in Korea as well as
on the other battlefields in Asia, whether cold wars or otherwise.
What happens there will be of great significance in determining
the future course of Japan.

Unfortunately enough the Western democracies are divided
on economic and political issues in the Far East; the maintenance of a strong Western policy in Asia is not guaranteed.
Moreover, the Japanese Government is pressed by circumstances in a more or less reactionary direction and a great many
Japanese have not yet found their spiritual stability and their
moral balance. It could be, therefore, that the obstacles to
communism in Japan will be easier to overcome in the future
than they appeared to be at the time of the coming into force
of the peace treaty.

Summarizing we find that communism can voice a more
modern, realistic and tangible appeal to the masses of the
Japanese people than extreme conservative nationalism. Secondly, the ultra right will lose its foreign supporters when it
starts to initiate the actual realization of its aims, while the
extreme left will secure an even more definite support from
foreign — communist — Powers, increasing in proportion to
its success.

Consequently one can say that the future danger from the
leftist side is, in fact, greater than the danger from the right,
notwithstanding the disadvantages for the Communists,
previously discussed.

The leftist danger would become alarmingly great, if certain
forces from the right — realizing the limitations of their

program — should compromise with the left on issues as the Emperorship, private enterprise and a few of their minor differences, and would join in a combined endeavor to create a leftist Japan. There are fewer obstacles to such a development than appear at first sight. The rightists' dreams of ultra-nationalism have much in common with those of the leftists; their systems of government are practically the same; their aims are not far apart — their joining forces is a practical possibility with frightening consequences, and their combined efforts would constitute a very serious threat to Japan and to the rest of the free world.

21. Cooperation between Free World and Japan Necessary for Growth of Democracy

What can the free world do to assist Japan in defying the dangers described above, and in what way can it favorably influence the developments in Japan?

As a beginning, the free world must abstain from *direct* interference in Japanese affairs, for such interference would only create unfavorable reactions.

The free world, on the other hand, has many *indirect* ways in which it can assist the Japanese nation on its road toward a true democracy. In the foregoing pages several indications have been given of the ways and means open to it in this respect. They may be summarized here. (1) The political parties in foreign countries can encourage contacts with their counterparts in Japan — the socialist parties of Europe in particular can exert a healthy influence; (2) educational leaders and students of Japan can be assisted in familiarizing themselves with education in other democratic countries — invitations can be extended, scholarships given and materials exchanged; (3) the public enlightenment of the Japanese people can be stimulated by foreign publications, by Japanese versions of foreign magazines, by radio broadcasts and by news from foreign news agencies; culture, art, science and literature can be sponsored through the exchange of cultural values; (4) the democratic women's organizations of the world can maintain close contact with their counterparts in Japan; (5) the labor movement in other countries can exercise an exceedingly important influence.

Through such contacts the people of Japan can be kept informed of the happenings in other parts of the world. Thus they will remain cognizant of the values of a free and democratic society, and they will be on guard against any encroachment on their rights and liberties. Dangerous situations developing in Japan can be more easily recognized and exposed so long as close contacts with the outer world are maintained. The outside press – and the real friends of Japan — will be able to follow the trend of events and will have an opportunity to criticize the wrong, stress the good and warn the Japanese against the occurrence of a growing reaction or a leftist tendency in their country. Totalitarianism does not breed in the open. Its favorable climate is secrecy and darkness. The democratic world can help Japan to keep her windows wide open to the sun of freedom and to light her remotest corners with the brightness of truth and liberty.

The free world, however, has to choose carefully the manner in which she exerts this influence and establishes and fosters these contacts. The cultural history of the world shows that when a sudden, sharp increase of communication and influence between nations occurs, and particularly when this influence is mainly of a one-sided character, friction, adverse feelings, and sometimes irritation are often created. This emphasizes the necessity of tact and restraint, especially in Japan where the occupation years have made the people somewhat over-conscious of foreign interference. This danger is accentuated by the continued stationing of American troops in Japan under the American-Japanese security pact. It will be strictly necessary for these troops to act as a "force in being" only; any assumption of a more direct role in Japanese affairs, and even an obvious demonstration of their presence in post-treaty Japan, might create dangerous tensions and might spoil the monumental work done in Japan during the occupation years.

In addition to the fostering of contacts between Japan and the free world, there is still another — equally important — field in which the free world can help Japan to develop her new democracy. Japan has to be accommodated in the economic structure of the free world. Place must be made for Japan's overseas trade and commerce, her international shipping and finance. The foregoing pages have stressed repeatedly that it is on the fulfillment of these conditions of economic equality that the democratic future of Japan largely depends. Wrongly understood self-interest on the part of the free world or fear of competition can easily lead to restrictive policies and a resentful attitude. Such behavior is not only contrary to the spirit of the San Francisco treaty, but would have disastrous consequences for the future of Japan and for the future of the world. The over-all political aim of establishing Japan's position as a member of the free world will, therefore, have to prevail over direct economic interests — as was the case in San Francisco. Japan has to be given a fair chance to develop a sound and independent economy, thereby enhancing her chances to develop a healthy and democratically inclined nation.

Not only the Western world, but also the Japanese people and their leaders face an enormous responsibility with regard to the future of Japan. They will have to demonstrate by their acts that they really want Japan to remain a member of the community of free and peace-loving nations. They will have to pursue a policy of dignified and purposeful cooperation with the free world. They will have to win back the respect and the good will of the outer world. They will have to take a definite stand against the inroads of communism. On the other hand, they will have to avoid antagonizing Asiatic nationalism, or freezing Japan's position with regard to future developments in Asia. The Japanese will have to be conscious of the necessity of the economic restoration of their country and make this restoration the primary aim of their national policy. At the same time, however, they will have to abstain from internationally unacceptable practices in trade competition, and they will have to make a sincere effort to implement the reparation clauses of the peace treaty. Moreover, the Japanese will have to retain — and even to restore — "things Japanese"; they will have "to reform some of the reforms" in order to make them better suited to Japanese circumstances. Yet, the Japanese have to maintain the new spirit, to foster the democratic way of life, and to oppose the return of militaristic, totalitarian, ultra-nationalistic tendencies. But most important of all, the Japanese people have — in the words of John Foster Dulles — "a new and historic opportunity to win honor in Asia". Said Dulles: "There is a confused situation which can be brought into order.

To do that calls for the finest qualities of which men are capable. Those who know the Japanese — as friend or foe — know that they can develop these qualities. However, they need to understand what it is that makes for true greatness. Greatness is not the ability to impose upon others what they do not want. Rather, it resides in the ability to help others to find the way to get what they want. If the Japanese do that — and they are capable of it — they can attain a leadership and influence in Asia which will be welcome". The goal set by Mr. Dulles implies not only a great responsibility; it sets forth a lofty aim and constitutes a great challenge.

22. *Future Challenges Japan and Free World*

During the post-war years a promising beginning has been made for Japan to become a trusted and respected member of the family of free, democratic and peaceful nations. MacArthur's intentions, voiced at the time of the surrender, have been realized. A great work has been performed.

The task, however, is not yet finished. The work must continue. The strengthening of the ties between Japan and the democratic nations and a further development of Japan along the road toward a true democracy, however, are only possible as the result of a genuine and constructive cooperation between the free world and Japan.

This is the great challenge facing both the free world and Japan.

The writer believes that the loftiness of the aim corresponds to the sweeping character of the challenge.

The purpose of this book has been to awaken the people of the free world and the people of Japan, and to call upon them to take up the challenge and to unite in an effort to build a democratic, peaceful, dignified and prosperous Japan, as a worthy member of a better world.

APPENDICES

BASIC POST-SURRENDER POLICY FOR JAPAN

The following directive, serial number 82, prepared by the Department of State to implement the policy adopted by the Far Eastern Commission on June 19, 1947 under the provisions of paragraph II, A, 1, of its terms of reference has been received from the State, War and Navy Departments for transmission to you for your guidance in accordance with paragraph III, 1, of those terms of reference:

This document is a statement of general policy relating to Japan after surrender. It does not deal with all matters relating to the occupation of Japan requiring policy determinations. Such matters as are not included or not fully covered will be dealt with separately.

PREAMBLE

Whereas on September 2, 1945, Japan surrendered unconditionally to the Allied Powers and is now under military occupation by forces of these powers under the command of General of the Army Douglas MacArthur, Supreme Commander for the Allied Powers, and

Whereas representatives of the following nations, namely, Australia, Canada, China, France, India, The Netherlands, New Zealand, the Philippines, the U.S.S.R., the United Kingdom, and the United States of America, which were engaged in the war against Japan, have on the decision of the Moscow Conference of Foreign Ministers met together at Washington as a Far Eastern Commission, to formulate the policies, principles and standards in conformity with which the fulfillment by Japan of its obligations under the Terms of Surrender may be accomplished;

The nations composing this commission, with the object of fulfilling the intentions of the Potsdam Declaration, of carrying out the instrument of surrender and of establishing international security and stability;

Conscious that such security and stability depend first, upon the complete destruction of the military machine which has been the chief means whereby Japan has carried out the agressions of past decades; second, upon the establishment of such political and economic conditions as would make impossible any revival of militarism in Japan; and third, upon bringing the Japanese to a realization that their will to war, their plan of conquest, and the methods used to accomplish such plans have brought them to the verge of ruin;

Resolved that Japan cannot be allowed to control her own destinies again until there is on her part a determination to abandon militarism in all its aspects and a desire to live with the rest of the world in peace, and until democratic principles are established in all spheres of the political, economic and cultural life of Japan;

Are therefore agreed:

To ensure the fulfillment of Japan's obligation to the Allied Powers;

To complete the task of physical and spiritual demilitarization of Japan by measures including total disarmament, economic reform designed to deprive Japan of power to make war, elimination of militaristic influences, and stern justice to war criminals, and requiring a period of strict control; and

To help the people of Japan in their own interest as well as that of the world at large to find means whereby they may develop within the framework of a democratic society an intercourse among themselves and with other countries along economic and cultural lines that will enable them to satisfy their reasonable individual and national needs and bring them into permanently peaceful relationship with all nations;

And have adopted the following basic objectives and policies in dealing with Japan.

PART I — ULTIMATE OBJECTIVES

1. The ultimate objectives in relation to Japan, to which policies for the post-surrender period for Japan should conform, are:

   a. To insure that Japan will not again become a menace to the peace and security of the world.
   b. To bring about the earliest possible establishment of a democratic and peaceful government which will carry out its international responsibilities, respect the rights of other states, and support the objectives of the United Nations. Such Government in Japan should be established in accordance with the freely expressed will of the Japanese people.

2. These objectives will be achieved by the following principal means:

   a. Japan's sovereignty will be limited to the islands of Honshu, Hokkaido, Kyushu, Shikoku and such minor outlying islands as may be determined.
   b. Japan will be completely disarmed and demilitarized. The authority of the militarists and the influence of militarism will be totally eliminated. All institutions expressive of the spirit of militarism and agression will be vigorously suppressed.
   c. The Japanese people shall be encouraged to develop a desire for individual liberties and respect for fundamental human rights, particularly the freedoms of religion, assembly and association, speech and the press. They shall be encouraged to form democratic and representative organizations.
   d. Japan shall be permitted to maintain such industries as will sustain her economy and permit the exaction of just reparations in kind, but not those which would enable her to rearm for war. To this end access to, as distinguished from control of, raw materials should be permitted. Eventual Japanese participation in world trade relations will be permitted.

Part II — ALLIED AUTHORITY

1. *Military Occupation*

There will be a military occupation of the Japanese home islands to carry into effect the surrender terms and further the achievement of the ultimate objectives stated above. The occupation shall have the character of an operation in behalf of the powers that have participated in the war against Japan. The principle of participation in the occupation of Japan by forces of these nations is affirmed. The occupation forces will be under the command of a supreme commander designated by the United States.

2. *Relationship to Japanese Government*

The authority of the Emperor and the Japanese Government will be subject to the Supreme Commander, who will possess all powers necessary to effectuate the surrender terms and to carry out the policies established for the conduct of the occupation and the control of Japan.

The Supreme Commander will exercise his authority through Japanese governmental machinery and agencies, including the Emperor, but only to the extent that this satisfactorily furthers judgment and discretion of the Supreme Commander, the Japanese Government may be permitted to exercise the normal powers of government in matters of domestic administration, or the Supreme Commander may in any case direct action to be taken without making use of the agencies of the Japanese Government.

After appropriate preliminary consultation with the representatives of the Allied Powers in the Allied Council for Japan, the Supreme Commander may, in case of necessity, take decisions concerning the removal of individual ministers of the Japanese Government, or concerning the filling of vacancies created by the resignation of individual cabinet members. Changes in the governmental machinery, or a change in the Japanese Government as a whole, will be made in accordance with the principles laid down in the terms of reference of the Far Eastern Commission.

The Supreme Commander is not committed to support the Emperor or any other Japanese governmental authority. The policy is to use the existing form of government in Japan and not to support it. Changes in the pre-surrender form of the Emperor institution and in the form of government in the direction of modifying or removing its feudal and authoritarian character and of establishing a democratic Japan are to be encouraged.

3. *Protection of United Nations Interests*

It shall be the duty of the Supreme Commander to protect the interests, assets, and rights of all members of the United Nations and their nationals. Where such protection conflicts with the fulfillment of the objectives and policies of the occupation, the government of the nation concerned shall be informed through diplomatic channels and shall be consulted on the question of proper adjustment.

4. *Publicity as to Policies*

The Peoples of the nations which have participated in the war against Japan, the Japanese people, and the world at large shall be kept fully informed of the objectives and policies of the occupation, and of the progress made in their fulfillment.

PART III — POLITICAL

1. *Disarmament and Demilitarization*

Disarmament and demilitarization are the initial tasks of the military occupation and shall be carried out promptly and with determination. Every effort shall be made to bring home to the Japanese people that part played by those who have deceived and misled them into embarking on world conquest, and those who collaborated in so doing.

Japan is not to have any Army, Navy, Airforce, Secret Police organization, or any Civil Aviation, or Gendarmerie, but may have adequate Civilian Police Forces. Japan's Ground, Air and Naval Forces shall be disarmed and disbanded, and the Japanese Imperial General Headquarters, the General Staff and all Secret Police organizations shall be dissolved. Military and naval material, military and naval vessels and military and naval installations, and the military, naval and civilian aircraft, wherever situated, shall be surrendered to the appropriate Allied commanders in their zones of capitulation of the Japanese troops and shall be disposed of in accordance with decisions of the Allied Powers already adopted or which may be adopted. Inventories shall be made and inspections authorized to insure complete execution of these provisions.

High officials of the Japanese Imperial General Headquarters and General Staff, other high military and naval officials of the Japanese Government, leaders of ultra-nationalist and militarist organizations and other important exponents of militarism and aggression will be taken into custody and held for future disposition. Persons who have been active exponents of militarism and militant nationalism will be removed and excluded from public office and from any other position of public or substantial private responsibility. Ultra-nationalistic or militaristic social, political, professional and commercial societies and institutions will be dissolved and prohibited.

The restoration, even in a disguised form, of any anti-democratic and militaristic activity shall be prevented, particularly on the part of former Japanese career military and naval officers, Gendarmerie, and former members of dissolved militaristic ,ultra-nationalistic and other antidemocratic organizations.

Militaristic, ultra-nationalistic and anti-democratic doctrines and practices, including para-military training, shall be eliminated from the educational system. Former career military and naval officers, both commissioned and non-commissioned, and all other exponents of militaristic, ultra-nationalistic and anti-democratic doctrines and practices shall be excluded from supervisory and teaching positions.

2. *War Criminals*

Stern justice shall be meted out to all war criminals, including those who visited cruelties upon prisoners of war or other nationals of members of the United Nations. Persons charged by the Supreme Commander, or appropriate United Nations agencies with being war criminals shall be arrested, tried and, if convicted, punished. Those wanted by another of the United Nations for offenses against its nationals, shall, if not wanted for trial or as witnesses or otherwise by the Supreme Commander, be turned over to the custody of such other nation.

3. *Encouragement of Desire for Individual Liberties and Democratic Processes*

Freedom of worship and observance of all religions shall be proclaimed and guaranteed for the future. It should also be made plain to the Japanese that ultra-nationalistic, militaristic and anti-democratic organizations and movements will not be permitted to hide behind the cloak of religion.

The Japanese people shall be afforded opportunity and encouraged to become familiar with the history, institutions, culture and the accomplishments of the democracies.

Obstacles to the revival and strengthening of democratic tendencies among the Japanese people shall be removed.

Democratic political parties, with rights of assembly and public discussion and the formation of trade unions shall be encouraged, subject to the necessity for maintaining the security of the occupying forces.

Laws, decrees, and regulations which establish discrimination on ground of race, nationality, creed or political opinion shall be abrogated; those which conflict with the objectives and policies outlined in this document shall be repealed, suspended or amended as required, and agencies charged specifically with their enforcement shall be abolished on appropriately modified. Persons unjustly confined by Japanese authority on political grounds shall be released. The judicial, legal and police systems shall be reformed as soon as practicable to conform to the policies set forth herein and it shall be the duty of all judicial, legal and police officers to protect individual liberties and civil rights.

Part IV — ECONOMIC

1. *Economic Demilitarization*

The existing economic basis of Japan's military strength must be destroyed and not be permitted to revive.

Therefore, a program will be enforced containing the following elements, among others: The immediate cessation and future prohibition of production of all goods designed for the equipment, maintenance, or use of any military force or establishment; the imposition of a ban upon facilities for the production or repair of implements of war, including naval vessels and all forms of aircraft; the institution of a system of inspection and control designed to prevent concealed or disguised military preparation; the elimination in Japan of those industries or branches of production which would provide Japan with the capacity to rearm for war; and the prohibition of specialized research and instruction contributing directly to the development of war-making power. Research for peaceful ends will be permitted but shall be strictly supervised by the Supreme Commander to prevent its use for war purposes. Japan shall be restricted to the maintenance of those industries which will sustain the level of economy and standard of living fixed in accordance with principles determined by the Far Eastern Commission, and consistent with the Potsdam Declaration.

The eventual disposition of those existing production facilities within Japan which are to be eliminated in accord with the program, as between transfer abroad and the purpose of reparations, scrapping, and conversion to other uses, will be determined, after inventory, in accordance with the principles laid down by the Far Eastern Commission or pursuant to the terms of reference of the Far Eastern Commission. Pending decision, no such facilities either suitable for transfer abroad or readily convertible for civilion production should not be destroyed, except in emergency situations.

2. *Promotion of Democratic Forces*

Organizations of labor in industry and agriculture, organized on a democratic basis, shall be encouraged. Other organizations in industry and agriculture, organized on a democratic basis, shall be encouraged if they will contribute to furthering the democratization of Japan or other objectives of the occupation.

Policies shall be laid down with the object of insuring a wide and just distribution of income and of the ownership of the means of production and trade.

Encouragement shall be given to those forms of economic activity, organization and leadership deemed likely to strengthen the democratic forces in Japan and to prevent economic activity from being used in support of military ends.

To this end it shall be the policy of the Supreme Commander:

a. To prohibit the retention in important positions in the economic field of individuals who because of their past associations or for other reasons cannot be trusted to direct Japanese economic effort solely towards peaceful and democratic ends; and

b. To require a program for the dissolution of the large industrial and banking combinations accompanied by their progressive replacement by organisations which would widen the basis of control and ownership.

3. *Resumption of Peaceful Economic Activity*

The policies of Japan have brought down upon the people great economic destruction and confronted them with economic difficulty and suffering. The plight of Japan is the direct outcome of its own behavior, and the Allies will not undertake the burden of repairing the damage. It can be repaired only if the Japanese people renounce all military aims and apply themselves diligently and with single purpose to the ways of peaceful living. It will be necessary for them to undertake physical reconstruction and basically to reform the nature and direction of their economic activities and institutions. In accordance with assurances contained in the Potsdam Declaration, the Allies have no intention of imposing conditions which would prevent the accomplishment of these tasks in due time.

Japan will be expected to provide goods and services to meet the needs of the occupying forces to the extent that this can, in the judgment of the Supreme Commander, be effected without causing starvation, widespread disease and acute physical distress.

The Japanese authorities will be expected, and if necessary directed, to maintain, develop and enforce programs, subject to the approval of the Supreme Commander, which are designed to serve the following purposes:

a. To avoid acute economic distress.

b. To assure just and impartial distribution of available supplies.

c. To meet the requirements for reparations deliveries.

d. To make such provision for the needs of the Japanese population as may be deemed reasonable in accordance with principles formulated by the Far Eastern Commission in the light both of supplies available and of obligations to other peoples of the United Nations and territories formerly occupied by Japan.

4. Reparations and Restitution

Reparations

For acts of aggression committed by Japan and for the purpose of equitable reparation of the damage caused by her to the Allied Powers and in the interests of destruction of the Japanese war potential in those industries which could lead to Japan's rearmament for waging war, reparations shall be exacted from Japan through the transfer of such existing Japanese capital equipment and facilities or such Japanese goods as exist or may in future be produced and which under policies set forth by the Far Eastern Commission or pursuant to the terms of reference of the Far Eastern Commission should be made available for this purpose. The reparations shall be in such a form as would not endanger the fulfillment of the program of demilitarization of Japan and which would not prejudice the defraying of the cost of the occupation and the maintenance of a minimum civilian standard of living. The shares of particular countries in the total sum of the reparations from Japan shall be determined on a broad political basis, taking into due account the scope of material and human destruction and damage suffered by each claimant country as a result of the preparation and execution of Japanese aggression, and taking also into due account each country's contribution to the cause of the defeat of Japan, including the extent and duration of its resistance to Japanese aggression.

Restitution

Full and prompt restitution will be required of all indentifiable property, looted, delivered under duress, or paid for in worthtless currency.

5. *Fiscal, Monetary, and Banking Policies*

While the Japanese authorities will remain responsible for the management and direction of the domestic fiscal, monetary, and credit policies, this responsibility is subject to the approval and review of the Supreme Commander, and wherever necessary to his direction.

6. *International Trade and Financial Relations*

Eventual Japanese participation in world trade relations shall be permitted. During occupation and under suitable controls, and subject to the prior requirements of the peoples of countries which have participated in the war against Japan, Japan will be permitted to purchase from foreign countries raw materials and other goods that it may need for peaceful purposes, and to export goods to pay for approved imports. Exports other than those directed to be shipped on reparations account or as restitution may be made only to those recipients who agree to provide necessary imports in exchange or agree to pay for such exports in foreign exchange usable in purchasing imports. The proceeds of Japanese exports may be used after the minimum civilian standard of living has been secured to pay for the costs of non-military imports necessary for the occupation which have already been made since the surrender.

Control is to be maintained over all imports and exports of goods and foreign exchange and financial transactions. The Far Eastern Commission shall formulate the policies and principles governing exports from and imports to Japan. The Far Eastern Commission will formulate the policies to be followed in the exercise of these controls.

7. *Japanese Property Located Abroad*

The clauses herein on reparations and references to this subject are without prejudice to the views of governments of the overseas assets issue.

8. *Equality of Opportunity for Foreign Enterprise within Japan*

All business organizations of any of the United Nations shall have equal opportunity in the overseas trade and commerce of Japan. Within Japan equal treatment shall be accorded to all nationals of the United Nations.

9. *Imperial Household Property*

Imperial household property shall not be exempt from any action necessary to carry out the objectives of the occupation.

TREATY OF PEACE

BETWEEN THE ALLIED POWERS AND JAPAN

Whereas the Allied Powers and Japan are resolved that henceforth their relations shall be those of nations which, as sovereign equals, cooperate in friendly association to promote to their common welfare and to maintain international peace and security, and are therefore desirous of concluding a Treaty of Peace which will settle questions still outstanding as a result of the existence of a state of war between them;

Whereas Japan for its part declares its intention to apply for membership in the United Nations and in all circumstances to conform to the principles of the Charter of the United Nations; to strive to realize the objectives of the Universal Declaration of Human Rights; to seek to create within Japan conditions of stability and well-being as defined in Articles 55 and 56 of the Charter of the United Nations and already initiated by post-surrender Japanese legislation; and in public and private trade and commerce to conform to internationally accepted fair practices;

Whereas the Allied Powers welcome the intentions of Japan set out in the foregoing paragraph;

The Allied Powers and Japan have therefore determined to conclude the present Treaty of Peace, and have accordingly appointed the undersigned Plenipotentiaries, who, after presentation of their full powers, found in good and due form, have agreed on the following provisions:

CHAPTER I — PEACE

Article 1

(a) The state of war between Japan and each of the Allied Powers is terminated as from the date on which the present Treaty comes into force between Japan and the Allied Power concerned as provided for in Article 23.

(b) The Allied Powers recognize the full sovereignty of the Japanese people over Japan and its territorial waters.

CHAPTER II — TERRITORY

Article 2

(a) Japan, recognizing the independence of Korea, renounces all right, title and claim to Korea, including the islands of Quelpart, Port Hamilton and Dagelet.

(*b*) Japan renounces all right, title and claim to Formosa and the Pescadores.

(*c*) Japan renounces all right, title and claim to the Kurile Islands, and to that portion of Sakhalin and the islands adjacent to it over which Japan acquired sovereignty as a consequence of the Treaty of Portsmouth of September 5, 1905.

(*d*) Japan renounces all right, title and claim in connection with the League of Nations Mandate System, and accepts the action of the United Nations Security Council of April 2, 1947, extending the trusteeship system to the Pacific Islands formerly under mandate to Japan.

(*e*) Japan renounces all claim to any right or title to or interest in connection with any part of the Antarctic area, whether deriving from the activities of Japanese nationals or otherwise.

(*f*) Japan renounces all right, title and claim to the Spratly Islands and to the Paracel Islands.

Article 3

Japan will concur in any proposal of the United States to the United Nations to place under its trusteeship system, with the United States as the sole administering authority, Nansei Shoto south of 290 north latitude (including the Ryukyu Islands and the Daito Islands), Nanpo Shoto south of Sofu Gan (including the Bonin Islands, Rosario Island and the Volcano Islands) and Parece Vela and Marcus Island. Pending the making of such a proposal and affirmative action thereon, the United States will have the right to exercise all and any powers of administration, legislation and jurisdiction over the territory and inhabitants of these islands, including their territorial waters.

Article 4

(*a*) Subject to the provisions of paragraph (*b*) of this Article, the disposition of property of Japan and of its nationals in the areas referred to in Article 2, and their claims, including debts, against the authorities presently administering such areas and the residents (including juridical persons) thereof, and the disposition in Japan of property of such authorities and residents, and of claims, including debts, of such authorities and residents against Japan and its nationals, shall be the subject of special arrangements between Japan and such authorities. The property of any of the Allied Powers or its nationals in the areas referred to in Article 2 shall, insofar as this has not already been done, be returned by the administering authority in the condition in which it now exists. (The term nationals whenever used in the present Treaty includes juridical persons).

(*b*) Japan recognizes the validity of dispositions of property of Japan and Japanese nationals made by or pursuant to directives of the United States Military Government in any of the areas referred to in Articles 2 and 3.

(*c*) Japanese owned submarine cables connecting Japan with territory removed from Japanese control pursuant to the present Treaty shall be equally divided, Japan retaining the Japanese terminal and adjoining half of the cable, and the detached territory the remainder of the cable and connecting terminal facilities.

Chapter III — SECURITY

Article 5

(*a*) Japan accepts the obligations set forth in Article 2 of the Charter of the United Nations, and in particular the obligations
  (i) to settle its international disputes by peaceful means in such a manner that international peace and security, and justice, are not endangered;
 (ii) to refrain in its international relations from the threat or use of force against the territorial integrity or political independence of any State or in any other manner inconsistent with the Purposes of the United Nations;
(iii) to give the United Nations every assistance in any action it takes in accordance with the Charter and to refrain from giving assistance to any State against which the United Nations may take preventive or enforcement action.

(*b*) The Allied Powers confirm that they will be guided by the principles of Article 2 of the Charter of the United Nations in their relations with Japan.

(*c*) The Allied Powers for their part recognize that Japan as a sovereign nation possesses the inherent right of individual or collective self-defense referred to in Article 51 of the Charter of the United Nations and that Japan may voluntarily enter into collective security arrangements.

Article 6

(*a*) All occupation forces of the Allied Powers shall be withdrawn from Japan as soon as possible after the coming into force of the present Treaty, and in any case not later than 90 days thereafter. Nothing in this provision shall, however, prevent the stationing or retention of foreign armed forces in Japanese territory under or in consequence of any bilateral or multilateral agreements which have been or may be made between one or more of the Allied Powers, on the one hand, and Japan on the other.

(*b*) The provisions of Article 9 of the Potsdam Proclamation of July 26, 1945, dealing with the return of Japanese military forces to their homes, to the extent not already completed, will be carried out.

(*c*) All Japanese property for which compensation has not already been paid, which was supplied for the use of the occupation forces and which remains in the possession of those forces at the time of the coming into force of the present Treaty, shall be returned to the Japanese Government within the same 90 days unless other arrangements are made by mutual agreement.

Chapter IV — POLITICAL AND ECONOMIC CLAUSES

Article 7

(*a*) Each of the Allied Powers, within one year after the present Treaty has come into force between it and Japan, will notify Japan which of its prewar bilateral treaties or conventions with Japan it wishes to continue in force or revive, and any treaties or conventions so notified shall continue in force or be revived subject only to such amendments as may be necessary to ensure conformity with the present Treaty. The treaties and conventions so notified shall be considered as having been continued in force or revived three months after the date of notification and shall be registered with the Secretariat of the United Nations. All such treaties and conventions as to which Japan is not so notified shall be regarded as abrogated.

(b) Any notification made under paragraph (a) of this Article may except from the operation or revival of a treaty or convention any territory for the international relations of which the notifying Power is responsible, until three months after the date on which notice is given to Japan that such exception shall cease to apply.

Article 8

(a) Japan will recognize the full force of all treaties now or hereafter concluded by the Allied Powers for terminating the state of war initiated on September 1, 1939, as well as any other arrangements by the Allied Powers for or in connection with the restoration of peace. Japan also accepts the arrangements made for terminating the former League of Nations and Permanent Court of International Justice.

(b) Japan renounces all such rights and interests as it may derive from being a signatory power of the Conventions of St. Germain-en-Laye of September 10, 1919, and the Straits Agreement of Montreux of July 20, 1936 and from Article 16 of the Treaty of Peace with Turkey signed at Lausanne on July 24, 1923.

(c) Japan renounces all rights, title and interests acquired under, and is discharged from all obligations resulting from the Agreement between Germany and the Creditor Powers of January 20, 1930, and its Annexes, including the Trust Agreement, dated May 17, 1930; the Convention of January 20, 1930, respecting the Bank for International Settlements; and the Statutes of the Bank for International Settlements. Japan will notify to the Ministry of Foreign Affairs in Paris within six months of the first coming into force of the present Treaty its renunciation of the rights, title and interests referred to in this paragraph,

Article 9

Japan will enter promptly into negotiations with the Allied Powers so desiring for the conclusion of bilateral and multilateral agreements providing for the regulation or limitation of fishing and the conservation and development of fisheries on the high seas.

Article 10

Japan renounces all special rights and interests in China, including all benefits and privileges resulting from the provisions of the final Protocol signed at Peking on September 7, 1901, and all annexes, notes and documents supplementary thereto, and agrees to the abrogation in respect to Japan of the said protocol, annexes, notes and documents.

Article 11

Japan accepts the judgments of the International Military Tribunal for the Far East and of other Allied War Crimes Courts both within and outside Japan, and will carry out the sentences imposed thereby upon Japanese nationals imprisoned in Japan. The power to grant clemency, to reduce sentences and to parole with respect to such prisoners may not be exercised except on the decision of the Government or Governments which imposed the sentence in each instance, and on the recommendation of Japan. In the case of persons sentenced by the International Military Tribunal for the Far East, such power may not be exercised except on the decision of a majority of the Governments represented on the Tribunal, and on the recommendation of Japan.

Article 12

(a) Japan declares its readiness promptly to enter into negotiations for the conclusion with each of the Allied Powers of treaties or agreements to place their trading, maritime and other commercial relations on a stable and friendly basis.

(b) Pending the conclusion of the relevant treaty or agreement, Japan will, during a period of four years from the first coming into force of the present Treaty

(1) accord to each of the Allied Powers, its nationals, products and vessels

(i) most-favored-nation treatment with respect to customs duties, charges, restrictions and other regulations on or in connection with the importation and exportation of goods:

(ii) national treatment with respect to shipping, navigation and imported goods, and with respect to natural and juridical persons and their interests — such treatment to include all matters pertaining to the levying and collection of taxes, access to the courts, the making and performance of contracts, rights to property (tangible and intangible), participation in juridical entities constituted under Japanese law, and generally the conduct of all kinds of business and professional activities;

(2) ensure that external purchases and sales of Japanese state trading enterprises shall be based solely on commercial considerations.

(c) In respect to any matter, however, Japan shall be obliged to accord to an Allied Power national treatment, or most-favored-nation treatment, only to the extent that the Allied Power concerned accords Japan national treatment or most-favored-nation treatment, as the case may be, in respect of the same matter. The reciprocity envisaged in the foregoing sentence shall be determined, in the case of products, vessels and juridical entities of, and persons domiciled in, any non-metropolitan territory of an Allied Power, and in the case of juridical entities of, and persons domiciled in, any state or province of an Allied Power having a federal government, by reference to the treatment accorded to Japan in such territory, state or province.

(d) In the application of this Article, a discriminatory measure shall not be considered to derogate from the grant of national or most-favored-nation treatment, as the case may be, if such measure is based on an exception

customarily provided for in the commercial treaties of the party applying it,
or on the need to safeguard that party's external financial position or balance
of payments (except in respect to shipping and navigation), or on the need to
maintain its essential security interests, and provided such measure is pro-
portionate to the circumstances and not applied in an arbitrary or unreason-
able manner.

(e) Japan's obligations under this Article shall not be affected by the
exercise of any Allied rights under Article 14 of the present Treaty; nor shall
the provisions of this Article be understood as limiting the undertakings
assumed by Japan by virtue of Article 15 of the Treaty.

Article 13

(a) Japan will enter into negotiations with any of the Allied Powers,
promptly upon the request of such Power or Powers, for the conclusion of
bilateral or multilateral agreements relating to international civil air transport.

(b) Pending the conclusion of such agreement or agreements, Japan will,
during a period of four years from the first coming into force of the present
Treaty, extend to such Power treatment not less favorable with respect to
air-traffic rights and privileges than those exercised by any such Powers at
the date of such coming into force, and will accord complete equality of
opportunity in respect to the operation and development of air services.

(c) Pending its becoming a party to the Convention on International
Civil Aviation in accordance with Article 93 thereof, Japan will give effect to
the provisions of that Convention applicable to the international navigation
of aircraft, and will give effect to the standards, practices and procedures
adopted as annexes to the Convention in accordance with the terms of the
Convention.

CHAPTER V — CLAIMS AND PROPERTY

Article 14

(a) It is recognized that Japan should pay reparations to the Allied Powers
for the damage and suffering caused by it during the war. Nevertheless it is
also recognized that the resources of Japan are not presently sufficient, if it
is to maintain a viable economy, to make complete reparation for all such
damage and suffering and at the same time meet its other obligations.

Therefore,

1. Japan will promptly enter into negotiations with Allied Powers so
desiring, whose present territories were occupied by Japanese forces and
damaged by Japan, with a view to assisting to compensate those countries for
the cost of repairing the damage done, by making available the services of the
Japanese people in production, salvaging and other work for the Allied
Powers in question. Such arrangements shall avoid the imposition of
additional liabilities on other Allied Powers, and, where the manufacturing
of raw materials is called for, they shall be supplied by the Allied Powers in
question, so as not to throw any foreign exchange burden upon Japan.

2. (I) Subject to the provisions of sub-paragraph (II) below, each of the Allied Powers shall have the right to seize, retain, liquidate or otherwise dispose of all property, rights and interests of

(*a*)   Japan and Japanese nationals,

(*b*)   persons acting for or on behalf of Japan or Japanese nationals, and

(*c*)   entities owned or controlled by Japan or Japanese nationals,

which on the first coming into force of the present Treaty were subject to its jurisdiction. The property, rights and interests specified in this sub-paragraph shall include those now blocked, vested or in the possession or under the control of enemy property authorities of Allied Powers, which belonged to, or were held or managed on behalf of, any of the persons or entities mentioned in (*a*), (*b*) or (*c*) above at the time such assets came under the controls of such authorities.

(II) The following shall be excepted from the right specified in sub-paragraph (I) above:

(i)   property of Japanese natural persons who during the war resided with the permission of the Government concerned in the territory of one of the Allied Powers, other than territory occupied by Japan, except property subjected to restrictions during the war and not released from such restrictions as of the date of the first coming into force of the present Treaty;

(ii)   all real property, furniture and fixtures owned by the Government of Japan and used for diplomatic or consular purposes, and all personal furniture and furnishing and other private property not of an investment nature which was normally necessary for the carrying out of diplomatic and consular functions, owned by Japanese diplomatic and consular personnel;

(iii)   property belonging to religious bodies or private charitable institutions and used exclusively for religious or charitable purposes;

(iv)   property, rights and interests which have come within its jurisdiction in consequence of the resumption of trade and financial relations subsequent to September 2, 1945, between the country concerned and Japan, except such as have resulted from transactions contrary to the laws of the Allied Power concerned;

(v)   obligations of Japan or Japanese nationals, any right, title or interest in tangible property located in Japan, interests in enterprises organized under the laws of Japan, or any paper evidence thereof; provided that this exception shall only apply to obligations of Japan and its nationals expressed in Japanese currency.

(III) Property referred to in exceptions (i) through (v) above shall be returned subject to reasonable expenses for its preservation and administration. If any such property has been liquidated the proceeds shall be returned instead.

(IV) The right to seize, retain, liquidate or otherwise dispose of property as provided in sub-paragraph (I) above shall be exercised in accordance with the laws of the Allied Power concerned, and the owner shall have only such rights as may be given him by those laws.

(V) The Allied Powers agree to deal with Japanese trademarks and literary and artistic property rights on a basis as favorable to Japan as circumstances ruling in each country will permit.

(b) Except as otherwise provided in the present Treaty, the Allied Powers waive all reparations claims of the Allied Powers, other claims of the Allied Powers and their nationals arising out of any actions taken by Japan and its nationals in the course of the prosecution of the war, and claims of the Allied Powers for direct military costs of occupation.

Article 15

(a) Upon application made within nine months of the coming into force of the present Treaty between Japan and the Allied Power concerned, Japan will, within six months of the date of such application, return the property, tangible and intangible, and all rights or interests of any kind in Japan of each Allied Power and its nationals which was within Japan at any time between December 7, 1941, and September 2, 1945, unless the owner has freely disposed thereof without duress or fraud. Such property shall be returned free of all encumbrances and charges to which it may have become subject because of the war, and without any charges for its return. Property whose return is not applied for by or on behalf of the owner or by his Government within the prescribed period may be disposed of by the Japanese Government as it may determine. In cases where such property was within Japan on December 7, 1941, and cannot be returned or has suffered injury or damage as a result of the war, compensation will be made on terms not less favorable than the terms provided in the draft Allied Powers Property Compensation Law approved by the Japanese Cabinet on July 13, 1951.

(b) With respect to industrial property rights impaired during the war, Japan will continue to accord to the Allied Powers and their nationals benefits no less than those heretofore accorded by Cabinet Orders No. 309 effective September 1, 1949, No. 12 effective January 28, 1950, and No. 9 effective February 1, 1950, all as now amended, provided such nationals have applied for such benefits within the time limits prescribed therein.

(c) (i) Japan acknowledges that the literary and artistic property rights which existed in Japan on December 6, 1941, in respect to the published and unpublished works of the Allied Powers and their nationals have continued in force since that date, and recognizes those rights which have arisen, or but for the war would have arisen, in Japan since that date, by the operation of any conventions and agreements to which Japan was a party on that date, irrespective of whether or not such conventions or agreements were abrogated or suspended upon or since the outbreak of war by the domestic law of Japan or of the Allied Power concerned.

(ii) Without the need for application by the proprietor of the right and without the payment of any fee or compliance with any other formality, the period from December 7, 1941, until the coming into force of the present Treaty between Japan and the Allied Power concerned shall be excluded from the running of the normal term of such rights; and such period, with an additional period of six months, shall be excluded from the time within which a literary work must be translated into Japanese in order to obtain translating rights in Japan.

Article 16

As an expression of its desire to indemnify those members of the armed forces of the Allied Powers who suffered undue hardships while prisoners of war of Japan, Japan will transfer its assets and those of its nationals in countries which were neutral during the war, or which were at war with any of the Allied Powers, or, at its option, the equivalent of such assets, to the International Committee of the Red Cross which shall liquidate such assets and distribute the resultant fund to appropriate national agencies, for the benefit of former prisoners of war and their families on such basis as it may determine to be equitable. The categories of assets described in Article 14 (a) 2 (II) (ii) through (v) of the present Treaty shall be excepted from transfer, as well as assets of Japanese natural persons not residents of Japan on the first coming into force of the Treaty. It is equally understood that the transfer provision of this Article has no application to the 19,770 shares in the Bank for International Settlements presently owned by Japanese financial institutions.

Article 17

(a) Upon the request of any of the Allied Powers, the Japanese Government shall review and revise in conformity with international law any decision or order of the Japanese Prize Courts in cases involving ownership rights of nationals of that Allied Power and shall supply copies of all documents comprising the records of these cases, including the decisions taken and orders issued. In any case in which such review or revision shows that restoration is due, the provisions of Article 15 shall apply to the property concerned.

(b) The Japanese Government shall take the necessary measures to enable nationals of any of the Allied Powers at any time within one year from the coming into force of the present Treaty between Japan and the Allied Power concerned to submit to the appropriate Japanese authorites for review any judgment given by a Japanese court between December 7, 1941, and such coming into force, in any proceedings in which any such national was unable to make adequate presentation of his case either as plaintiff or defendant. The Japanese Government shall provide that, where the national has suffered injury by reason of any such judgment, he shall be restored in the position in which he was before the judgment was given or shall be afforded such relief as may be just and equitable in the circumstances.

Article 18

(a) It is recognized that the intervention of the state of war has not affected the obligation to pay pecuniary debts arising out of obligations and contracts (including those in respect of bonds) which existed and rights which were acquired before the existence of a state of war, and which are due by the Government or nationals of Japan to the Government or nationals of one of the Allied Powers, or are due by the Government or nationals of one of the Allied Powers to the Government or nationals of Japan. The intervention of a state of war shall equally not be regarded as affecting the obligation to consider on their merits claims for loss or damage to property or for personal injury or death which arose before the existence of a state of war, and which may be presented or re-presented by the Government of one of the Allied Powers to the Government of Japan, or by the Government of Japan to any of the Governments of the Allied Powers. The provisions of this paragraph are without prejudice to the rights conferred by Article 14.

(b) Japan affirms its liability for the prewar external debt of the Japanese State and for debts of corporate bodies subsequently declared to be liabilities of the Japanese State, and expresses its intention to enter into negotiations at an early date with its creditors with respect to the resumption of payments on those debts; to encourage negotiations in respect to other prewar claims and obligations; and to facilitate the transfer of sums accordingly.

Article 19

(a) Japan waives all claims of Japan and its nationals against the Allied Powers and their nationals arising out of the war or out of actions taken because of the existence of a state of war, and waives all claims arising from the presence, operations or actions of forces or authorities of any of the Allied Powers in Japanese territory prior to the coming into force of the present Treaty.

(b) The foregoing waiver includes any claims arising out of actions taken by any of the Allied Powers with respect to Japanese ships between September 1, 1939, and the coming into force of the present Treaty, as well as any claims and debts arising in respect to Japanese prisoners of war and civilian internees in the hands of the Allied Powers, but does not include Japanese claims specifically recognized in the laws of any Allied Power enacted since September 2, 1945.

(c) Subject to reciprocal renunciation, the Japanese Government also renounces all claims (including debts) against Germany and German nationals on behalf of the Japanese Government and Japanese nationals, including intergovernmental claims and claims for loss or damage sustained during the war, but excepting (a) claims in respect of contracts entered into and rights acquired before September 1, 1939, and (b) claims arising out of trade and financial relations between Japan and Germany after September 2, 1945. Such renunciation shall not prejudice actions taken in accordance with Articles 16 and 20 of the present Treaty.

(d) Japan recognizes the validity of all acts and omissions done during the period of occupation under or in consequence of directives of the occupation authorities or authorized by Japanese law at that time, and will take no action subjecting Allied nationals to civil or criminal liability arising out of such acts or omissions.

Article 20

Japan will take all necessary measures to ensure such disposition of German assets in Japan as has been or may be determined by those powers entitled under the Protocol of the proceedings of the Berlin Conference of 1945 to dispose of those assets, and pending the final disposition of such assets will be responsible for the conservation and administration thereof.

Article 21

Notwithstanding the provisions of Article 25 of the present Treaty, China shall be entitled to the benefits of Articles 10 and 14 (a) 2; and Korea to the benefits of Articles 2, 4, 9 and 12 of the present Treaty.

CHAPTER VI — SETTLEMENT OF DISPUTES

Article 22

If in the opinion of any Party to the present Treaty there has arisen a dispute concerning the interpretation or execution of the Treaty, which is not settled by reference to a special claims tribunal or by other agreed means, the dispute shall, at the request of any party thereto, be referred for decison to the International Court of Justice. Japan and those Allied Powers which are not already parties to the Statute of the International Court of Justice will deposit with the Registrar of the Court, at the time of their respective ratifications of the present Treaty, and in conformity with the resolution of the United Nations Security Council, dated October 15, 1946, a general declaration accepting the jurisdiction, without special agreement, of the Court generally in respect to all disputes of the character referred to in this Article.

CHAPTER VII — FINAL CLAUSES

Article 23

(a) The present Treaty shall be ratified by the States which sign it, including Japan, and will come into force for all the States which have then ratified it, when instruments of ratification have been deposited by Japan and by a majority, including the United States of America as the principal occupying Power, of the following States, namely Australia, Canada, Ceylon, France, Indonesia, the Kingdom of the Netherlands, New Zealand, Pakistan, the Republic of the Philippines, the United Kingdom of Great Britain and Northern Ireland, and the United States of America. The present Treaty shall come into force for each State which subsequently ratifies it, on the date of the deposit of its instrument of ratification.

(b) If the Treaty has not come into force within nine months after the date of the deposit of Japan's ratification, any State which has ratified it may bring the Treaty into force between itself and Japan by a notification to that effect given to the Governments of Japan and the United States of America not later than three years after the date of deposit of Japan's ratification.

Article 24

All instruments of ratification shall be deposited with the Government of the United States of America which will notify all the signatory States of each such deposit, of the date of the coming into force of the Treaty under paragraph (*a*) of Article 23, and of any notifications made under paragraph (*b*) of Article 23.

Article 25

For the purposes of the present Treaty the Allied Powers shall be the States at war with Japan, or any State which previously formed a part of the territory of a State named in Article 23, provided that in each case the State concerned has signed and ratified the Treaty. Subject to the provisions of Article 21, the present Treaty shall not confer any rights, titles or benefits on any State which is not an Allied Power as herein defined; nor shall any right, title or interest of Japan be deemed to be diminished or prejudiced by any provision of the Treaty in favor of a State which is not an Allied Power as so defined.

Article 26

Japan will be prepared to conclude with any State which signed or adhered to the United Nations Declaration of January 1, 1942, and which is at war with Japan, or with any State which previously formed a part of the territory of a State named in Article 23, which is not a signatory of the present Treaty, a bilateral Treaty of Peace on the same or substantially the same terms as are provided for in the present Treaty, but this obligation on the part of Japan will expire three years after the first coming into force of the present Treaty. Should Japan make a peace settlement or war claims settlement with any State granting that State greater advantages than those provided by the present Treaty, those same advantages shall be extended to the parties to the present Treaty.

Article 27

The present Treaty shall be deposited in the archives of the Government of the United States of America which shall furnish each signatory State with a certified copy thereof.

SECURITY TREATY BETWEEN THE UNITED STATES OF AMERICA AND JAPAN

Japan has signed a treaty of peace with the Allied powers. On the coming into force of that treaty, Japan will not have the effective means to exercise its inherent right of self-defense because it has been disarmed.

There is danger to Japan in this situation because irresponsible militarism has not yet been driven from the world. Therefore, Japan desires a security treaty with the United States of America to come into force simultaneously with the treaty of peace between Japan and the United States of America.

The treaty of peace recognizes that Japan as a sovereign nation has the right to enter into collective security arrangements, and further, the Charter of the United Nations recognizes that all nations possess an inherent right of individual and collective self-defense.

In exercise of the rights, Japan desires, as a provisional arrangement for its defense, that the United States of America should maintain armed forces of its own in and about Japan so as to deter armed attack upon Japan.

The United States of America, in the interest of peace and security, is presently willing to maintain certain of its armed forces in and about Japan, in the expectation however, that Japan will itself increasingly assume responsibility for its own defense against direct and indirect aggression, always avoiding any armament which could be an offensive threat or serve other than to promote peace and security in accordance with the purposes and principles of the United Nations Charter.

Accordingly, the two countries have agreed as follows:

Article I

Japan grants, and the United States of America accepts the right, upon the coming into force of the treaty of peace and of this treaty, to dispose United States land, air and sea forces in and about Japan. Such forces may be utilized to contribute to the maintenance of international peace and security in the Far East and to the security of Japan against armed attack from without, including assistance given at the express request of the Japanese Government to put down large-scale internal riots and disturbances in Japan, caused through instigation or intervention by an outside power or powers.

Article II

During the exercise of the right referred to in Article 8, Japan will not grant without the prior consent of the United States of America, any bases or any

22

rights, powers or authority whatsoever, in or relating to bases or the right of garrison or of maneuver, or transit of ground, air or naval forces to any third power.

Article III

The conditions which shall govern the disposition of armed forces of the United States of America in and about Japan shall be determined by administration agreements between the two Governments.

Article IV

This treaty shall expire whenever in the opinion of the Governments of the United States of America and of Japan there shall have come into force such United Nations arrangements or such alternate individual or collective security dispositions as will satisfactorily provide for the maintenance by the United Nations or otherwise of international peace and security in the Japan area.

Article V

This treaty shall be ratified by the United States of America and Japan and will come into force when instruments of ratification thereof have been exchanged by them at Washington.

In witness whereof the undersigned plenipotentiaries have signed this treaty.

Done in duplicate at the city of San Francisco, in the English and Japanese languages, this eight day of September, 1951.

INDEX